D0340261

Marginalized in the Middle

ALAN WOLFE

MARGINALIZED

in the middle

THE UNIVERSITY OF CHICAGO PRESS / CHICAGO & LONDON

Alan Wolfe is chair of the Department of Sociology at
Boston University.

The University of Chicago Press, Chicago 60637
The University of Chicago Press, Ltd., London
© 1996 by The University of Chicago
All rights reserved. Published 1996
Printed in the United States of America
05 04 03 02 01 00 99 98 97 96   1 2 3 4 5
ISBN: 0-226-90516-0 (cloth)
      0-226-90517-9 (paper)

Library of Congress Cataloging-in-Publication Data

Wolfe, Alan, 1942–
    Marginalized in the middle / Alan Wolfe.
      p.   cm.
    Includes bibliographical references (p.   ) and index.
    1. Social problems.   2. Criticism.   3. Sociology.   4. Intellectual
life.   I. Title.
    HN27.W65   1996
    361.1—dc20   96-3324

For David Riesman

Contents

Acknowledgments

About 80 percent of this book appeared as essays and reviews in *The New Republic, Society, Partisan Review, The Wilson Quarterly,* and *The Public Interest,* as noted below. My strongest debt is to editors at those publications who worked with me, sometimes line by line, on the text, especially Ann Hulbert and Leon Wieseltier. Steve Lagerfeld also deserves considerable credit.

In some ways this book began almost thirty-five years ago when I took a course in college on social criticism. The first book we read was *The Lonely Crowd,* and I distinctly recall understanding immediately that I was going to be a social scientist. I did not meet David Riesman until I moved to Boston in 1992; now, having lunch from time to time with him is one of life's special pleasures. I am delighted he did not take offense at my desire to dedicate this book to him.

Sanford Levinson and Morris Dickstein both persuaded me that my essays would stand up in a book format. I hope they are right. Woody Powell and Michael Schudson supported the project with enthusiasm and inside-dopester criticism. The comments of Mark Hulliung proved enormously helpful. This book also enabled me to work together with Doug Mitchell. I am not the only sociologist to testify to that treat. He is a national resource for our discipline. My wife Jytte Klausen is a critic's critic—literally.

* * *

Chapter II rearranges material from three of the author's articles: "The Culture of Cultural Studies," *Partisan Review* 63, no. 3 (1996); "The Feudal Culture of the Postmodern University," *The Wilson Quarterly* 20 (Winter 1996), pp. 54–66, and "Two Cheers for Professionalism: The 1960s, the University, and Me," in Steven Macedo, ed., *Reassessing the 1960s* (New York: W. W. Norton, forthcoming.

Chapter III is a revised version of "Realism and Romanticism in Sociology," *Society* 32 (January-February 1995), 56–63.

Chapter IV is a revised version of "The New American Dilemma," *The New Republic*, April 13, 1992, pp. 30–37.

Chapter V is a revised version of "The Gender Question," *The New Republic*, June 6, 1994, pp. 27–34.

Chapter VI is a revised version of "Dirt and Democracy," *The New Republic*, February 19, 1990, pp. 27–31, and "The Return of the Melting Pot," *The New Republic*, December 31, 1990, pp. 27–34.

Chapter VII is a revised version of "The Age of Anxiety," *The New Republic*, November 20, 1995, pp. 33–34.

Chapter VIII is a revised version of "School Daze," *The New Republic*, February 8, 1993, pp. 25–33.

Chapter IX is a revised version of "The Mothers of Invention," *The New Republic*, January 4 and 11, 1993, pp. 28–35.

Chapter X reorganizes material from "Not Quite in Our Genes," *The Public Interest* 118 (Winter 1995), 106–14; "Only Connect," *The New Republic*, October 4, 1993, pp. 33–38; and "Psychology on Our Minds," *The Public Interest* 122 (Winter 1996), pp. 115–18.

Chapter XI is a revised version of "She Just Doesn't Understand," *The New Republic*, December 12, 1994, pp. 26–34.

Chapter XII rearranges material from "The Professor of Desire," *The New Republic*, June 3, 1991, pp. 29–35 and "Aron's Rod," *The New Republic*, April 16, 1990, pp. 35–39.

Chapter XIII is based on "The Feudal Culture of the Postmodern University," *The Wilson Quarterly* 20 (Winter 1996), pp. 54–66, and "The Good, the Bad, and Gingrich," *The New Republic*, May 1, 1995, pp. 35–41.

I thank all of the editors of the above publications for permission to reprint the materials indicated.

MARGINALIZED IN THE MIDDLE

Social Criticism's Golden Age

So long as there has been society, there has been social criticism. Myth, literature, art, and religion have inspired visions that stood in sharp contrast to the received wisdom of their day, and, in so doing, rebuked the practices and institutions of the world around them. Try to find the first social critic, and your search will take you back to the origins of human history.

But social criticism also takes a distinctly modern form, insisting not only that there are many possible worlds but that those worlds are there to be created if we have but the determination and facts. The modern critic finds her society wanting not merely because it fails to live up to the brilliance of someone's imagination but also because it does not live up to its own ideals. To right the wrongs, the critic appeals not to a supernatural power or to an enlightened prince but to reason, the good sense of ordinary people, or norms of justice. Above all else, the events which inspire modern social criticism have a specific character. They cannot result in fatalism, or else there is no role for the critic. But nor can they be routine adjustments in the flow of historical time, for then there is nothing to criticize. The modern world has seen more than its share of such earth-shattering but not necessarily inevitable events—reason enough why modernity and social criticism move hand in hand.

Not even America, which long considered itself immune from the plagues of history, has escaped this preoccupation with social criticism. American social criticism has a distinguished history: Melville's *The Confidence Man*, Mark Twain's depiction of the "Gilded Age," Transcendentalist respect for nature, the antislavery movement, *Uncle Tom's Cabin*—all established a voice of concern about the path America seemed to be taking. Those worries reached their crescendo in protest against World War I. Randolph Bourne became America's quintessential social critic, embodying—in person, in style, and in ideas—the heroic stance of dissent against large-scale social forces which threaten to render individual autonomy superfluous. Social criticism in the Bournean mode was defined by the contrast between world-shaping events on the one hand and the power of the word on the other. But Bourne's voice was as archaic as it was powerful; his was a nineteenth-century lament, having more in common with Thoreau than it would with the later social science of C. Wright Mills and David Riesman.

In his anguish at World War I, Bourne could never have foreseen World War II—let alone the Holocaust, totalitarianism, and the cold war. Events of that magnitude, each following the other without letup, made individual protest seem futile. Something else was required when nothing else would do. Short of a response, but desperately in need of explanations, twentieth-century social criticism, at least in America, turned to social science. If we could not adequately respond to the evils, we could at least theorize about their causes: ideas about capitalism, prejudice, the military-industrial complex, and mass society flourished in the aftermath of the events that inspired them. The idiosyncratic protest of the artist gave way to the clinical dissection of the social scientist.

Robert and Helen Lynd began the process by studying a typical American community,[1] giving rise not only to Robert Lynd's reflections on the purposes of social science knowledge[2] but to an entire tradition of implicitly criticizing the country's values by looking at "small town in mass society" or "democracy in Jonesville."[3] Margaret Mead and Ruth Benedict undertook the same project in reverse; rather than exposing our peculiarities at home, they tried to demonstrate the superiority—or at least the equivalence—of cultures abroad.[4] Refugee intellectuals added to the mix, as they tried to understand American social practices, such as conformity or consumption, through the lens of fascist or communist experience.[5] C. Wright Mills brought a particularly American version of Marxism to social criticism,[6] but Freud was the inspiration for more social criticism during this period than Marx. Not only were David Riesman and the anthropologists influenced by him, but Erich Fromm, Karen Horney, Bruno Bettelheim, Norman O. Brown, Lionel Trilling, Philip Rieff, and Erik Erikson would have been included in any list of America's most prominent social critics.

Social criticism reached far beyond the academy. That overused term "New York intellectual" included not only literary critics but writers who concentrated on primarily social and political themes: Paul Goodman, Jane Jacobs, Lewis Mumford, Dwight Macdonald. Critical ideas about American society spilled out from the small literary magazines into the general culture. To borrow an expression from Macdonald, social criticism was once so popular that it became midcult. Vance Packard or Betty Friedan could crack the best-seller lists with ersatz sociology, while Hollywood, in films like *Blackboard Jungle* and *Rebel Without a Cause*, made passing critical commentary on American social institutions. The politics of the 1950s may have been conservative, but the culture was increasingly radical. And what made it radical was the transmission of social science insights to the general culture. Social science was every-where. Whether the subject was sexuality, the atom bomb, delinquency, suburbia, or the family—and whether the genre was a novel, a film, an essay, or an ethnographic study—social criticism and social science were increasingly linked.

The 1950s and 1960s constituted a "golden age" for social criticism. In invoking this term, I do not mean that a critical imagination flourished in the years after World War II in a more expansive way than ever before. My point, rather, has as much to do with the term "social" as with the term "criticism," for during this period skepticism toward American institu-tions was tightly linked with the accumulation of social knowledge and the use of social science techniques, all written in ways to tap the interest of the informed reader and concerned citizen. This was a period when majors in sociology expanded, when academic writers such as John Kenneth Galbraith could reach huge audiences, when the unconven-tional ideas of the social scientist became, in Galbraith's phrase, the new conventional wisdom. Never before had social scientists been so optimis-tic that their diagnoses of the American condition were correct and their cures workable; never again, when the mood changed, would that opti-mism return.

Looking back on this period forty years later, which a more somber mood in America forces one to do, the three elements which combined to make social criticism flourish—a faith in social science, a belief in de-mocracy, and a strong sense of political commitment—all seem to work at cross-purposes. Given the tensions between them, one has to wonder, not why the golden age passed, but how it ever happened at all.

Social science gave legitimacy to social criticism. A prophetic voice is off-key to a modern social critic; it was not God to whom the critic turned to register injustice but Fact. The appeal of the social critic was to a devia-tion from the norm, and the norm was established by empirical analysis. Unlike the prophet, the modern social critic's indictment will be dis-missed if his methodology is flawed. Struggling to win the masses, the social critic also has to still the doubts of the experts. It is often forgotten that most classic works of social criticism were self-conscious about their research: *The Lonely Crowd* was supplemented by *Faces in the Crowd*,[7] the latter presenting the interviews upon which the former was based, while C. Wright Mills, who condemned "abstracted empiricism," nonetheless took methodology seriously and advised students about the best ways of doing it.[8] European social critics remained primarily philosophers, religious thinkers, or novelists; Sartre and de Beauvoir defined the genre. American social critics built on disciplines, such as sociology, which themselves had become quintessentially American. Even when European social critics moved to America—one thinks of Theodor Adorno—they dropped dialectics in favor of interview schedules.

But if social criticism was rooted in social science, it also wanted to reach a large audience. To reach a large audience, social criticism had to be dramatic—even oversimplified. Nuance and respect for complexity, however crucial for social science scholarship, could not be among the first priorities of the social critic. Social critics did not generally write in scholarly journals for other academics; although they may have drawn upon such work, they presented their analyses in books and in articles for general-interest publications. Social critics thus tended to be mavericks within their disciplines; indeed, they often indicted their discipline as part of their indictment of society. Whatever marginalization they may have felt in academia was made up by their identification with history or the right cause. Academics were, in Noam Chomsky's phrase, "mandarins," leaving the critics as the genuine democrats.[9] Social criticism's objective was to give voice to the populace against the rule of the experts, which uncomfortably included the expertise of the critic himself. No prominent social critic of the 1950s and 1960s quite figured out how to be a social scientist and a democrat at the same time.

This task was made even harder when the social critic was motivated by political passion. Of necessity, the social critic could not accept too sharp a distinction between facts and values; ideological commitments drove social criticism from the start. Yet such commitments, rather than linking democracy with expertise, alienated the critic from both. On the one hand the American critic sought ideological clarity in a country whose population is usually suspicious of ideology; the social critic was far more likely to receive support for his ideological positions from European social theorists than from residents of "Jonesville." On the other hand, the social critic's ideological commitments ran counter to the legitimacy conferred by social science, a legitimacy rooted precisely in the notion that whatever social science is, it is not ideology. Democracy, social science, and ideology all combined to make modern social criticism possible, yet all conspired to make modern social criticism difficult.

Caught between so many contrasting imperatives, one has to ask: is social criticism possible? Is it desirable? I believe that the answers to both questions are positive—but only to the degree that social criticism moves beyond the sensibilities that defined it for so long. It is important to re-visit the golden age of social criticism, not to emulate it, but to learn from it. We are mistaken, I will try to show throughout this book, if, with Russell Jacoby, we believe that the passing of the New York intellectuals meant the death of a powerful critical consciousness.[10] Not only were the approaches and ideas of the critics of that time flawed, but the critical sensibility and explanatory power of the best social criticism of today is insufficiently appreciated. Social criticism is more than possible; it happens all the time. Looking for it in the wrong place in the wrong way, we often fail to see it right under our noses. Once we begin to see it for what it is, we are in a better position to understand what makes it effective.

The Critic as Hero

Although the golden-age social critic left behind the nineteenth-century voice of individual protest in favor of the scientific advice of the clinician, he often could not help striking a heroic pose. Central to the radical vision of the social critic was the notion that American society was in the process of becoming so stultifying that only a critical stance could, if not save it, then at least bear witness to a more authentic vision. At it most extreme, this image of the critic as hero took the form of an existential revolt against authority—C. Wright Mills on his motorcycle or Allen Ginsberg shocking bourgeois propriety. But an even better illustration of the critic as hero comes not from the extremes but from the always moderate voice of Irving Howe. Published in *Partisan Review* in 1954, "This Age of Conformity" is in many ways the quintessential text of the golden age of social criticism, even though it was written neither by a social scientist nor by a beatnik.[11]

The conformity to which Howe alludes is not, as one might first expect, that of suburban tract developments or organization men. Howe is rather anticipating what would later be called neoconservatism, the movement of his intellectual contemporaries to the right. Filled with references to the key words of yesterday's sociology—mass society, mass culture, the war economy, bureaucracy—Howe writes that "today the zeitgeist presses down upon us with a greater insistence than at any other moment of the century (38)." Intellectuals ought to be resisting such pressures, but not only do they have their own temptations, modern society also demands their allegiance. An avant-garde sensibility, one that is modernist in culture and radical in politics, is the best defense against the age of conformity. We have had such moments in the past: the Greenwich Village bohemians, the glory days of *Partisan Review*. Howe did not find this spirit very alive in the 1950s; his essay is gloomy, his prognosis doubtful. Still, Howe had no doubt what we need: "the idea of a mind committed yet dispassionate, ready to stand alone, curious, eager, skeptical. The banner of critical independence, ragged and torn thought it may be, is still the best we have (49)."

There is a tendency to look back on this period and lament the passing of this kind of critical sensibility; Howe's heroic vision of dissent remains the norm for those inspired by the political movements which erupted ten years after his essay was published, even though Howe himself was critical of those movements when they occurred. Seeking to understand the intellectual roots of 1960s activism, Andrew Jamison and Ron Eyerman speak of the "breathing spaces" which social critics "carved out of the postwar American landscape."[12] Compared to Mills, "a scrappy public thinker, who was also a professor," today's academic sociologists, writes Russell Jacoby, "are first professors and rarely, if ever, public intellectuals."[13] Christopher Lasch, whose views of the 1960s were anything but nostalgic, nonetheless lamented, shortly before his death, that social criticism is "the one form of intellectual activity that would seriously threaten the status quo and the one form that has no academic cachet at all."[14] Lasch's death seemed to underscore the point, depriving America of one of the few academics who could write for general audiences on large subjects with passionate moral fervor.

Yet writers in this tradition are too quick to romanticize the golden age of social criticism. Many of the "classics" of 1950s social criticism have not stood the test of time. Margaret Mead was not a scrupulous ethnographer; the case against her portrait of Samoan adolescence made by Derek Freeman is devastating.[15] Erich Fromm is generally dismissed as an oversimplifier. The shrill tone of a Herbert Marcuse grates on the contemporary ear. Mills was as pompous and bombastic as he was prophetic. Noam Chomsky's sense of moral superiority established in the 1960s could not survive his defense of Holocaust deniers' rights to free speech in the 1980s, let alone his soft spot for Pol Pot. Dwight Macdonald, as even his sympathetic biographer testifies, could be irresponsible, sometimes anti-Semitic, and incapable of writing a major book.[16] Not all the brilliant European refugees understood the society they had made their new home; Hannah Arendt's arguments against federal intervention in the Little Rock schools revealed considerable ignorance about American history and culture. Freud's influence was incredibly far-reaching, yet it is increasingly recognized that the entire Freudian enterprise, however fascinating metaphorically, is anything but science. Even *The Lonely Crowd*, in my opinion one of the outstanding books of the period, makes far too much not only of psychoanalytic ideas but also of mass conformity; ordinary Americans were far less "other-directed" than Riesman and his collaborators made them out to be.

The politics of social criticism have also changed. Mills and others of a heroic disposition envisioned the critic as a loner, railing against bourgeois society in a desperate effort to hold it to a higher standard. But, despite occasional invocations of that stance,[17] the image of the heroic critic has become blurred. As Michael Walzer observes, a critic too alienated from the society under criticism cannot be effective; belonging comes before bemoaning.[18] Furthermore, the political roles have been reversed. At a time when radical academics, firmly entrenched in university life, dismiss conservative critics of themselves as "marginal intellectuals," a substantial segment of the critical urge comes from the right.[19] As I will show in the chapter which follows, this reversal of political roles has changed the texture of social criticism significantly—and probably for the better.

Critics, moreover, have become more modest in their criticism, reflecting the obvious fact that confidence in the alternatives to liberal capitalism has noticeably diminished. One can no longer wait for Lefty; the notion that a society will come to exist in which oppression, inequality, and sexual restraint no longer exist is simply not believable, although American society did accomplish the last of these goals in the 1960s. As the alternative wanes, respect for what exists waxes; yesterday's social critic is today's neoconservative. This modesty is only partial; it is now on the right where one is most likely to find the kind of no-holds-barred, know-it-all ideological smugness once associated with the left, a tendency which conservative intellectuals no doubt attribute to the conclusion that they must be right. (I would urge modesty on them.) But, with that exception, social critics are more likely to understand that they are part of the society being criticized and that, consequently, their own ideas are fair game for their own theories. That understanding produces a kind of criticism that is less sweeping but also more deserving of respect.

If social criticism has changed, so has the society which receives it. One reason critics could adopt for themselves the mantle of heroic dissent was that they seemed so marginal to what C. Wright Mills called the great American celebration. But America is not in as celebratory a mood as it once was. It would be an exaggeration to claim, as many conservative writers do, that the critics have the public stage while the defenders of American institutions have become the marginalized minority, but there is some truth in the charge—at least in the university and the popular-culture industry. Ideas about racial injustice, the inequities of the nuclear family, and corporate mistreatment of the environment—once treated as radical notions—have become a new conventional wisdom, even as American politics has turned to the right and corporate power has reasserted itself. What Lionel Trilling famously called the "adversial culture" seems to have changed sides;[20] if *Dissent* were founded today, it would probably be started by right-wing intellectuals.

Even more important than a society's receptivity to criticism is the direction from which criticism comes—and the direction in which it aims. Social critics in the heroic mode assumed that the elites had an interest in suppressing criticism while dissident groups would naturally be attracted to the "critical spirit."[21] But now it is on the left, especially among those concerned with "identity politics," where one finds worries about excessive criticism. Large portions of the American left are attracted to a therapeutic ethic, which finds value in everyone's statements or ideas; from such a perspective, criticism can be psychologically dangerous—a threat to society's overall mental health.[22] Cultural relativism urges us not to criticize practices or ideas that seem to us wrong. A certain strand of feminist thought finds criticism to be an essentially male activity; women, we have been told, seek cooperative, not conflictual, relationships.[23] Political correctness is premised on the idea that we ought not criticize those who are oppressed, even if we know that what they are doing and saying deserves criticism. The alleged decline of standards in America—known to every academic as grade inflation—reveals a propensity not to criticize too harshly. Self-esteem, not criticism, is the objective of school guidance counselors, even, sometimes, of politicians.[24] Some writers hold that American society, with its emphasis on competition and reward-giving, pays too much attention to criticism and too little to mutual support.[25]

Under such conditions, the critic necessarily becomes a critic of other critics, focusing attention on the alternatives as much as on the society against which the alternatives are offered. In an odd way, it becomes the critic who appeals to established values, historical traditions, old-fashioned standards, and well-tested rules. When we think of a critic now, we are more likely to think of Frederick Crews, who attacks Freud's ideas as untrustworthy, rather than the Freudian-inspired therapist urging people to recover childhood memories of abuse.[26] When social criticism was discouraged from the top, the critic looked to the future. When it is frowned upon from below, the critic tends to look to the past. There are problems with both approaches, if either the past or the future is viewed in arcadian terms, but, for seriousness of purpose, the latter is preferable to the former, for the past offers guidelines based on events that were real, whereas criticism based on events that have not yet taken place offer no check against critical grandeur.

Given these changes in both criticism and society, it makes sense to treat the social criticism of the golden age as a subject of intellectual history, not as a form for contemporary emulation.[27] I believe that there is much of value in the tradition, especially the attempt, however flawed in practice, to base criticism on original empirical research about the society. But I also think that reflections on the nature of social criticism— indeed, of criticism itself—are in order. We need to know more about what social criticism is. Or, as befits a critic, we ought also to know what criticism is not.

Criticism and Polemic

Critics, unlike apologists, rarely have nice things to say. Every critic, of course, is an apologist in waiting; it makes little sense to invest in an attack unless there is something one is prepared, at some time and in some place, to defend. But, at least in the here-and-now, critics are driven by anger, disappointment, a sense of injustice, a hatred for hypocrisy, jealousy, hope, and similar emotions which, however different from each other, are all in opposition to pleasant-minded acceptance. Without bones to pick and faults to find, there is no criticism. If it is true, as Ian Shapiro has claimed, that democracy is "an ethic of opposition" as well as "a system of government," then criticism is surely a crucial component of democracy.[28]

Because the critic's work is so crucial, the major threat to social criticism would seem to come from quietism; critics are no longer critics when unfairness, bad faith, or sloppy thinking no longer move them—or when fairness and good faith move them to restrain their criticism. This obvious truism misses a more subtle threat to criticism, however, for when anger gets out of hand, when the rage is uncontrolled and exaggerated, the critic is no longer engaged in criticism. He has turned to polemic, which is a very different thing.

Edward Said is a critic, one known not only for his interpretations of novelists such as Joseph Conrad, but also for his strongly held political views on imperialism and the Arab-Israeli conflict.[29] In many ways, Said seems the very embodiment of the critic as dissident. His left-wing politics, no matter how ubiquitous in the academy, are outside the mainstream of American opinion. When another critic therefore writes of Said like this:

> I disagree with him so fundamentally on issues both of theory and history that our respective understandings of the world— the world as it is now, and as it has been at many points over the past two thousand years or so—are simply irreconcilable, which then leads, inevitably, to differences of local interpretation and local reading so numerous that one essay cannot name them all . . .

we naturally think we are listening to a neo-conservative or a defender of the West. We are not. Said's critic in this case is Aijaz Ahmad, and he is criticizing Said from the left.[30]

What "irreconcilable" differences exist between Ahmad and Said— both of whom are leftists, side with third-world revolutions against the West, support the Palestinians, and read literature as political documents? Roughly, as far as I can tell, these: Said, with his taste for high culture, not only likes Matthew Arnold but fails to understand a writer like Ranajit Guha. In Ahmad's writings, one sees polemic gone so wild that it loses touch with the obvious reality that whatever differences exist between Said and Ahmad are not only minor but also marginal.

Polemicists constantly fight a losing psychological battle; they write in anger to show how much they disagree with certain ideas, but the very depth of their anger displays a deep concern with those ideas. Polemicism is bad criticism because it cannot face up to its own respect for what it attacks. Its inauthenticity deprives it of what criticism must have: credibility. The polemicist implicates himself in his own critique. He becomes at one with his opponent, depriving himself of whatever detachment might give his criticism a ring of truth. Although the polemicist wants us to take his criticism seriously, he does not aim to persuade. His audience is merely a means to get to his target. Display is what counts. Hence the polemicist attacks his opponent without engaging his opponent. The reading is preordained, the substance of the critique understood by all parties before it is even delivered. One of the odder aspects of the polemic is how it rarely touches the individual or idea under attack; criticism this vigorous, this obviously one-sided, cannot be taken seriously. There is no alternative but polemic in response—that, or silence. (I prefer silence).

The eye of the polemicist wanders in either of two directions: toward those very close (as in Ahmad's dismissal of Said) or those far away. In the former case, the polemicist exaggerates minor differences; in the latter, she finds a common ground that does not exist. In *Who Stole Feminism?* Christina Hoff Sommers claims to be a feminist. There once existed a reasonable and responsible kind of feminism, Sommers claims, in comparison to which contemporary versions are pale shadows.[31] But Sommers's claim to feminist credentials lacks as much authenticity as Ahmad's assertions of difference with Said. There is little actual sympathy for the historical situation of the feminists with whom she claims identity, and even less understanding of how radical they were in their own time, how exposed they were to the nineteenth-century equivalents of Christina Hoff Sommers. One has to wonder: if Sommers had not made the relatively crude rhetorical ploy of solidarity with those she attacks, would her attack have actually been more balanced? For in asking the reader to accept that she really is a feminist, Sommers undermines the credibility of her polemic against feminism. Greater straightforwardness in the one area might have made for greater straightforwardness in the other. As it is, her book suffers from inauthenticity in both its praise and its condemnation.

Avoiding polemic in no way implies avoiding anger at ideas and practices the critic finds anathema. Quite the contrary, for furious polemic is psychologically very close to fawning praise. The critic, unlike the polemicist, must establish credibility, and since very few things in the world are either all good or all bad, credibility is usually undermined by too doctrinaire a tone. But not always; some things in the world are all bad (even fewer are all good), and on those rare occasions an uncompromising stance can have its virtues—all the more reason to avoid polemic wherever possible, so as to make it more effective where necessary. Ideologues have little interest in credibility, which is why the polemical style is so congenial to those of fixed political belief. When the ideologue writes, it is not the critic's words which appear on the page but the words of the political position the critic represents. Ideological thought, not only of the Marxist stripe, tends to view individuals as pawns of larger social forces, as good a way as any of deflecting attention from whether what the critic has to say is credible or not.

Polemic is not limited to politics. Philosophers, who make a living out of turning minor differences into major disputes, surely are the undisputed masters of polemic, especially when their concerns are narrow and technical. Literary critics can get more worked up over which novels belong in the canon than political critics can get exercised over who should qualify for public assistance. Although the polemical style, which is bad criticism, is even worse literature, literary critics find themselves attracted to it; Morris Dickstein writes of Philip Rahv, a master polemicist, that he "could write as if he were drawing up a position paper for a party meeting, excommunicating writers rather than criticizing them."[32] Little has changed in that respect since the days of the New York intellectual; it is not because he is a professor of law that Stanley Fish is so disputatious, but because he is a professor of English. If American intellectual life has had a particularly dogmatic and unrepentant tone this past few years, it may be because it has been dominated by humanists rather than social scientists or political theorists.

Nonetheless, polemic is usually associated with political writing and political beliefs. While it is understandable that political disagreements can lead to such strong feelings, it is also the case that polemical writing is *less* appropriate for political criticism than for any other kind. Politics, we know from Max Weber, is always about violence; the same is true of political writing. No one should enter into political or social criticism without a sense that someday their words may be used by others. One can never have control over how they are used, of course; that is true of all writing. But political writing is a special category. Political and social criticism, even if negative, is advice. It is directed either to those in power today or those who may be in power someday. If ever found useful, it will be because it serves an agenda, even if the critic did not have one.

Weber insisted on recognizing the violence behind all politics because of his strong belief in an ethics of responsibility. Responsibility is also important to the social critic, for polemical political writing is violence squared: a violent tone devoted to potentially violent ends. One has to ask of the polemical critic: if the world you do not like were to replaced by one you did like, how would you act? I would be skeptical of the actions of anyone, no matter what their political point of view, who can find nothing but fault in what they criticize. No one in the world of ideas has yet to reach that stage of perfection.

Social criticism has to maintain its critical stance without lapsing into polemic. We expect conservatives and liberals not to like each other's ideas, but there is no reason for them to write about each other unless they find some merit in those ideas. When he wrote that "criticism requires critical distance," Michael Walzer pointed out the dangers of feeling so alienated and rejected by the society that one believes there is no need for criticism.[33] But the critic is "connected," again in Walzer's phrase, not only to society but also to what is under criticism. That connection is determined by the critic's interest in writing about something; I cannot imagine spending the time reading and thinking about a subject, even reading and thinking about books which I will not like, without being interested enough to explore. At the very least, I owe my subjects thanks for stimulating me to write; not every book can inspire a response, and the books I surely have felt the most negative about are those that, after reading, I declined to review. There is a kind of ethnographic identification involved in criticism—however much distance from the subject is required for effective commentary, a certain amount of sympathy is also required for authenticity.

The social critic is also connected to the discipline of criticism. Social criticism has been in existence long enough to have developed its own traditions and to have evolved its own commitments. While the critic may fancy himself a lone voice in the wilderness, he is also at the mercy of all the critics that have come before him. "Most social critics, if they are any good at all, live without a handbook," Walzer has written.[34] This is not quite true. It would be impossible for any critic practicing today not to be guided by the mistakes and successes of critics in the past. The plot of social criticism is as simple as plots come: there is society, there are alternative standards, and the critic judges the former negatively in the light of the latter. Social criticism has become a genre; it has rules and conventions strictly enough defined that creativity enters, if it enters at all, in refinements of the craft: new evidence about social practices, reinterpretations of the alternatives, explorations about judgment.

A third kind of connection—of a particularly ambiguous sort—exists between the social critic and reality. Unlike literary critics, social critics deal not with works of the imagination but with real-world experience. Both are tied to what they analyze; the literary critic is suspect for not being an artist, even when the critic (Matthew Arnold, T. S. Eliot) is an artist. That tension can be resolved, to the satisfaction of the critic if no one else, by arguing for equality between criticism and literary creativity, as some forms of French literary theory do. But social critics do not have that alternative; they are tied to what they analyze in a different way. Equality between the critic and the policy-maker is impossible, for the latter—especially in matters of war and peace, but also in domestic issues such as health care or education—takes direct responsibility for the consequences of his ideas in a way the critic never can. Social criticism requires its own kinds of responsibility, both to truth and to the consequences of the criticism; policy-maker and critic are joined to the degree that they deal with a world in which consequences matter. Their responsibilities, however, differ in degree; the buck does not stop with the critic, but with those he criticizes.

Because social critics deal with real-world problems and policies, they have an obligation to connect their criticism with the world around them. The bane of "golden age" social critics was their inability to keep in balance their respect for what was with their preference for what should have been. So different are the sensibilities involved in advocating and describing that one could easily conclude that it is impossible to reconcile them. But that would be an unfortunate conclusion. In fact, advocacy and description can work to each other's benefit.

Criticism can hardly be effective if it gets reality wrong; the critic must develop respect for what his methods find or he will have no credibility. One can get away with a sermon—once. But the critic who keeps finding the same reality in book after book—and, lo and behold, a reality which just happens to conform exactly with the critic's own political positions—will have lost all claims not only to scientific objectivity but also to criticism. Condemning one world, he will be praising the one we have lost—or the one we have not yet gained. The same sharp edge which gives his criticism power in dealing with what exists turns into mush when it comes to what he would like to have exist. Having left science behind, he becomes only half a social critic, removing from his gaze the worlds he likes in order to focus exclusively on those he hates. Utopias of the past need discoverers, while utopias of the future need popularizers; neither needs critics.

In a similar way, good criticism can inform good science. For all its limits, the social criticism of the golden age has lasted longer, and given us more insight into society, than most of the self-consciously scientific sociology of the 1950s. In retrospect, it is difficult to say who had the monopoly on utopia: the radicals who thought that America could achieve equality and abolish exploitation or the positivists who thought a social science modeled on physics was just around the corner. Knowledge is not necessarily gained because the social scientist proclaims objectivity; our current knowledge of family dynamics has been strengthened by feminist criticisms of the family, just as our understanding of the persistence of racism is sharpened by an awareness of how wrong racism is. Indignation is as good a motive for science as curiosity. It is, after all, not the motive which finally counts but the results. A deeply ingrained longing for a better world can, if disciplined, shed considerable light on this imperfect one.

There is no theory that will inform the social critic how to bring the tension between description and advocacy into line. The critic who is also a social scientist must be simultaneously aggressive and modest, involved and detached, radical and conservative, a scholar and an essayist, a scientist and a clinician—all at the same time. Perhaps this makes criticism more an art than a science, but I prefer to think of social criticism as a science requiring the sensibilities of an artist.

Think criticism, and one is likely to think of all those things I have been arguing that social criticism is not: polemical, engaged, and speculative. But that is just another way of saying that modern social criticism has outgrown the models that gave it birth. The golden age of social criticism of the 1950s was quite different from the earlier social criticism of the 1930s: one worried about depression, the other about affluence; one was primarily economic, the other psychological. It follows that social criticism at century's end cannot, and ought not, model the social criticism of thirty years ago. Would-be social critics who look to the writers of the golden age are not likely to be persuasive: their arguments will be too predictable, their politics too tired, their missionary zeal too false, their nostalgia too unrealistic, their utopia too untrustworthy. America needs social criticism, but it does not necessarily need the kind it once had. Social critics always run the risk of their society changing more rapidly than they do.

The View from the Center

As opposed to marginal intellectuals standing on the left sideline, the social critic now exists all across the American cultural field. Enough of America's social practices and institutions have been influenced by the values of the 1960s to make the conservatives of today sound like the C. Wright Millses of yesterday; the term "the liberal establishment," once a source of condemnation from the left, has become a routine expression of denunciation from the right. Who more appropriately can lay claim to the title of "social critic"? The defender or the attacker of affirmative action? The apologist for or the critic of single-parent families? The protector of social security or the reformer? Liberals have held sufficient power since the 1960s to generate significant criticism; it is conservatives like Newt Gingrich who now speak the language of revolution, while political radicals discover themselves as dispositional conservatives, using unfamiliar, even uncomfortable, language to defend institutions, such as the university, which have been good to them.

At the same time, America remains a conservative country, with enough of a conservative politics to allow liberals and radicals to be social critics as well. There may no longer be a military quite as all-powerful as the one that prompted Mills's ire, but we have enough of an industrial complex left to keep alive the faith of radical decentralizers and populists. Ecologists now constitute the single most effective, and popular, source of anticorporate sentiment in America. The Reagan years reversed trends toward greater equality in America, furnishing considerable material for social critics. Even many who believe that affirmative action is problematic public policy also believe that Americans have obligations to minorities who have suffered discrimination at the hands of majorities. As conservatives win political battles and cut down the size of government, they will surely encourage social critics from the left to address once again issues of poverty and opportunity. After their resounding electoral victory in 1994, conservatives are beginning to taste the responsibilities of power and liberals can once more enjoy the joys of dissent.

Because America is unlikely to be as conservative as liberals believe or as liberal as conservatives assert, we need social criticism from all points on the political spectrum. More than that: we need social critics willing to learn from both directions. Tomorrow's social critic should be someone who cares deeply enough about her society to understand and appreciate its leading ideas and dominant institutions, yet who, precisely because of that caring, is willing to elaborate and defend a standard against which those ideas and institutions can be judged. Neither attack nor apologia will do. This may sound like a formula for balance and sweet reason inappropriate to the role of a critic, a willful adaptation of what Jules Feiffer once satirized as "the radical middle." That may well be true, but the critic who tries something like this will also meet opposition from both ends. Those who defend what is being criticized will find the critic insufficiently appreciative, while those who want to replace one ideology with another will find the critic insufficiently angry. Such a critic will be marginalized in the middle rather than isolated at the extremes.

Marginalized in the middle is perhaps the best place for the social critic to stand, for the middle looking out gives a clearer perspective than the sidelines looking in. One usually thinks of the center as solid and the extremes as precarious, but in the ideological climate of today the reverse seems more accurate; the extremes of right and left know where they stand, while the center furnishes what is original and unexpected. There will always be social critics. But they will always stand in different places. What else could a social critic expect?

THE CHANGING POLITICS OF SOCIAL CRITICISM

From Left to Right

The left has no monopoly on social criticism, but few were aware of this by now self-evident fact during social criticism's golden age. "This age of conformity," after all, was dominated by McCarthyism, racial segregation, the cold war, business influence, and the Eisenhower presidency—all of which seemed to call for criticism from only one side of the political spectrum. In 1952, when *Partisan Review* published "Our Country/Our Culture"—its coming to terms with America—the word went out to putative social critics: too many intellectuals, especially those of a literary bent, were finding life in America too pleasant. [1] Their retreat was the bugle call for social criticism's advance. The flame of social protest would be kept alive by social scientists of a radical persuasion, who would continue to shed light on inequality, war, and injustice, no matter how conservative the rest of the country, including its leading academics, became.

This picture was never quite true, even for its time. Some critics of the "golden age," especially those inspired by Freud, were anything but leftist; one thinks of David Riesman or Philip Rieff. Others who would (often incorrectly) come to be called neoconservatives, such as Daniel Bell, were writing books that seemed to fit the label of social criticism. Norman O. Brown thought of himself as a man of the left, but, as I will try to show later in this book, his rejection of liberalism increased his sympathy for right-wing, even fascist, writers. Still, both the advocates and the critics of social criticism during its golden age had little doubt that criticism and left-wing radicalism went together. Protest automatically meant protest from the left. No self-respecting conservative, it was believed, had any reason to protest anything.

Whether accurate or not for its time, an identification of criticism with the goals of the left no longer makes sense at all. In the 1990s, social criticism is far more vigorous on the right than anywhere else. Ideas hostile to some of the dominant institutions of American society—organized religion, the foundations, Hollywood, the universities, even, on rare occasions, big business—come from conservative authors and politicians. Like the earlier generation of leftists, they write in popular magazines, think in terms of public policy, try to apply the findings of social science research, and sometimes reach best-seller status. Conservatives once thought of themselves as "remnants," the odd men out of American thought, doomed to the fate of speaking a truth that few would want to hear.[2] Now, suffering from all the problems of too many talk shows, they are the ones who have to find the appropriate balance between what their intelligence tells them and what the general public wants to hear.

Meanwhile, on the other end of the political spectrum, radicals have become increasingly defensive. Things are not really so bad as the critics charge, one is likely to hear them saying. The world is complicated. It requires experts, not critics. Radicals defend professionalism and write in ways the general public can barely understand; in some cases, they hold the general public in contempt. As their words fall on deaf ears in the culture at large, radicals prepare, like conservatives before them, for the long haul; some day, their truths, widely ignored now, will be found to have validity. For the moment, however, their disposition has become just as much one of complacency as the temperament of the right has become one of criticism.

Two American institutions in particular stand out as sites for this reversal of political roles: the university and the culture industry. Moreover, this reversal is most apparent when those institutions come together in efforts by academics to understand popular culture—what goes, in contemporary lingo, under the name of "cultural studies." Arguments over the university and the media provide a feel for how deep the changes in the politics of social criticism have become, as well as what some of the implications of those changes might be.

Radicals in the Professional University

Inspired by the writings of such social critics as Paul Goodman and C. Wright Mills, the student radicals of the 1960s attacked not only the military-industrial complex but the university as well. Clark Kerr's notion of a "multiversity" seemed to say it all; the university was complicit in the power arrangements which radicals believed had to be overturned—if not abolished. No wonder that the protest which erupted in Berkeley in 1964 was directed against the academy. And no wonder that it spawned few successful academics. David Lance Goines has tried to identify everyone arrested at Sproul Hall at Berkeley on December 3, 1964. His list includes some who made careers as politicos, such as Los Angeles City Council member Jackie Goldberg, and others, like Goines himself or Barbara Garson, who would achieve fame in nonacademic pursuits. Yet I could find no more than 10 out of the 825 who have achieved even a modicum of academic renown.[3] Myra Jehlin, then an activist graduate student, was not arrested; the list of those who were includes Stephen Gillers, now an NYU law professor, Stephanie Coontz, a feminist historian, and Randall Collins, a distinguished sociologist. But that's about it.

There surely are reasons why young political activists at that time would find the academy an unattractive career option. A maddening calm dominated university culture, one that simply could not be ruffled by considerations of social justice, demands for relevance, or a preference for substance over process. Between those whose lives were shaped by depression and war and those growing up in the affluent society lay a chasm. The former—cautious in all things, pleased with the security (although not the low pay) of academic employment, and suspicious of causes and extremism—could only look with dismay, if not fury, at the high expectations and impatience for results that characterized the latter. If one extrapolated these trends to a later time, the conclusion would have been clear: radicals would criticize the university as an impossibly reactionary institution, and conservatives, who rose to the defense of the university in the 1950s and 1960s, would become its staunchest supporters.

Yet the exact opposite took place. These days conservatives delight in pointing out the shortcomings of the university. Charles Sykes's *Profscam* summarizes the indictment; professors are ripping everyone else off. They should teach more. Their English should be understandable. Their research should be less esoteric. They ought to spend more time with undergraduates. They should be in their offices more often. It is absurd that they get one year in seven off. They should keep their politics out of the classroom and their hands off their students. (Yes, Sykes has three pages on sexual harassment, and they are righteous with feminist indignation). "Faculty members are locked in place through tenure and they wield the moral authority of 'academic freedom' like a mighty engine of destruction," Sykes writes. "No reform can be implemented without the consent of the faculty, because the professors can simply refuse to do anything they don't like."[4]

Martin Anderson catalogues many of the same failings identified by Sykes, but, if anything, he ups the rhetorical level. Anderson is especially fond of the word "corruption." Professors are politically corrupt because they do not like Republicans and personally corrupt because the engage in hanky-panky with students (another conservative for feminism), while universities are institutionally corrupt because administrators exaggerate overhead costs and build expensive football facilities.[5] And since the one thing that professors have the most power over is what they teach, conservative criticisms of the curriculum are really criticisms of the faculty. Roger Kimball has no doubt who is responsible for the decline of the canon; "the faculty was, in the end, to blame for the demise of the Western culture course at Stanford."[6] Even the Speaker of the U.S. House of Representatives is convinced that "campuses are run for the benefit of the faculty, not the students," for "college and university faculties have developed a game in which they have lots of petty power with very little accountability."[7]

If the right attacks, the left must perforce defend. Sounding remarkably like the very people the left once criticized, Cary Nelson and Michael Bérubé, self-described "loyal, card carrying" leftists, write that "lecture courses have their place even in the humanities." There is nothing wrong with esoteric scholarship: "the public does not understand that knowledge in the humanities must be produced as well as transmitted." There is faculty stagnation, but this "is not the same thing as the so-called 'deadwood' problem."[8] Nelson and Bérubé do admit that the university has problems, which distinguishes them from some of their colleagues. Ernest Benjamin, general secretary of the American Association of University Professors, gives no ground at all. "Elimination of tenure . . . will not increase the number of available positions," he writes. "Nor can we improve teaching by increasing teaching loads."[9] The task is, in fact, not to change anything in the modern university; instead, as Linda Ray Platt, professor of English at the University of Nebraska and recently president of the AAUP, writes: "the faculty must develop a new narrative of our own and find ways to carry it to the public."[10] One could hardly imagine a more conservative language, even if those speaking it think of themselves as leftists of one sort or another.

This shift in political stance has had important implications for the practice of social criticism. Leftists have done quite well in academic life. The radicals of the early 1960s may have rejected the whole business of academia as inherently corrupt, but those born five to ten years later, for whom Vietnam and Watergate, not demands for student power, were the defining events, found the modern university very much to their liking.

(Andrew Ross, a leading figure in cultural studies, was eight years old when Berkeley erupted). Ensconced in humanities departments, they devoted themselves to epistemological, rather than actual, revolutions. As their focus shifted to an attack on the privileges spawned by race and gender, their attitudes toward the university shifted from unease to full acceptance. We can see just how conservative these radicals became when we look at what they have to say about the professionalization inherent in the contemporary university.

An academic professional can be understood as a person who is committed to specialization in a particular discipline, engaged in producing work to be read primarily by other professionals, committed to a career in which the rewards are long-term, devoted to self-governance and critical of any outside interference, preoccupied with questions of method, and convinced that amateurs are unable to do what professionals do best, precisely because they lack the commitments just described. Each of these elements—more triumphant in the academy after the left's triumph within it than they were when the university was far more conservative—are, ironically for adherents to a movement inspired by the critics of the 1950s and 1960s, hostile to the conditions that make for effective social criticism.

Academic professionals thrive in disciplines. When the tale of the left's triumph in the academy is told and retold, the two most prominently mentioned institutions are the Modern Language Association and the Duke University English department. Both, of course, are tied to an academic discipline. Nor are they tied to just *any* discipline. English literature represents not only the language itself but the entire culture fashioned by that language. We know, thanks to Gerald Graff's history, that the hows and whys of English departments have always been contested, but the debates of the past were narrow in scope.[11] Everyone accepted, until relatively recently, that whatever they might not be, English departments were one thing: elitist. Those who taught English were by definition holdouts from mass society, guarding the language and its literature against the corruptions of the quotidian.

In an age of deconstruction, that quaint image of the English department is long dead. But it is still worth remarking how everything was deconstructed but the department. Although a substantial part of the early New Left critique of the university focused on specialization as a particular evil, academic leftists, once out of graduate school, outspecialized their mentors. Gone was the early New Left's demand for interdisciplinary approaches to knowledge; as Stanley Fish would put it, "Being interdisciplinary is so very hard to do."[12] Even those whose careers flourished in brand-new academic disciplines, such as black studies or women's studies, mocked the organizational characteristics, if not always the academic standards, of the traditional disciplines.

Professional associations flourished along with departments. Much has been made of the politicization of the Modern Language Association, but before it could become a prize worthy of capture it first had to expand in size and scope. Academic professional associations were transformed from *gemeinschaft* to *gesellschaft* as radicals came to power in the academy; indeed the American Sociological Association, reflecting its professional understandings of these matters, changed its name from the American Sociological Society and moved to Washington in the early 1960s.[13] Not only did these organizations develop professional staff, financed by ever-increasing membership dues, they also broke up into specialized units, each reflecting a particular tendency within the field. When disciplines were dominated by a few departments, academic professional associations were relatively unimportant. But as departments proliferated, trips to the annual meetings became, for the aspiring professional, a necessity. It was all part of the long march through institutions.

Professionals write for other professionals. Whatever the value of this activity, it is far different from the atmosphere of social criticism which inspired the early 1960s generation. Andrew Jamison and Ron Eyerman trace the "seeds of the 1960s" back to fifteen critics of the previous decade, from Rachel Carson and Erich Fromm to Lewis Mumford and James Baldwin.[14] All were either nonacademics entirely or academics living on the margins of their disciplines.[15] And virtually none of them have been reproduced among those inspired by their ideas. There are, within today's crop of academic writers, a number who are read outside of their professional discipline: Richard Rorty, Henry Louis Gates, Edward Said, Stephen Jay Gould, Michael Walzer, Cornel West, and Martha Nussbaum are examples. All of them, unlike the earlier generation, obtained tenure at elite universities. Only Camille Paglia comes to (my) mind as an example of an intellectual working in a nonelite institution who reaches an audience as large as those of a Herbert Marcuse or a Margaret Mead. And Paglia herself is often identified as a neoconservative; whether true or not (I do not believe it is), Paglia has more in common with nonacademics such as Roger Kimball than she does with the academic feminists at the Ivy League university in her city.

Academic radicals like to brag about their frank careerism. The general idea seems to be that one is absolved of unseemly behavior by not only confessing to it but by relishing it. This "dirty little secret" rhetorical style particularly fits Stanley Fish, academia's bad boy, who believes that he has struck a fatal blow at bourgeois society by acting bourgeois.[16] Yet Fish speaks for a generation; when leftists maintain that the personal is political, they mean not only that decisions made in private have public consequences but that public positions have private motivations. Having ridden the postwar wave of economic growth into comfortable positions with enviable job security, radicals come to terms with earlier vows of purity or poverty by acknowledging the reality of their success. They will not, like an earlier generation of academics, pursue a career while denying ambition. They will make their career the touchstone of their ambition.

Self-governance is at the heart of professional self-definition; physicians think of themselves as physicians to the degree that they, and not oversight agencies, make the key decisions involving care. Peer review is the particular form that academic professionalism takes. Only colleagues in a similar field should judge the competence of a candidate for tenure. Departments, not obtrusive administrators, determine who joins the ranks. The best work is that which passes tests of blind submission and blind review. In short, faculty, like professionals everywhere, pride themselves on their autonomy. They owe the public no obligations, and the public, in return, should keep its nose out of their business. Interestingly enough, however, if faculty autonomy has become a cornerstone of contemporary professionalism, as Nathan Glazer suggests, university autonomy has not. The Berkeley radicals demanded that government keep out of academic affairs; to them, the university was a sanctuary, roughly like a church, and state legislators had no business telling professors and students what to do. By contrast, the state of New Jersey has, until very recently, funded an office charged with insuring that issues of race, class, and gender are introduced into the curriculum of the state's institutions of higher education. Similarly, Leonard Jeffries of City College had little trouble appealing to outside agencies, including the courts, when his university stripped him of his department chairmanship. Very little of the agenda of the academic left—from affirmative action to sensitivity training—can be accomplished without the regulation of universities by political agencies. Faculties are increasingly autonomous within institutions which are not.

Academic professionals are especially preoccupied with questions of method, sometimes to the point where substance drops out of their work altogether. In the social sciences, the survival of quantitative methods is quite unexpected. There was, in the minds of a previous generation of social critics, an association between reliance on quantitative methods and the war in Vietnam; both were unseemly products of a technocratic mentality bent on using human subjects to further the designs of autocratic elites. Luddism characterized the 1960s *zeitgeist;* the revolt against academic complacency and irrelevance took the special form of a revolt against positivistic methods.

A glance at any of the leading social science journals indicates that quantitative methods, since that time, have become even more ubiquitous than they were then. What was unexpected was how many former leftists would contribute to their hegemony. Some Marxists criticized every aspect of bourgeois society except counting; they would use the tools of the social sciences to demonstrate the persistence of class inequalities. Radical economists turned, not to the early Marx, but to neo-Ricardians who believed that one could actually measure the falling rate of profit or the rate of surplus value. Those whose work was not primarily quantitative nonetheless developed a methodological self-consciousness; they would prove that historical or qualitative methods were methods nevertheless. Just as leftist English professors developed a more arcane and theoretically driven style than the New Critics and philologists who preceded them, radical social scientists could crunch numbers as well as anyone else. The clash between the attack on method and entrenched ways of conducting academic life was no contest; the latter won, hands down.

The concluding impact of all these trends is to reenforce the professional's historic disdain for the amateur and, at the same time, to increase the distance between the university and the world around it.[17] Whatever else the university became as the academic left reached its prominence, it is not a place that welcomes generalists. Indicative of the mood among leftist academics is a pamphlet called *Speaking for the Humanities*—an effort on the part of six prominent humanists, sponsored by the American Council of Learned Societies, to justify the changes which the 1960s generation brought to American English departments. Its authors find themselves advancing the cause of specialization in ways that would make Clark Kerr blush. Humanistic thought "must be free to pursue questions as far as possible without knowing what general use or relevance the answers might prove to have," these humanists write. The clear message of *Speaking for the Humanities* is that "belle lettrists" and advocates of the "gentlemanly ideal" have no standing to contest the "competence of the best scholars in the humanities today," which is "remarkable."[18] It is as if the authors of this document had Lionel Trilling and other critics of the 1950s in mind, not only to criticize their politics but also their understanding of the nature of the intellect.

No wonder, then, that the culture of social criticism has not only shifted from left to right, it has also shifted from the academy to the world of independent think tanks, journalists, and free-lance writers. Martin

Anderson sees a benefit in this; conservative critics, unprotected by tenure, face a competitive world which forces them to sharpen their ideas and develop their writing style, while left-wing academics, given the cartel arrangements called tenure, never test themselves against the market, which means that, no matter how much they write for each other, they never find themselves writing for anyone else.[19] There is some obvious truth in this charge. Professional history departments have little room for narrative storytellers with large audiences, just as English departments are unwelcome to John Gross's "man of letters."[20] A literary humanist named John Kenneth Galbraith, who also happened to be an economist, could never have gotten tenure at Harvard if he had been born fifty years after he was. These days a C. Wright Mills would run into trouble at Columbia, not because his ideas were too far to the left, but because, too popular, they were insufficiently rigorous.

Yet, as I will argue in the concluding chapter of this book, the idea that the universities, captive of the specialists, is no longer a place for social critics is not quite right. Not only is the work produced in think tanks and by independent journalists easily as ideological as that produced in university English departments, not all academic specialization is bad. When done right, attention to methodology and respect for the demands of logic and evidence can improve social criticism, not work against it. The problem is that, when done wrong, academic work produced by the current conditions of university life can easily turn complacent.

An interesting example of this complacency is provided, not by the mandarins of high theory and European fashion so predominant in the English departments of elite universities, but by a self-consciously populist effort, often led by academics at the less than top universities, to focus on America and its everyday culture. In this field created and sustained by the academic left, one in which conservatives need never apply, we find a lack of critical perspective, an acceptance of capitalism, and a stunning complacency in face of violence and ugliness. This field is called cultural studies.

The Culture of Cultural Studies

Inspired mostly by British writers such as Raymond Williams, Richard Hoggart, and Stuart Hall, cultural studies examines the ways in which popular culture shapes ordinary people's perceptions of the world—and how it presumably provides tools of "resistance" against the hierarchies of advanced capitalism. Although borrowing from its own coterie of Continental thinkers, especially Pierre Bourdieu and Michel Foucault—let alone the theorists of the Frankfurt School—cultural studies is refreshingly humanistic compared to the deterministic logic of poststructuralism. It is less pompous and can, at times, even display a sense of humor. Bad writing is endemic in the contemporary academy; nevertheless, enthusiasts for cultural studies, unlike deconstructionists, at least recognize the importance of writing in ways accessible to the uninitiated.

The rise of cultural studies is a reaction among the politically engaged against the defeatism inherent in poststructuralism. Cultural studies advocates are committed, not to the didactic seminar, but to the explicit politicization of the classroom. The typical academic task of the poststructuralist is to read a single text, usually a written one, deeply and intensively, while for the cultural studies enthusiast it is to jump from one (often visual) text to another, making startling, if not always sensible, connections between them. If deconstructionists find allies in departments of philosophy, cultural studies reaches out to sociology, anthropology, film studies, communication, and schools of education. For the former, multiculturalism is primarily epistemological, rooted in a theory about the perspective of the Other; for the latter, multiculturalism is more like the ethnically balanced slate of a political machine. Not only are cultural studies enthusiasts more likely to write about rap music, Malcolm X, or Nike commercials than to comment on de Man or Heiddeger, notable among their ranks are such African-Americans as Cornel West, bell hooks, and Michael Eric Dyson.

There is a missing generation in cultural studies. Some of its prominent representatives, such as Stanley Aronowitz, were political activists in the 1960s, or even earlier. But most of its well-known participants came to maturity long after the heyday of the New Left. Cultural studies combines those who never lost their taste for Marxism with those for whom Marxism remained doubly forbidden fruit: frowned upon not only by the culture as a whole but also by academic leftists more attracted to theory than to political commitment. Revised to make race and gender coequal with class as categories of oppression, cultural studies engages itself with the twenty-first century in culture while upholding the nineteenth century in politics. Its ideal of a cultural product is science fiction or cyberspace, while its ideal of a political concept is the class struggle or Gramsci's notion of hegemony.

One does not generally find in cultural studies tortuous efforts to justify the impossibility of justification as one does in postmodernism and its various offshoots. For this reason alone, its lack of philosophical pretension is an advantage; it rarely claims to be anything other than an effort to keep "progressive" politics alive among faculty and students. But the self-conscious Marxism of cultural studies is also an oddity in a post-Marxist world. Cultural studies is important, not because of its critique of popular culture, but because it so readily accepts, and celebrates, popular culture. In so doing, cultural studies turns the social criticism of the golden age on its head. Its task is to welcome as subversive the very capitalism social critics once denounced as conformist.

Cultural studies is haunted by the ghosts of the anti-Stalinist intellectuals who contributed to "Our Country/Our Culture." They, too, felt a tension between their political and their cultural commitments, one that was eventually resolved when their taste for high culture weakened to the point of nonexistence their inclinations to Marxism. Cultural studies reverses this aspect of a previous generation's ideas; Marxism will be kept alive by praising the achievements of what used to be called mass society. The intellectuals of the cold war may have had their failings, but self-hatred was not among them. Intellectuals were defined by their respect for intellect. Even the one intellectual usually faulted for his ready enthusiasm to join in attacks on American society, Dwight Macdonald, was second to none in his distaste for the culture produced by nonintellectuals. (He knew, having worked for them.) Underneath the increasingly tenuous commitment to socialism on the part of these intellectuals was a nightmare worse than capitalism: a society in which the masses would have no respect for the life of the mind.

Cultural studies by contrast takes as its premise, not the culture's lack of respect for intellectuality, but intellectuality's lack of respect for the culture. Cold war intellectuals may have moved away from the "neo-aristocratic critique of mass culture" associated with Eliot or Ortega, Andrew Ross writes, but they nonetheless retained a strong fear that the popular culture "would lend itself to ever greater forms of social control and an increasing monopolization of all channels of opinion and information."[21] But this one-sided view, Ross continues, overlooks the "resentments born of subordination and exclusion" (231) usually embodied in the products of popular culture. There is no secret why intellectuals make this mistake; they like the world to be rational and purposeful. The popular, by contrast, "is perhaps the one field in which intellectuals are least likely to be experts" (232).

Respect for popular culture inevitably brings with it a certain disrespect for the mind. This is not only acceptable, it can even be an advantage. The left must, above all else, be popular, writes Michael Bérubé: "a preachy left that situates itself safely above stupid, reactionary movies

and their stupid, reactionary meanings, can be—*and has been*—very easily lampooned as a 'politically correct' left of somber, humorless mor-
alizers."[22] Andrew Ross is even more explicit in attempting to reposition
the left's attitude toward the stupid. A new generation of left-wing intellectuals faces a new, and contradictory, task: "encouraging resistance to
the privileges of 'smartness,'" even if in so doing "they find themselves
lined up against the order of cultural capital which is the basis of their
own authority as contestants in the social world" (213).

In this campaign against smartness, nothing is too dumb for cultural
studies. "Roll Over Beethoven" is the anthem;[23] whatever the literati once
denounced, cultural studies will uphold: romance novels, Star Trek,
heavy metal, Disneyland, punk rock, wrestling, Muzak, *Dallas*. If the
Rosenberg letters represented for Leslie Fiedler and Robert Worshaw an
irresistible combination of Marxist clichés and cultural *kitsch*, then it is
important to stress, as Andrew Ross does, that these letters "challenge the
assumption that effective political statements cannot be communicated
in a language that lacks the ring of posterity, and therefore that political
sentiments, to be persuasive, require trained intellects or populist rheto-
ricians" (28). If shopping centers were for an earlier generation of Marxists symbols of the fetishism of commodities, then contemporary
advocates of cultural studies, such as Meaghan Morris, find them "over-
whelmingly and constitutively paradoxical," embodying uniformity on
the one hand and, on the other, a tendency to "dissolve at any one point
into a fluidity and indeterminacy that might suit any philosopher's delir-
ium of an abstract femininity."[24] If Rambo can be seen as little more than
a money-maker, he also represents, argues William Warner, the vulnerability of the American male at a time when masculinity is brought
into question; besides, as Douglas Kellner writes, he has "long hair, a
head-band, eats only natural foods, . . . is close to nature, and is hostile
toward bureaucracy, the state, and technology."[25]

Enthusiasts for cultural studies are the first to admit that popular culture is not always pretty; its images can be violent, pornographic, racist,
and militarist. But popularity must be respected for its own sake; if a
product sells, and sells hugely, there must be something to it. There is, in
this sympathy for the popular, something to be respected: unlike feminists against pornography, who denounce an ugliness they do not like
(and who, according to Ross, therefore sound like the cold war intellectuals of a previous generation), writers in the tradition of cultural studies
are more likely to try and discover why pornography has appeal—and
not just to men. Doing this, however, often requires rather complicated
gymnastics. And, truth be told, cultural studies stumbles badly. To claim,
as endless writers in this tradition do, that Madonna serves feminist goals

by challenging the border between masculine and feminism represents little more than celebrity envy.[26] It a short step from that position to sympathy for sadomasochism or even to the argument of Shannon Bell, who finds that feminist critics of prostitution, the ultimate form of women's degradation, silence prostitutes by insisting on a difference between routine and illicit sex.[27] It is hard going for the left to respect a culture which shows so little respect for the left.

Perhaps the most painful example of the inability of cultural studies to deal with ugliness is bell hook's treatment of "gangsta rap." Feminists must be "bold and fierce" in their condemnation of black rapsters who preach violence against women, she claims. But we should also recognize that the white power structure has an interest in having black music "stir up controversy to appeal to audiences." Gangsta rappers are just dupes of the machinations of white elites. Therefore, as hooks inelegantly concludes:

> our feminist critiques of black male sexism fail as meaningful political interventions if they seek to demonize black males, and do not recognize that our revolutionary work is to transform white supremacist capitalist patriarchy in the multiple arenas of our lives where it is manifest, whether in gangsta rap, the black church, or in the Clinton administration.[28]

When Republicans such as William Bennett have no qualms denouncing the profitable products of a huge corporation such as Time-Warner, while a self-professed Marxist just cannot quite find the right denunciatory language, the politics of cultural criticism have shifted indeed.

Agonies such as these are a product of cultural studies' certainty that the popular culture is popular. But how do we know that it is? The mere fact that people buy something does not mean that they like it, or even use it. The sociology of the popular is terra incognita; since the days of Paul Lazarsfeld, sociologists have been trying to understand the phenomenon of the mass audience, and with little success. But cultural studies enthusiasts, unrestrained by a sociologist's need for data, spin imaginative interpretations of what *Hustler* magazine or AIDS iconography means to those who read or see them. If we only knew. The fact is that there is as little basis for concluding that popular culture is a source of resistance to the dominant order as there is for believing that it is a prop of the dominant order. Cultural studies is what happens when literature professors wander into the territory of sociologists without a map; as Michael Schudson points out,[29] cultural studies, as it moved across the Atlantic and away from the more sociological perspectives of Stuart Hall and

Richard Hoggart, lost its old-fashioned socialist respect for working-class sensibility, its connectedness to real experience, and even its genuine appreciation of high culture. Cultural studies in Great Britain, facing an underdeveloped sociological tradition, filled a social science gap, while cultural studies in America, facing competition from sociology, moved away from the social sciences to humanities departments increasingly inclined to pass over classic texts in favor of popular artifacts.

For this very reason, cultural studies also takes the popularity of popular culture far more seriously than the purveyors of popular culture do. Those who write the soap operas and market the punk rock are guided by little else than their relentless quest for something that will turn a profit. Postmodernists in their own fashion, they operate by no core principles and subscribe to no theories of human nature or the proper organization of society. They would be the first to recognize that there is no message in their message, other than half-hearted efforts at product differentiation. They can never be sure that their contributions to popular culture will ever make it past the wastebasket and into the video stores. When their products are successful, they usually have little idea why. If they are interested, and they generally are not, they could consult advocates of cultural studies, who are busy making an effort to supply the meaning and rationale for their work which they themselves do not possess.

Cultural studies thus operates as a vanguard party for the media elite. In Australia, where cultural studies flourishes, its enthusiasts, no longer able to find work in the university, are, according to Meaghan Morris, "virtually forced to work in the media or in the bureaucracy or increasingly in the private sector."[30] No such corresponding shift in occupational affiliations has happened in the United States, but the day may well come. "A media-conscious left, a left that knows how social signs can be appropriated and reappropriated, may be capable of deliberately wrestling cultural meanings away from the New Right on its own ground" (146), writes Bérubé. Why wait? Cultural studies can begin right now to present itself in media-like fashion: its books, sound-bite scholarship, tend to be collections of smaller articles rather than sustained arguments; its titles are meant to grab attention ("Pop Goes the Academy: Cult Studs Fight the Power"); its language strives for, even if it often fails to accomplish, inside-dopesterism; its conferences are usually packed and feature the academic equivalent of rock stars; illustrations are favored and books are packaged brilliantly; and the treatment of what is under investigation resembles fan magazines more than disinterested inquiry. Social critics of the golden age retreated with horror from the crassness of the popular; conformity, the organization man, the mass media's treatment of the family—these products of popular culture inspired its critique. Not so among the enthusiasts for popular culture; theirs is not an effort to study the mass media but to imitate them.

Cultural studies not only loves the popular, it tends to be contemptuous of high culture—especially those forms of high culture which nourish intellectuals and social critics. Intellectuals, Andrew Ross writes, are those who "patrol the ever-shifting borders of popular and legitimate taste, who supervise the passports, the temporary visas, the cultural identities, the threatening 'alien' elements, and the deportation orders, and who occasionally make their own adventurous forays across the border" (5). Cultural studies strives for something even more ambitious than an occasional venture into enemy territory: not to cross the border between higher and lower standards, but to abolish the border completely. Marxists thought that one class could abolish all classes; the intellectuals of cultural studies want to see a world in which intellectuals no longer exist. One of the golden age social critics, Richard Hofstadter, went out of his way to remind us that America has never been a country particularly attracted to ideas.[31] But anti-intellectualism, in Hofstadter's treatment, was especially a movement of the right. No doubt he would be as surprised as anyone to find a decided anti-intellectualism stemming from the academic left.

The anti-intellectualism which inevitably accompanies a celebration of popular culture is particularly strange given the brouhaha over political correctness, the most recent chapter in the right's campaign to attack the left by attacking professors and their peculiarities. Cultural studies is obsessed by the attack on political correctness, even if the leading lights of the movement were not, like defenders of Derrida and de Man, the objects of that attack. This obsession is no doubt explained, as cultural studies readily admits, by the eerie similarity that the right bears to the popular culture defended by the left. The conservative political tradition has surely been a thoughtful one, but few would claim that the era of Newt Gingrich is one of its great moments of intellectual depth. The Republican "Contract with America" is more a cultural than a political product: market-tested, easy to swallow, simplistic. No wonder that cultural studies shares common ground with the New Right on a number of points: respect for irrationality, a preference for particularism, and the desire—successful in the case of Gingrich, a complete failure in the case of cultural studies—to achieve popularity by appealing to emotions rather than to logic and evidence.

From the standpoint of this common ground, one might expect cultural studies to treat the attack on political correctness with a knowing wink: we understand that you could not care less about what is taught in literature courses, that your real objective is a political one, they could say to the right, for the same is true of us; if anything, we have less respect for pretentious academic posturing than you do. But no, when it comes to political correctness, cultural studies once again disappoints. Acknowledging that the right has identified something real—"I'm not going to pretend that versions of these caricatures don't exist in American universities" (14), Bérubé writes—he, like many of his colleagues, delivers a tired defense of the academic left, premised on the assumption that, in Paul Lauter's terms, the attack on PC has been led by right-wing "flacks" and "fifth-column" liberals within the academic world.[32] The one thing missing in Lauter's analysis is any sense that critics of political correctness might actually have something important to criticize.

By stripping the debate over political correctness of any content, cultural studies approaches the problem as one of rhetoric, strategy, and image. The right, these writers argue, does a better job of making its points stick, not because its critique is accurate, but because the right is unified and never concedes a point. The left fails in its strategy because it doesn't understand that the right plays by hard-ball rules which are uncomfortable to well-meaning leftists; the right lies, for example, while the left never does. It therefore all comes down to image: the left simply has to do a better job of explaining its position. The major problem with the position is this: in embracing popular culture so enthusiastically, how can cultural studies defend an institution such as the university, which exists to promote the life of the mind?

What might seem like a contradiction resolves itself when one examines the ways in which cultural studies makes its defense. Bérubé, who argues that the left is ill-advised to defend an intelligent high culture against a popular low culture, turns around and accuses the right of anti-intellectualism because it is scornful of cutting-edge literary theory; it is surely an odd sensibility that elevates academic writing as better embodying the life of the mind than the poetry of Eliot or Pound. Paul Lauter writes that "it is because I have a certain faith in the value of intellectual work and in the academy that I have helped begin an organization called—perversely it seems to some—the Union of Democratic Intellectuals" (85). But it turns out that even this "certain" faith is compromised; for him, intellectual work "does not cease with the final footnote. It takes us into communities, into politics; into organizing, in short" (86). Through arguments like these, what might have been a contradiction becomes no contradiction at all; cultural studies' defense of higher learning is not a defense of intelligence but of academic scholasticism on the one hand and political organizing made possible by the modern university on the other. It is precisely because such unintelligent things go on in universities that a movement such as cultural studies, which prizes the low and dumb, can support them so enthusiastically.

If this sympathy for low culture means an end to social criticism as we have known it, so be it, argue some of those identified with cultural studies. "The mantle of opposition no longer rests upon the shoulders of an autonomous avant-garde," Andrew Ross writes, in language resonant of the end-of-ideology thesis. "Neither the elite metropolitan intellectuals who formed the traditional corpus of public tastemakers or opinion-makers; nor the romantic neo-bohemians who shaped the heroic Nietzschean image of the unattached dissenter . . . nor the organic party cadres whom Lenin shaped after the model of the 'professional revolutionary'" can serve as a force of resistance to advanced capitalism. Echoing Daniel Bell, Ross finds hope only in one place: "it has been scientific intellectuals rather than humanists who have been at the forefront of this professional activism" (210).

There is no reason, according to Ross, to lament the end of ideology and, with it, the passing of what he calls "the universal intellectual" (229). Future contestations will be over the body, not the mind, and the new politics of identity—especially movements organized around gays, women, and blacks—are primarily bodily in nature. Academics, under such conditions, are best off jettisoning their obsolete beliefs in intellectual criticism and joining the action. Even the vanguard party must go, and, as Michael Bérubé writes, so will most of the elements of classic Marxism, leaving only "sugar-free, low-cholesterol, no-fat decaffeinated Marxism lite" (141). Cultural studies announces what has been obvious for some time: the American left, having become quite comfortable in its academic respectability, would rather join the culture than fight it. Social criticism may have been radical in its time, but in the postmodern 1990s it is just one more vestige of an all too cerebral society doomed to wither away. The age of the highbrow critic is over; long live MTV.

Social Criticism Beyond Politics

The cause of the left may be worse off without its monopoly on social criticism, but the cause of social criticism is better off without its monopoly by the left. There would seem to be an inevitable cycle associated with the politics of social criticism. Inspired by a political vision, social criticism comes to invest in its particular understanding of the world. As it does, it becomes defensive: it must hold on to an understanding of the society it likes to denounce, even as the society changes, for only then does the social critic occupy a familiar role. No matter how radically America is changing, critics from the left insist that it really hasn't changed that much at all: it is still capitalist, still patriarchal, still racist—all the things these critics have to insist the society is, in order for their criticism still to hold water.

The increasingly tired conservatism of the left's social criticism is ultimately responsible for the shift in political energy to the right. But one can already begin to detect the same dynamic which undermined the left taking place on the other side. Conservatives, having found political correctness, cannot let it go, recycling the same incidents over and over in increasingly frenzied tones. Just as radicals insist that racism and patriarchy always win, conservatives conclude that the forces of multiculturalism never lose—even, oddly enough, when they do. For twenty years, neoconservatives tried to keep the spirit of the 1960s alive, all for the sake of denouncing it. In the 1990s, conservatives finally have their chance to repeal the policies they detest; if successful, they will surely prepare the way for the left's return to preeminence among social critics.

The relationship between social criticism and politics is not a simple one. Those who defend tradition, believe in authority and obedience, and assign a relatively low priority to reason and argumentation are not going to find social criticism to their liking. In this broad sense, social criticism, a product of Enlightenment values, belongs to the liberal tradition. But the liberal tradition is not the exclusive property of the left. The American left in the 1990s has found itself advocating a politics of group identity, which often involves suppressing criticism in favor of solidarity. When liberals give up on liberalism, what are conservatives to do?

The obvious answer is for conservatives to put themselves into a mood of opposition. But this is as uncomfortable for them as advocating group solidarity is for liberals. To defend the rule of elites, conservatives have to write popular books. Their case for religious belief is made in a decidedly secular manner. Forceful and articulate women defend the traditional family. A movement often attracted to anti-intellectualism—John Stuart Mill called conservatism the "stupid party"—lays claim to the mantle of academic freedom. They attack affirmative action in the name of egalitarian and meritocratic values they never believed in before. There is a lesson to be learned here: Liberals tend to be dismayed when conservatives are on the offensive as social critics. They ought to realize that conservative ends are being justified by liberal means, perhaps the greatest testimony to the power of liberal ideas in a presumably conservative age.

Although social criticism belongs to the liberal tradition, it would be a mistake to equate the urge to criticism with a position in current political wars between left and right. Social critics are far better off staking their criticism on the distance society travels from relatively timeless liberal principles, such as equality, fairness and, compassion. Because such ideals are timeless, societies are unlikely ever to meet them, always giving the critic something to say. And anything worth saying will always include not only criticism of the society which fails to meet those goals but also criticism of those who argue for and advance those goals, whatever political disposition they may have at any particular moment. The breakdown of the left's monopoly on social criticism is an opportunity—for the left as well as the right.

REALISM AND ROMANTICISM IN SOCIAL CRITICISM

Social Criticism's Heart and Head

Two contrasting styles of criticism are available to those seeking to understand, and thereby to change, the society around them. The critic can be begin with the proposition that the existing society is so corrupt, its practices so decadent, its institutions so warped, that the only effective criticism is one of passionate rejection. The critic's vocation is to denounce and, in so doing, to express longings that will be visionary, imaginative, hopeful. Social critics who speak in this voice resonate with romanticism. Only someone prepared to look beyond the injustice of today to the utopia of tomorrow can truly claim to be critical.

Despite the obvious appeal of romanticism, a substantial number of social critics reject it in favor of realism. To change society, they claim, critics first have to get reality right. The vocation of the critic is not denunciation but explanation. Social criticism in the realistic mode is strongly linked to social science. Collect the data, examine the history, interview individuals, get the facts—nothing speaks more eloquently about the injustices of society than precise documentation of its inequities. A new society is not willed into being by painting pretty pictures of an arcadian future. It comes about when the people affected by society's distorted priorities understand how things came to be the way the are—the first step in trying to make them different.

Of all the ways in which the politics of social criticism have shifted, one of the most striking involves the changing tone of criticism itself. As they have with respect to the virtues of the specialized university, right and left have switched sides on the issue of realism. There was a time when radicalism and realism worked together. In contrast to theological or aristocratic versions of the world, in which the real conditions of, say, the urban proletariat, were considered irrelevant to what was proper or necessary, realism took the form of a sociological equivalent of Zola's *Ger-*

minal. The social surveys of nineteenth-century Britain and the blue books which formed the basis of Karl Marx's library research were realistic in this sense; factual descriptions of the world as it is would require only minimal preaching or partisanship, for those facts would, in and of themselves, constitute a radical indictment of society.

But realism is no longer automatically associated with the left. Faced with real-world problems such as perpetual poverty, out-of-wedlock births, criminal violence, or addictive behavior, the tendency of some radical social critics is to explain away rather than to explain. This refusal to look at reality takes primarily political and epistemological forms. For some, the real world is a trap; to look it directly in the face is impossible, for what we think of as reality is only a construct, a Potemkin village assembled by people so that they can live with what the social scientist takes, even if the subject does not, to be oppressive or intolerable conditions.[1] For others, political considerations compel a turn away from reality; merely to discuss pathological behavior among the poor constitutes a form of "blaming the victim."[2] It is not that such behavior is subject to different interpretations, one radical, the other conservative. It is more that such behavior is not subject to any interpretation, for to admit its existence is itself understood to be a symptom of conservative politics. This is a long way from the realism of Karl Marx.

Romanticism has undergone a similar political transformation. Like the romantic poets, romantic social critics were once nostalgic critics of capitalism, invoking the solidarity of *Gemeinschaft* in preference to the coldness of *Gesellschaft.* Conservative romanticism was more a European, specifically a German, phenomenon than an American one, and it lasted well into the twentieth century in the ideas of Martin Heidegger, Hans Freyer, and Arnold Gehlen.[3] But there was nonetheless an American form of the conservative critique of modernity, invoking the virtues of the small-town compared to the city.[4] Somewhat lost in the shuffle that passes for intellectual fads in America has been a condemnation of modernity in terms similar to the critique now offered by the left—but coming, in this case, from the right.[5]

Nostalgia still exists; one finds its expression in one of the most widely read contemporary critiques of modernity, *Habits of the Heart.*[6] But these days romanticism is more likely to be Rousseauian in its condemnation of convention and worship of nature. Sociological romanticism is a cry of protest against the mechanization of life in a bureaucratic and industrial society. It is a product of the New Left rather than the Old Left, for its focus is not so much on material conditions and real world outcomes as on culture, personality, and the self—aspects of society that cannot be captured by tables and charts but require probing into subconscious processes invisible or irrelevant to the realist. It does not look backwards to the organic harmony of the preindustrial village, but forward to a utopia in which repressive desublimination will be abolished. Its objective is authenticity, the creation of conditions under which people can overthrow social convention and achieve the genuineness which is truly theirs.

The social critics of the golden age, inspired by a heroic vision of dissent, were often romantic in inclination but realistic in methodology. Torn between heart and head, social critics aimed to accumulate data about the real world as a way of trying to bring about a new one. It was a tricky balance to maintain, one which was often lost. Social criticism today is more far likely to express romantic longings than provide realistic investigations. This, I believe, is a mistake. As much as it may fuel the imagination of the critic to begin with an ideal world against which to contrast this one, both social science and social criticism are improved when the facts of this world constitute the starting point for contemplating others. Realism focuses a critical sensibility by disciplining it against utopian longings that ultimately have no critical edge. Romanticism is a slippery guide to understanding, and without understanding, there can be no effective social criticism. Social criticism can take a major step forward by going backward to its roots in a realistic tradition.

The Romantic Moment

The driving force of romantic social criticism is an attack on bourgeois values. At one level, this is hardly new. With the exception of Herbert Spencer, sociology developed in opposition to utilitarianism and other forms of "economic" theorizing about society. Sociology would put in the emphasis on community, morality, and meaning—all of which economics left out. Middle-class values were not to be taken for granted but to be explained as the by-product of something else: displaced Protestantism, the revenge of the locals against the cosmopolitans, anti-intellectualism, and resentment against progress.

Given this hostility toward bourgeois values, it followed that sociology, and the social critics inspired by it, has long been attracted to what used to be called "deviance." Durkheim established the modern sociological practice of looking at the behavior of people who could not or would not adjust to norms. In our century, this side of sociology flourished. "Chicago school" sociologists studied hobos and other products of urban displacement.[7] One entire tradition of sociological inquiry has made the unconventional its major focus; symbolic interactionism, a way of understanding how people themselves participate in the creation of the symbols that govern their lives, developed a taste for the exotic: mental institutions, juvenile delinquents, tattoo parlors, funeral homes, prostitution.[8] For numerous sociologists, "outsiders" were the natural subject matter of the field.[9] Because so much of social criticism is so strongly tied to sociology, it was a short step from the study of outsiders to calls for a rejection of the society that created the need for outsiders. A book like *Talley's Corner*—a quintessential effort to bring to life a group of inner-city black males who were also outsiders in the culture of middle-class, white America—could only be read as an indictment of the inequalities that permitted the existence of the conditions it described.[10]

Although firmly committed to portraying the lives of the excluded and the marginalized, the sociology and social criticism of the 1950s were not necessarily romantic. Realists as well as romantics write about the underside of urban life; comparing the sociology of the Chicago school with the contemporary fiction of Theodore Dreiser, one cannot always tell whose Chicago is more gripping. It is not whether outsiders are given attention which differentiates the realist from the romantic but the way outsiders are understood. In a realist mode, the injustice of excluding the outsider is that, if permitted inside, he would be as conventional as anyone else; marginality is not to be praised but to be overcome. Erving Goffman's world portrays everyone as a confidence man, which means that the outcast is as bourgeois as everyone else, calculating the means to achieve any particularly desired end.[11] Interpreted this way, social criticism's taste for the exotic during the golden age represented not an attack on bourgeois values but an appreciation of the plasticity of bourgeois experience. So deeply entrenched are middle-class values that they envelop those who have been excluded from middle-class life.

This unacknowledged respect for bourgeois values is a far cry from more contemporary sociological efforts to present, and to justify, behavior and lifestyles that flout conventional proprieties. Romanticism in contemporary social criticism is anthropological rather than sociological, extending what Richard Shweder has called "anthropology's romantic rebellion against the Enlightenment."[12] The fascination with the exotic in contemporary social criticism is not so much an appreciation of those who are different as a celebration of the fact of their difference. Outsiders are portrayed, not to welcome them to bourgeois morality, but to hold them up as alternatives to the conventional. By their very existence, the marginalized stand in condemnation of the society which marginalized them. The social critic's task is to give voice to what makes them different, for criticism comes by simply acknowledging their existence. From this perspective, the more exotic the better; indeed, hobos and tramps seem quaint and conventional compared to the transsexuals and transvestites praised by contemporary feminist theorists for their "difference." In their search for the exotic, contemporary social critics resemble Jean Gênet more than Theodore Dreiser; the excluded are to be glorified, not transformed.

Works dealing with the inner city provide more representative examples of romantic social criticism than works dealing with gender. If the social critic is to identify with the one feature of inner-city life most feared by the conventional middle class, his choice would surely be gangs. Gangs seem to stand for everything the middle class is against: violence, lack of respect for property, the failure to get and keep a job, sexual license, anomie. Gangs, from a romantic perspective, cry out not for explanation or condemnation but justification.

The "classic" approach to gangs involved an attempt to understand them as a response to the social disorganization of the city.[13] But, as Martín Sánchez Jankowski points out, that approach downplays the behavior of the actual individuals who join gangs.[14] To understand such individuals, Jankowski decided to study gangs at close range, which he did by establishing contact with gang leaders in three American cities. Gangs being what they are, they were not inclined to trust a sociologist in their midst—unless the sociologist passed a test. As Jankowski describes his ritualistic introduction to the gang world, he was frequently "set up" to report illegal behavior to the authorities by gang members. When he proved his reliability by not reporting their illegal activities, Jankowski came to be trusted, which enabled him to observe gang behavior in action. Thus the sociologist, like the subjects he studies, becomes an outlaw, defying bourgeois convention—in this case the duty to report a crime—in order to establish his romantic credentials.

Observing gang members at close range, Jankowski discovered rebels against bourgeois order. To be sure, gang members, like the society to which they are opposed, are rationally self-interested, but their individualism, in contrast to the conformism of bourgeois society, is "defiant." This defiance, Jankowski argues, puts into perspective two aspects of gang behavior which would otherwise be puzzling: criminal activity and violence. The former, which Jankowski calls "crude economic activity"— he has in mind muggings, holdups, small burglaries—is not, as most people believe, a product of gang ritual and gang solidarity. Crime, rather, represents the defiance of individual members of gangs who act self-interestedly. "Because individual members constantly seek their own interest and usually have few resources to undertake large projects, they are motivated to undertake this type of activity. Most of the crude economic activity recorded by the authorities as gang related crime is thus in actuality done by individual gang members acting on their own, and this is a direct outgrowth of the defiant individualist character" (133).

Much the same can be said about violence. Conventional opinion misunderstands the nature of gang violence, Jankowski argues: "The general public's persistent questions about why young people become involved in violence, and frustration at gang members' seeming lack of resource for their participation in violence, indicate how widespread the public's failure to understand the gang violence phenomenon is" (137). For violence is one of the ways in which defiant individuals express themselves: "Much of the violence attributable to gangs is, in fact, committed by members of gangs acting as individuals rather than as agents of the organization" (141). Such violence is no doubt vicious, but it is not irrational. An example is provided by gang involvement in prostitution:

> . . . many members of gangs have set up their own prostitution businesses. If other pimps attempt to hinder them, gang members will often attack their prostitutes. In the majority of cases, the individual gang members see themselves as attacking the property of the competing pimps. This rationale makes them psychologically able to deny the guilt associated with attacking people, which they rationalize as being a natural part of business. Within this rationalization is the idea that female prostitutes are property and not individuals to be respected. This is another example of the fact that gang members are, by and large, similar to others in society who view and/or treat women as property. (158)

Gang violence, in short, is functionally necessary if gangs are going to do their work. "If the organization is to maintain itself, it must allow for some individual expressions of violence" (176).

All the characteristics of the romantic style are present in this analysis. If the self-interest of gang members appears similar to the self-interest of the capitalist, it also captures the narcissism of the romantic hero, whose romantic *weltschmerz*, Lillian Furst writes, "resides in that solipsistic self-absorption that entraps him in a vicious circle. . . . Eventually he reaches a depth of self-involution where his introverted sense of self completely distorts his perception of outer reality so that he sinks even further into himself."[15] The romantic rebel, therefore, is not really a rebel against society, however much he may disdain society's conventions, for his hostility, which can easily turn into self-hatred, serves no particular end, and certainly not the end of social reform, but becomes an excuse for its own self-perpetuation.

Jankowsi's seeming indifference to violence also resonates with the romantic's moral vision. Irving Babbitt argues that the Rousseauian romantic "is fascinated by every form of insurgency."[16] Bourgeois morality is one more symptom of the emptiness of bourgeois life. The proper moral code is not one which emphasizes right and wrong. Nor is it given to typically Protestant moral virtues such as self-control and personal responsibility. "The underlying assumption of romantic morality," Babbitt continues, "is that the personal virtues, the virtues that imply self-control, count as naught compared with the fraternal spirit and the readiness to sacrifice oneself for others" (141). Jankowski's gang members gave lip service to these romantic ideals; gang members were called "brothers" and loyalty to the family was constantly praised. But these romantic ideals had a difficult time surmounting the selfishness of gang behavior. "It is interesting," Jankowsi writes, "that gangs (as organizations) attempted to utilize a concept having to do with family, because most gang members would not really trust their own biological brothers to the degree that they attempted to get members to trust each other" (87). By the late twentieth century, the heroic romanticism of the outlaw had become the ersatz romanticism of the urban gang.

From a romantic point of view, it is also important that gang members come from the poorer segments of society. For many European romantics, borrowing an idea that originated in the Middle Ages, both the upper class and the lowest class were blessed. As César Graña writes, "One class was, so to speak, Godlike and the other Christlike, but both belonged to the transcendental order of things and revealed in their lives great teachings and great purpose."[17] All this, of course, was meant to contrast with the impoverished spirituality of the middle class, which occupied the full space of the profane even as the classes on each side touched on the sacred. Jankowski's urban poor are not quite this noble, but romanticism nonetheless enters into his account of why they are not ignoble. Our society spins a "folkloric myth" about gangs, Jankowsi argues. We are told that gangs are violent, antisocial, that they are involved in "undermining the morals and values of the society as a whole" (308). These myths are not true. "The vast majority are quite intelligent and are capable of developing and executing creative enterprises," Jankowski writes of gang members. They are no more sadistic than any other group in society; in fact, they are likely to be less so. They are not even necessarily criminal, for their activities are "labelled" illegal by society; they are, in fact, "similar to the law-abiding 'best and brightest' in our society" (312).

To the degree that romanticism is a powerful force in contemporary social criticism, it is likely to be accompanied, as it is in Jankowski's case, with ethnographic and qualitative research methods rather than with quantitative ones. The romantic world is not one which appreciates averages and norms; it seeks truth by establishing the extremes against which the norm can be judged. This creates a paradox for the romantic social critic. By their very marginality, the subjects of romantic ethnography cannot be taken as representative of the society in which they exist, but romantic critics are obviously as interested in the society that makes the margins as they are in the margins themselves. How does the critic move from the particular to the general, from local description to a truth more compelling than local description can provide? One answer, at least in Jankowski's case, is through theory.

At first glance, theory would seem to have little in common with romantic longings. Whereas romanticism often invokes a world of organic harmony, theory presupposes a world of rational inquiry and universal truth. Romanticism protests the elimination of the particular by the stultifying and leveling powers of modernity, but theory seeks uniformity and subsumes local realities under general laws. Romanticism appreciates the spontaneous and the irrational; theory has no room for the unexplainable. Romantics are poetic, while theorists aim for scientific validity. Yet despite these radical differences, many works of romantic social criticism tend to be self-consciously theoretical. This is most clearly seen in literary studies, where, under the influence of postmodernism, theoretical abstraction has reached a level that would surely shock C. Wright Mills—the great critic of abstract theory in the sociology of the 1950s. It can also be found in writings by feminist theorists on gender, which can move back and forth from the particular to the universal with astonishing ease. And it is found in a book like Jankowski's, for although Jankowski lived with and wrote about particular gangs and their members, he also wants to tell us something about the larger problems of poverty, inequality, race, and ethnicity.

Jankowsi has theoretical objectives; his first chapter is called "A Theory of Gang Behavior and Persistence." In this way, his work stands in odd contrast to classics of urban ethnography, such as *Street Corner Society* or *Talley's Corner*.[18] Those books made their indictment of society indirect; by recounting powerful local stories of particular people in particular situations, they aroused the sympathies of the reader in a way similar to the novelist's capacity to make larger statements through the

details of particular situations. But Jankowsi's characters are not especially interesting and their stories leave no lasting impression with the
reader. This is because they serve not as individuals in their own right but
as representatives of larger didactic points.

No vivid characterization emerges from Jankowski's book, for, in the
final analysis, the description of particular gang members and their behavior is not his objective. His purpose is to expose what, to him, are the
hypocrisies of American society by showing how gangs mirror all the virtues that Americans, in middle-class contexts, admire: individualism, organization, entrepreneurship. Gang behavior is "different only in scale,
not in kind, from competitive behavior observable in the corporate
world" (312–13), Jankowski writes. Whether true or not, the fact is that
Jankowski has not studied corporations, only gangs. To make the comparison, he has to move from what he knows at close range to unconvincing remarks culled from Max Weber. Gangs, Jankowski concludes,
manifest the spirit of capitalism, even though, by his own admission, they
lack the two features which Weber identified as crucial to that spirit: self-
denial and worldly asceticism. This is theory moving well beyond description, indeed, moving in opposition to description.

It is possible for a work of social science to be romantic, descriptive,
and theoretically grounded; Eric Hobsbawm's treatment of romantic
rebels meets all three criteria.[19] But this can only be achieved when the
instincts of the critic are subordinated to the skills of the social scientist.
The better trained the historian, the more acute the ethnographer, the
more sophisticated the data analyst, the more persuasive their social
criticism is—for the criticism comes from the results of the research, not
the hectoring of the author. To the degree that the critic allows untested
and unexamined theoretical instincts to override social science stric-
tures, by contrast, the resulting social criticism is often flat, unpersuasive, predictable. In Jankowski's treatment of gangs, the romantic urge to
protect them and the theoretical urge to explain them away trump the
realistic desire to understand them for what they are. By combining a romantic condemnation of the society that creates the outcasts with a theoretical account of the society's failures, the romantic social critic leaves
the reader wondering, not only whether his political judgments are trust-
worthy, but also whether his social science can be taken at face value.

As tempting as romantic rejection may be for the social critic, it is a
temptation that serves neither the cause of criticism nor the cause of
social science. Nonetheless, romanticism flourishes in contemporary social criticism—and well beyond the arenas of race and gender. Educational theorists, the true heirs of Rousseau, envision schools that will
remake personalities. Enthusiasts for immigrants romanticize cultural

differences. Unseemly realities such as pornography will be wished away. Conflict and disagreement can be overcome by communitarian longings. Ecological awareness can make us whole again. In the 1950s and 1960s—when capitalism was unregulated, racial segregation was ubiquitous, gender discrimination pervasive, and war an ever-present reality—social criticism retained its links to reality. In the 1990s—when real progress has made been made on all fronts of concern to the social critics—criticism itself becomes more romantic, more passionate, more condemnatory, and, as a result, less persuasive, at least to those who need to be persuaded. That, to say the least, is an odd outcome for forty years of social criticism.

The Realist Alternative

In contrast to romantic critics, realistic social critics try to understand the world around them, no matter how distasteful, politically objectionable, or immoral that world may be. Realism, as much a genre as romanticism, has its own style, themes, theories, and methods.

First of all, realists, like romantics, begin with the particulars of time and place. What makes people real is that they live within the boundaries that define their reality for them. In order to capture aspects of reality, the social scientist usually visits the particular place in which the people he wants to study live and work, in order to understand the real conditions of their lives. Many classics in realistic sociology, not surprisingly, were named after specific places: Middletown (actually Muncie, Indiana), Levittown, Canarsie.[20] This is a feature that realistic sociology shares with realistic fiction; both are attempts to paint portraits of very particular places. Even the quantitatively oriented social scientist with realistic inclinations tries, as much as possible, to collect data about specific communities and societies, not global or universal trends; William Julius Wilson writes primarily about Chicago, even though he, like Martín Sánchez Jankowsi, wants to make larger points about America.

It is not only a particular place that is important to the realistic temperament, but also, and especially for social critics, a place that is in the process of dissolution: Herbert Gans's West End now bears as much resemblance to the neighborhood he studied as Manchester today resembles the city that became so important for Engels. Because time passes, it is important for realistic purposes to capture the limits imposed by particular times. History for that reason has been an ally of realistic social criticism, as indeed it was for realistic novelists; in their concern for the details of everyday life during particular periods, historians have been attracted to the same distinctive features of group identity that attracted the urban sociologists of the 1920s. The realist does not imagine people living in a timeless condition; getting the period details right is the first, and for some, the only, requirement of a realist sensibility.

If realists and romantics both begin with particulars, they quickly diverge from there. In contrast to the romantic strain in social criticism, which focuses upon the outcast and the marginal, realism aims to capture the daily life of bourgeois classes, even if those classes are excluded from political participation or conditions of economic equality. The working class, one of the most bourgeois of all classes in its emphasis on productivity and just rewards, has been the favorite class of both realistic sociology and realistic history, just as Marx favored the workers over the more exotic lumpenproletariat. "While no areas are barred to the realist," George Becker writes about novelists in this tradition, "he has staked out his major claim in the area of ordinary lower-class experience, if for no other reason than that this was the subject matter which had never been adequately treated and was, preponderantly, that which was most accessible to him."[21] Realist fiction and realist sociology both study the respectable, even if, due to conditions beyond their control, the respectable find themselves treated by their society as outcasts.

It follows that realists seek to understand not the marginal exception but the representational rule. "Thus in realism there is a movement from Frye's 'high mimetic' mode to his 'low mimetic,' to a range of ordinary human beings, to the average, or, more accurately, to that portion of humanity which constitutes the mode in statistical terms" (50), Becker writes of realism in literature. Realism in social criticism is also attracted to the statistical norm; quantitative methods are more likely to be found among realists than among romantics. Survey research methods have become routine in social science and are often criticized for not accurately representing the complexities of public opinion. Whatever the merits of such a critique, though, survey methods have their origin in the efforts by Victorian social critics such as Charles Booth to grasp the conditions of real life in London.[22] In the United States, social reform efforts such as Hull House in Chicago or the photographic expressions of Jacob Riis were closely tied to realistic conceptions of social science which gathered statistics in the hopes of portraying life as it was lived. "The picture is the thing," Dreiser wrote of his fiction (cited in Becker, 59). For the social critic as well as the novelist, objectivity is enough; the pictures will tell the whole story. Social science is more than compatible with social reform; it is social reform.

There are, nonetheless, qualitative traditions associated with realism as well. Herbert Gans's ethnographic work can be read as a sharp rejoinder to the romanticism so popular among cultural critics of the 1950s. Unlike, say, a Dwight Macdonald, whose romantic longings for a more authentic society took the form of a biting critique of lower-middle-class cultural tastes, Gans wanted to show that the real people who lived in the houses made of ticky-tacky were human and deserved sympathy.[23] Qualitative methods were understood to be democratic in a cultural and not just a political sense. Those who lead ordinary lives do not generally leave behind them monuments of the culture they create; ethnographers, in writing about them, would do it for them.

Finally, realists usually emphasize the tragic side to life. Unlike the romantic hero, who bends every effort to escape the dictates of fate, realistic tragedy is a product of the tension between the individual's will and the larger social forces that frustrate that will. The events which move realistic social criticism are not a crisis of conscience within any particular character but large-scale events such as economic depressions, plant closings, natural disasters, and victory or defeat in war. A pessimistic strain runs throughout sociological realism. Events tend to be viewed as having inevitable outcomes. Those outcomes are often the opposite of what individuals themselves intend—the unintended consequences of purposive social action, as Robert Merton called the phenomenon. To the degree that realistic social scientists are attracted to theory, it is usually to one or another version of structuralism; individuals are viewed as products of the conditions that define their lives. It is not one of the primary objectives of realism to make explicit value judgments; the novel, as Stendahl put it, should have the objectivity of a court record. But there nonetheless tends to exist, in realistic social criticism, a mood which pays particular attention to the ways in which large forces continually frustrate individual efforts to develop character or take charge of one's own fate.

Just as writings on race illustrate the romantic inclinations of today's social critics, they also illustrate the realistic tendencies of the social critics of the golden age. Black Americans never doubted whether they lived in America, but they often had good reason to doubt whether they existed in the sociological portraits taken of America, especially those which took the small towns of the Midwest as the norm. The study of race relations in America therefore developed in a fully realist mode, from the early relationship between Robert Park of the University of Chicago and Booker T. Washington to that enormous collective project of social research which resulted in the publication of *An American Dilemma*.[24] Indeed one of the defining moments of contemporary realism took place when the U.S. Supreme Court, in 1954, ruled segregated schools unconstitutional in *Brown v. Board of Education*. For that decision joined together legal realism and sociological realism in a firm alliance; the courts would look behind formalities to the actual legal conditions in the land, and they would use social science evidence to help them in their investigation.

Realism traditionally has been the friend of excluded groups, since the first task of such groups was to gain the recognition in description that they knew they already had in reality. In contemporary America, realism continues to characterize the way many writers treat race; Elijah Anderson's *Streetwise* is in the qualitative tradition of the Chicago school while William Julius Wilson's work is more quantitative, but both are quintessentially realistic in their efforts to describe the conditions of inner-city poverty as graphically as their methods allow.[25] Anderson and Wilson both take pains to emphasize the fact that poverty and racial concentrations are bourgeois tragedies; inner-city residents would like nothing more than to lead lives of decent respectability, and in the recent past many of them did, but large-scale economic transformations have resulted in the perpetuation of self-destructive behavior.

I will treat controversies around race at much greater length in the chapter that follows. But it is worth emphasizing here how realistic writers such as Anderson and Wilson have been criticized as apologizing for conditions they ought to be denouncing. Many writers on race either romanticize inner-city poverty or explain self-destructive behaviors as understandable responses to conditions outside the control of the individuals who engage in them.[26] Realism, they argue, is a dangerous urge, one that not only can provide ammunition to those who want to condemn the behavior of minorities, but that can also provide sympathy for the prejudices of majorities. Caught between a realistic desire to bring minorities into the picture and a fear of the consequences of doing so, a book like Andrew Hacker's *Two Nations* verges back and forth from a classic nineteenth-century statistical portrait of reality to a romanticization of the differences between whites and blacks.[27] In the end the romantic wins.

Although I will argue in favor of realism and against romanticism throughout much of this book, realism is by no means a perfect mode of social criticism. Just as the romantic can lose the sharpness of particular characters for the sake of a larger theoretical point, realism's affiliation with structuralist theories produces a surprisingly unmoving tragic sensibility. Yes, large-scale economic forces have created a tragic situation for inner-city black males, but a genre which tends to absolve individuals from the responsibility for their actions is not going to present a convincing account of American urban poverty. Nor is it always the case that the data-driven nature of realistic social science and social criticism can resolve, or even clarify, contentious social issues. We know, thanks to work in the realistic tradition, that housing segregation is still omnipresent in America,[28] but that does not tell us whether the benefits of increased residential integration outweigh the difficulties it would produce in electing black office-holders. Realism is a necessary condition for social criticism, not a sufficient one.

Moreover, the romantic is right to believe that realism will moderate the social critic's indignation. To be sure, the realist does not confuse analysis with advocacy; the description of something is not the same as its justification. Realists are, if anything, more confident critics than romantics, for they generally have few doubts that their research will uncover the faults they are sure are there. But there the problem enters, for what happens if they do not find the faults? Realists agree to test their indignation against reality. In so doing, they must be prepared to tone down their voice if reality proves other than expected. Respect for reality inevitably adds nuance, acknowledges complexity, and questions utopian alternatives. That is why the romantic condemns the realist: how can one retain one's critical sensibility if one comes to appreciate what one ought to denounce? To which the realist can only respond: if my picture of reality is right, it will persuade; if it is wrong, it does not deserve to persuade.

There is, finally, such a thing as too much realism. Comfortable with the world as it presently exists, realism can easily lead to a complacent conservatism that drops all pretense at social criticism. Indeed realism is often the preferred style for those who question the indictments of social critics of any sort; the realities of "human nature," conservatives often claim, make impossible a society of greater equality, racial harmony, gender fairness, or ecological balance. Men are born like that. That's the way the cookie crumbles. Whites will never accept blacks. The language of realism is common enough in American culture; it is the language of those who like the world as it is. But realism cannot be pursued as an end in itself; for the social critic at least, it is a starting point, not a destination. If one believes that respect for reality teaches nuance and complexity, then realism transformed into dogma loses all claims to reality.

Realism is not a political outlook on the world. Nor is it a prewritten script. Nor does it require a particular methodology. If the world changes, so must the realist. Realism can even, in the right doses, benefit from occasional forays into romanticism; style, like politics, benefits from respect for its opponents. What makes social criticism different from literary criticism, however, is that the only societies worth criticizing are those which actually exist. For the social critic, reality has to come first.

The Return to Realism

A commitment to realism is a commitment to being old-fashioned, in almost any of the meanings of the term. Realistic fiction and realistic painting are no longer in style. Legal realism speaks to the concerns of a bygone era. The idea that we can capture reality, even by the words we speak, is considered hopelessly naive by today's philosophical avant garde. Even in international relations, *realpolitik* is undermined both by a businesslike insistence on the profit of the firm over the power of the state *and* an idealistic stress on a moral and ethical foreign policy.

If realism is increasingly considered passé, so is the golden age of social criticism—indeed of social science itself. Social science classics are now considered irrelevant by both the empirical and the postmodern tendencies in contemporary social science. Those committed to abstraction believe that the social science classics are part of the history, not the theory, of their disciplines and are as relevant to current work as Ricardo and Malthus are to current economic model-building. Those committed to postmodernism, feminism, or the politicization of social science view the classic works as irrelevant to the needs of the constituencies for whom they speak. As social science in the grand tradition goes, so does social criticism. Critics of the golden age felt the need for a realist methodology to persuade others of radical truths. Now those truths have become so accepted that realism is no longer required. Who, after all, believes that there is no such thing as a power elite or that institutions such as the schools are less than perfect? Old-fashioned social criticism, to the postmodern ear, sounds—old-fashioned.

It would be a mistake to return to the realism of social criticism's golden age, but it would not be a mistake to rethink the relationship between realism, social science, and social criticism. Intent on dismissing the possibility of reliable knowledge, certain that the marginalized possess a truth unavailable to the conventional, attracted to literary theory rather than social science, convinced that the popular has more to teach than the refined—all that is faddish in the academy pushes those who write about issues of equality and inequality, justice and fairness, difference and sameness into a romantic style which, in the name of criticism, loses its ability to explain and persuade. Realism, in a less than perfect world, remains the best ally of social critics. One of the more puzzling aspects of the world they criticize is that so many putative critics fail to recognize that truth.

TALKING ABOUT RACE

Beyond Black and White

No other issue in American life raises more complications for the social critic than race. Four or five decades ago, this was not the case. When legal segregation resulted in morally unambiguous forms of racism and discrimination, the role of social criticism was as simple as it was essential: one attacked racism in unambiguous terms and invoked the ideals of a society in which skin color became irrelevant. Because segregation was so wrong, its critic was nearly always right. Such a situation called for eloquence and passion more than analysis and explanation: Martin Luther King Jr.'s speeches, not Gunnar Myrdal's *An American Dilemma*. The texts from social criticism's golden age that stand up best on the subject of race are sermons or novels rather than social science tomes.

The situation could not be more different today. Racial conflict in America is fueled by conditions of inner-city life so at odds with the American dream that they have inspired a host of moving novelistic and ethnographic accounts;[1] but they also raise disturbing questions about the responsibility of individuals for their own fate which cannot be resolved by blaming circumstances. Black intellectuals are no longer in agreement, if ever they were, about what could be called "the civil rights agenda," which has been criticized with great effect by black conservatives. America has become more multicultural, but "minorities" are as likely to disagree with each other as they are with "majorities"—there is no "rainbow coalition" in America. Most important of all, the issue of race is no longer as morally simple as it was when segregation ruled: white racists still exist, but so do black demagogues; racial classification is defended by those who claim to be inheritors of the ideal of a color-blind society; and no one has a credible solution for sorting out how poverty and social class interact with race to produce a reality just as "wrong" as legal segregation, but one without a constitutional solution.

Under these conditions, there is still a role to play for the "classic" social critic, the person who would hold American society up to a model of full racial equality and judge it wanting. Among recent writers, Andrew Hacker best represents that model.[2] But so puzzling have the dynamics of race in America become that, in order to accomplish his objective, Hacker engages in generalizations about race that, at least to the economist Glenn Loury, seem indistinguishable from the racism that once justified second-class status for African-Americans.[3] When a white liberal speaks in favor of white racism as the explanation for America's two nations, while a black conservative denounces him, the time has come to move beyond black and white in the way we talk about black and white.

In this environment, the social critic's posture necessarily changes from the one established during the golden age. For one thing, there is more breathing room for the social critic, who can now rightfully criticize not only American society for its failures but also the groups challenging racial inequalities for their mistakes; surely the mantle of a social critic would apply to Shelby Steele, who is anything but sanguine about the motives and intentions of many who believe they are fighting for a more racially just society.[4] For another, the story told by the critic will have to be more morally nuanced, while taking cognizance of more complex social realities. If we no longer can be sure whether, in the name of racial progress, we want segregated housing and neighborhoods (to elect more black officials), segregated colleges and universities (to give blacks greater self-confidence) segregated families (so that whites will not, in adopting black children, practice cultural "genocide" on the blacks' heritage), and segregated knowledge (so that black students will have a stronger sense of black accomplishment), then the plot thickens dramatically with respect to social criticism.

It can hardly be surprising, when so little is certain, that talk about race is marked by charges of bad faith and betrayal. Yet the same uncertain atmosphere makes it possible to move toward a more realistic understanding of racial inequality and why it persists. If ever a subject cried out for more realism and less romanticism, it is the subject of race.

The Obsolescence of the Classical Critic

Andrew Hacker's *Two Nations* is a passionate effort to revive moral condemnation as the appropriate language for a discussion of race. For

Hacker, moral condemnation begins with numbers; he presents statistics which demonstrate that blacks are likely to be poorer than whites; to live in neighborhoods that whites choose to avoid; to suffer numerous debilitating diseases out of proportion to their share of the population; to live in other than two parent families; to engage in crime; to be unemployed; to receive less, and inferior, education; to go to prison; to work in the public sector; to receive welfare; and to die a violent death. When three times as many blacks as whites are unemployed, or when the chance of living in poverty is similarly three times greater if one is black than white, the case that blacks have seemingly made little progress in America seems confirmed.

Hacker's statistics, however, do not tell the whole story and in some cases tell the wrong story. *Two Nations* is an old-fashioned kind of book in the sense that it makes race, and only race, the determining factor in explaining differences between black and white. Yet the most interesting developments have been taking place not between the races but within them. Social scientists have discovered that a considerable reduction in the educational and occupational differences between blacks and whites took place since 1960; for example, 55 percent of black Americans were below the poverty line in 1959, compared to 34 percent in 1970.[5] Although considerable segregation in housing and education remained, the gains made by black Americans were "widespread and significant" in educational attainment, better jobs, and higher salaries.[6] The relatively rapid rate by which the gap between black and white was closing began to slow down in the 1980s;[7] still, the overall picture since the passage of the Civil Rights Act of 1964 was one of considerable improvement.

Of even greater importance, however, is not the difference between whites and blacks but the differences which emerged among blacks. The economic slowdowns of the 1970s left some black wage earners relatively well-off and others without jobs, producing "a significant number of prime working-age black families with incomes above $40,000 and a significant number of black families with incomes below $10,000."[8] By 1980, black males between the ages of 25 and 34 with some college education earned 80–85 percent of what whites with the same characteristics earned, while uneducated blacks were often unemployed and unemployable.[9]

An even more stunning development within the black community was the emergence of a sharp gender difference. In some occupations, minority women actually earned more than white women with similar education, while the differences between black and white men were "persistent" and "substantial."[10] Young African-Americans who have not completed high school, many of them products of single-parent families, are in desperate straits,[11] but, given the emergence of a vibrant middle class, not all black Americans are.[12] Because he compares blacks with whites rather than with each other, Hacker misses most of these developments and interprets them incompletely when he spots them.

Consider how Hacker deals with the sensitive subjects of sex and marriage. By the age of 15, 68.6 percent of black girls have had sexual intercourse, while among whites the percentage is 25.6 percent. Of the former, 40.7 percent become pregnant by age 18 compared to 20.5 percent of the latter. Not surprisingly, 63.7 percent of black births in 1988 were out of wedlock compared to 14.9 percent of white births. On the face of it, these numbers are astonishing and suggest that each race possesses quite different cultural attitudes toward sex and marriage. Not wanting to reach such a conclusion, Hacker compares percentage increases between the races. It turns out that in 1950 17.2 percent of all black households were headed by females compared to 5.3 percent for whites, or, in terms of a ratio, 3.2 times more for the one than the other. In 1990, those figures had increased to 56.2 percent and 17.3 percent, respectively, but stood in exactly the same ratio of 3.2. Furthermore, in 1950 there were 9.2 times more out-of-wedlock births among blacks than whites, whereas in 1988 the ratio had dropped to 4.3. Because "white births outside of marriage have been climbing at an even faster rate" than black ones, Hacker concludes that there is no use "lecturing only one race on its domestic duties" (72).

The problem is that Hacker is creating a ratio out of ratios, a procedure so far removed from the actual world as to be little more than a statistical artifact. The "improved" ratio between blacks and whites is a function of the increase in the absolute number of black families in trouble; the ratio between blacks and whites has to decrease, given any white increase, because there is a finite number—every single black child born in America—beyond which the comparison cannot go. What Hacker has discovered is a statistical artifact; as a ratio reaches its upper limit, it can no longer increase at the same high rate it did before it approached the limit. Charles Booth, that great Victorian cartographer of poverty, said of his opponents: "In the arithmetic of woe, they can only add or multiply, they cannot subtract or divide."[13] Hacker multiples and divides but rarely adds and subtracts.

As serious as this technical objection may be, the conclusions that Hacker draws from his comparisons are even more problematic. Fertility and illegitimacy would be charged subjects even if racial and class differences did not exist, but when they do, public discussions of their consequences require a greater appreciation for moral complexity than Hacker shows. We should, as he rightly suggests, never lecture one race on its domestic duties, but we most certainly should be concerned with the sexual behavior of *individuals*. Americans have decided that the very poor ought to be given income support paid for by the taxes of everyone else, even if our commitment is far lower than that of other countries. This support, commonly called welfare, in all likelihood does not cause higher rates of fertility and illegitimacy—certainly there is precious little academic evidence to that effect.[14] But because welfare exists, those whose tax money makes it possible have every right to be concerned by the statistics cited by Hacker; fertility patterns that are subsidized by others will inevitably be viewed differently than fertility patterns that are not. Focusing on race as the cause of untoward behavior is racist; focusing on untoward behavior, even if disproportionately manifest among specific groups, is common sense. Hacker too often ignores the difference.

Questions of fertility and illegitimacy inevitably lead to a discussion of the conditions facing the very poor. Those conditions have reached a stage of desperation wildly at odds with the promise of a humane and secure social order. They kill, often at a tragically early age, those who live under them. They are destructive to hardworking, law-abiding parents trying to raise children amidst them. They warp the character and altruism of middle-class people who come in contact with them. They are dangerous to those who stand in the way of the random bullets that are a byproduct of them. They are corrosive of the values of those trying to escape them. We cannot understand how race relations in America have changed without paying special attention to what has been called "the underclass."

When we turn our attention to the underclass, we must introduce a new kind of social criticism, for the classic model—with its emphasis on the power of racism perpetuated against innocent victims—no longer applies. This more realistic social criticism will be as unafraid to look at the reality of inner-city life as it is to look at the real causes of inner-city poverty. Two social scientists—Christopher Jencks and Elijah Anderson—provide more appropriate models for the role of social critic in an age of racial complexity than Andrew Hacker.

Few social scientists have spent as much time trying to understand the size and nature of the poorest segment of the American population as Christopher Jencks. Jencks believes—it is a passion with him—that social scientists provide objective numbers which can help resolve contentious debates over politics and morality. Masterful in the way he frames problems, collects data, and explains what he is doing to the reader, Jencks is careful to show which kinds of problems have gotten worse, which have stopped getting worse, which have gotten better, and which have stopped getting better. His instinct is to avoid any simple answer to the question of whether the "underclass" is growing, but he nonetheless, almost in spite of himself, tells us anyway: urban poverty among blacks *has* changed and *is* more intractable.[15]

Consider the problem of unemployment. Jencks argues that the unemployment rate tells us little, since it does not include those so discouraged that they have stopped looking for work, which by itself is a fairly good definition of the problem we would like to measure. Instead, Jencks examines the number of black men in their early twenties who were neither working nor in the armed forces; this figure increased from 8 percent from the 1965–69 period to 26 percent in the 1980–83 period before declining to 21 percent. More young black men, in a word, are idle than ever before. Furthermore, as we have seen, they are also not marrying. Countering these trends are some more hopeful signs: educational attainment increased among blacks over the past two or three decades, while the pattern of violent crime shows too many ups and downs to reveal a consistent pattern. But the overall picture is one in which the worst poverty in America is no longer a function of getting older, nor the by-product of frictional unemployment. Poverty, rather, has to do with people's behavior, which leads Jencks to argue, in contrast to Hacker, that "we can at least stop disparaging the moral rhetoric that black leaders must use if they are to make a dent in such problems" (142).

Elijah Anderson's study of two adjacent neighborhoods of an East Coast city also documents deteriorating conditions among the worst-off black Americans.[16] Anderson's examination of the process of "gentrification" is a perfect device for examining questions of race and class in American life, for included within the neighborhoods he examines are upper-middle-class whites, prosperous blacks, white ethnics, a Korean grocer, former hippies and community organizers, and poor blacks. Through extensive interviews and field notes, Anderson provides a realistic and convincing account of what it takes to be "streetwise" in a "mixed" urban area.

Like Jencks, Anderson is meticulous about not reaching for dramatic conclusions. He too lets his facts speak for themselves, even though his data are ethnographic rather than statistical. And those data are powerful indeed. No one, it would seem, is more aware of how the urban ghetto has changed than those who live within it. A generation ago, urban black neighborhoods contained their share of "old heads"—defined by Anderson as "a man of stable means who believed in hard work, family life, and the church" (3). Despite the importance at one time of these old heads, "a new role model is emerging and competing with the traditional old head for the hearts and minds of young boys. He is young, often a product of the street gang, and at best indifferent to the law and traditional values" (3).

Young black males—dressed in the "urban uniform" of jogging suits, expensive sneakers, broad caps, sunglasses, and heavy gold chains—are portrayed with enormous empathy by Anderson. They face a "cultural catch-22": to be accepted among their peers, they must adopt the street mannerisms that, to whites, label them as dangerous and threatening. It is to his credit that Anderson humanizes those who, for many whites, are something less than human. But the problem remains. Young black males with little to do but get into trouble are the main reason why, in Anderson's "Northton," "There's a different kind of black man today" (73). Considering how nostalgic white Americans tend to be for lost worlds of community, it is refreshing to hear one of Anderson's subjects talk about "the old days" when "everybody stayed dressed on weekends" and "they were all in school." "But see," this older black male concludes, "the new batch didn't go to school. . . . We don't have the heroes no more" (239).

No other aspect of life in "Northton" is more chilling than the influence of drugs, particularly crack cocaine. Indeed those looking for a technological answer to what has changed among the urban black poor will find it in the ability to turn cocaine into a smokeable substance capable of giving an intense, extremely addictive, and very short high. Crack cocaine destroys everything that makes a viable community possible. Friendship and trust are turned into encounters for hooking new addicts. Children "backstab" their parents by promising to do better, only to "mess up" as soon as they can. Crack "zombies," in Anderson's account, are more desperate, and more dangerous, than what used to be called "junkies" or "dopies." For one thing, they approach crime with "a new boldness"; as Anderson writes, "they seem to lack a sense of reality and the immediate consequences of their behavior" (88). Drug dealers take special pride in turning the better girls—the ones who are too proud for the streets—into "coke whores," who will do anything for a puff on "the glass dick" (88). The old heads and strong women of Northton look on in shock and dismay as crack establishes a new status hierarchy in the community. "These drugs are ruining the community," one old head told Anderson. "They done ruined it. People break into each other's cars, they walk the street, might knock you in the head. They trying to get that dope" (100).

Neither Anderson nor Jencks is out to develop a worst-case scenario. Both are careful to insist that much of what they find is due to class, not race. Each finds sources of strength in the black community. (For Jencks, it is increasing levels for educational attainment; Anderson describes the efforts of one resident determined to halt the effects of crack cocaine.) Yet precisely because both men are social science realists, their accounts are more convincing than Hacker's. Consider just one point of comparison: teenage mothers. The chances that an inner-city black teenager who gives birth can rise out of poverty are close to nonexistent. Anyone concerned with the life chances of such a person would want to warn her of the dangers she faces if she is sexually promiscuous, does not use birth control, and is unwilling to have an abortion. What, then, is the appropriate language to use in this situation?

Hacker's language is sentimental:

> They believe that having a baby to love will provide a focus for their lives. Given the surroundings so many of them have known, life offers few other options. So the act of reproduction becomes a way to validate yourself as a productive human being. Also, it offers a sphere of independence, including selecting its clothing and deciding how late it can stay up at night. Not least is the freedom to choose—or, even better, to make up—the baby's name. (78)

If this picture seems unrealistic, Anderson fills in the appropriate details; sexually active by the age of twelve, girls in "Northton" often have their first babies by the age of fifteen or sixteen. The father, who months ago spun dreams of consumption and leisure, wanders off with other males, bragging about his sexual exploits and leaving the girl to turn to her own family and peer group for support. The "baby club" thus becomes an element of life in "Northton," as girls praise each other's babies and give what support to each other they can. But there is a harsh, competitive edge to these encounters; the baby having become the only thing of value in a girl's life, "the young mother often feels the need to dress her baby in the latest and most expensive clothes 'that fit' (rather than a size larger that the baby can grow into)" (125). After a while, the baby, so important to the young mother, becomes a burden, an obstacle to fun and further sexual adventure. But mothers and sisters can tire of the work involved, creating a special role for grandmothers, some of them in their mid-thirties, who "may simply informally adopt the baby as another one of her own" (128). Obviously this is not the whole picture. There are stable families in even the most desperate neighborhoods, and some fathers will accept paternity. But the overall pattern is one that seems destined to produce infants who, in fifteen years, will reproduce the despair of their own childhood.

There is an important lesson for social criticism in these diverse treatments of race in America. Social science usually tells a more nuanced story than moral condemnation. Jencks and Anderson are social scientists of very different stripes: one quantitative, the other qualitative. Yet their methodological differences disappear in the face of their commitment to getting reality right. That reality does not fit a sermonizing mode. As important as it may be to place blame where blame is due—surely white racism is responsible for persistent housing segregation or the disproportionately small number of blacks in certain job categories—the argument that only one race is at fault for the problems facing blacks lacks the authenticity necessary for a serious discussion of how further progress can occur.

Explanations of Racial Disparity

It is one thing to describe what has happened but a far more difficult one to account for why it did. Three general explanations of why the conditions of life for the black urban poor are so miserable can be found in the social science literature. They can be characterized as the white racism view, the structural account, and the moral character emphasis.

That white racism is the single most important reason for black poverty is a point of view that received more or less official recognition with the report of the Kerner Commission, established in 1968 by President Johnson to investigate the reasons for black rioting.[17] Depending on which version of the theory one chooses, the general line of argument runs as follows. Slavery was only an extreme form of the fear whites have toward blacks. The legal segregation that followed slavery has broken down, but it has been replaced by an unofficial, but nonetheless powerful, form of racism that leads whites to take any measures necessary to preserve their sense of superiority to blacks. At the psychological level, white fears about blacks are irrational and stereotypical reactions that seek simple answers to complex problems. At the social level, white choices about housing and schools reflect a desire to protect racial homogeneity, even when to do so is counter to economic self-interest. At the political level, the 1980s and 1990s constituted a counter-revolution in which reactionary politicians brazenly manipulated symbols such as Willie Horton to mobilize the anger of white ethnics, thereby permitting them to redistribute income to the rich. Blacks, therefore, cannot be blamed for the problems they face. Any changes that have to be made will have to come from whites, who will have to give up the privileges that come with the color of the skin.

Andrew Hacker adopts the white racism theory to account for black poverty. "From slavery through the present," he writes, "the nation has never opened its doors sufficiently to give black Americans a chance to become full citizens" (23). Hence segregated housing is "residential apartheid" that is "imposed" on blacks in ways different from those affecting any other ethnic or racial group (35). American schools "focus mainly on the achievements of white people" (40). Moreover, schools are segregated because of "the attitudes and actions of white parents, who have made it clear that they will accept integration only on the most minimal of terms" (162). Hypertension, asthma, and AIDS—all of which affect the black community disproportionately—are "not simply due to poverty" but also reflect "the anxieties that come with being black in America" (46). "The strains that come with being black put extra burdens on a marriage" (75), and therefore contribute to high rates of female-headed households and out-of-wedlock births. Because "it is white America that has made being black so disconsolate an estate," Hacker concludes that "the question for white Americans is essentially moral: is it right to impose on members of another race a lesser start in life, and then to expect from them a degree of resolution that has never been demanded from your own race?" (218–19).

No one can disagree with Hacker's assertion that "something called racism obviously exists" (19). Patrick Buchanan is only the latest of a line of politicians that instinctively understand white fears and play directly to them. Ugly, demeaning episodes erupt on even the most liberal campuses and in suburban neighborhoods proud of their tolerance. The instinct to protect white turf in New York is as powerful as it is primitive.[18] We are obsessed by race, always and at all times aware of the racial composition of those around us.[19] Yet the argument for white racism as the cause of what has gone wrong among the urban poor increasingly wears thin as social scientists investigate the complexity of human behavior. Two areas in particular illustrate the limits of too intense a focus on white racism: crime and resistance to affirmative action.

If there is any one reason why whites distance themselves from blacks, it is because they fear violent crime. In 1990, according to Hacker, 61.2 percent of all arrests for robbery, and 54.7 percent of all arrests for murder and manslaughter, were of blacks. This means that blacks were arrested five times more than their percentage of the population for the one crime and four and a half times more for the other. Now arrest rates do not measure crime per se, for not all criminals are arrested, and police forces generally show a tendency to arrest blacks more willingly than whites. Still, surveys of victims in general match the arrest ratios for the most violent crimes (except rape); 69.3 percent of those surveyed by the FBI in 1989 said that those who robbed them were black, while 53.1 percent of all murders committed in 1990 were by blacks. It is obviously a manifestation of racism for a white person to believe that every black male walking toward him is going to commit a robbery or a murder. But is it racism, given these differences in the racial composition of crime, to choose to live in a neighborhood that has a reputation for safety—even if in choosing a mostly white neighborhood, one abandons the worst areas in the inner city primarily to poor blacks? For most parents of small children, for elderly people, for anyone but the most altruistic and idealistic, for the middle class of both races, there can only be one answer.

Yet Hacker offers another. From his perspective, whites tend to ignore crime by members of their own race and focus disproportionately on black criminality. This enabled the Republican Party to rely on Willie Horton to help elect George Bush in 1988. After all, Hacker writes, Michael Dukakis "had not been directly aware of Horton's eligibility for a furlough" (179) when the man was released from prison. But the Willie Horton episode, as Thomas and Mary Edsall have pointed out, symbolized liberal blindness toward crime more than it did racism.[20] Horton was a first-degree murderer who killed a seventeen-year-old gas station attendant. Dukakis, in 1976, vetoed a bill that would have excluded first-degree murderers from the state's furlough program—itself a product of liberal concern with prisoners' rights. On his tenth weekend furlough, Horton broke into a home, cut the man he found there twenty-two times and raped his fiancée when she returned home. Republicans were no doubt cynical in their use of the Horton issue, but it was not irrational for white voters to respond. They sensed that those who attribute white fears of black criminals to the psychological disposition of the former rather than the actual behavior of the latter are incapable of having an honest discussion of the relationship between race and crime.

Nor can resistance to affirmative action be attributable to white racism, if for no other reason than the appearance of doubts among blacks as well as whites.[21] Christopher Jencks helps us understand why affirmative action is too complex a policy to be treated in simple liberal (or conservative) terms. On the one hand, affirmative action did not necessarily produce dramatic new employment possibilities for blacks; Jencks demonstrates, rather, that affirmative action helped perpetuate a dual labor market among black males: those with steady jobs were helped, but a greater number of black males could not find steady jobs. At the same time, the political resistance to affirmative action among whites increased because most people knew of cases where whites were passed over for blacks. "As a result," Jencks writes of affirmative action, "both whites and blacks now see themselves as victims of discrimination" (58), an outcome difficult to square with the proposition that affirmative action failed because racist whites did not want blacks to find jobs. Now that a national campaign against affirmative action has become a reality, there will inevitably be efforts to see it as a new manifestation of white racism. Yet a policy never subject to national debate—and one, moreover, adopted in spite of specific assurances during the passage of the Civil Rights Act that it would never occur[22]—requires a debate at some point; racism may be an element in the opposition to affirmative action, but it is only an element.

Racism, in short, remains a powerful force in American society, and we would be foolish to deny its importance. But you cannot explain a variable with a constant; if whites are, and have always been, racist, neither the deterioration among very poor blacks nor the improvement among middle-class blacks makes sense. The white racism theory is especially unable to deal with the latter of these developments. Those who adhere to such a thesis generally put themselves in the position of denying that any real progress in race relations has been attained. Sometimes this denial of progress becomes absurd, as when Hacker writes, with considerable illogic: "While lynchings are no longer used as means of control, anxieties over interracial sex have far from abated" (62). At other times, the theory is highly selective. Hacker argues, for example, that the more the Democratic Party incorporates black constituencies and black concerns, the more it becomes a minority party in presidential elections. One can blame that on white racism, but it is also the case that black officeholders may prefer holding more seats in a minority party than fewer seats in a majority party—a phenomenon for which racism cannot be the explanation.

A second category of explanations for the persistence of black poverty is structural, emphasizing the loss of jobs in the black community as a result of large-scale change in the economy. All such accounts exist in the shadow of the work of William Julius Wilson, who has demonstrated meticulously, street by street, how factory closings in Chicago have devastated lives in the underclass. Wilson's thesis is that the mismatch between jobs and workers is the primary cause of what we are witnessing; jobs exist in the suburbs, black workers in the city. The costs of bringing the two together are too high, and urban blacks pay those costs.[23]

Lawrence Mead, a New York University political scientist, has serious reservations about such structural theories. Mead believes that unemployment in urban black ghettos is part of "a watershed in America's experience, and increasingly that of the West as a whole."[24] Out of the Great

Depression emerged a political configuration in which the distribution of work became the major issue facing the country; some had more, at higher wages, and some had less, at lower wages. Labor and capital fought bitterly over how jobs and wages would be distributed, but they all agreed that jobs were the key. No longer. Mead posits a "new politics of poverty," one that accompanies the existence of a class unlikely ever to be anything but poor. It is not the distribution of work, but whether work itself can be required, that defines this new politics. "On the whole," Mead writes, "the immigrant poor of old were poor *despite* work, while the current poor are needy for *lack* of it" (6). Those who do not work, unlike those who work for low wages, are dependent on taxpayers. The new politics of poverty thus shifts from a struggle between capital and labor to issues involving government and taxation.

With this shift, issues of character and capacity become part of the politics of dependency. Americans, Mead believes, are wedded to what he calls the "competence assumption" (19–21). If you are viewed as in charge of yourself, you will not generally need the beneficence of others. If you are incompetent through no fault of your own, you can expect others to help you. But if you are competent and unwilling to take charge of your life, no one can be expected to be your keeper. The new politics of poverty turns against those who fail the competence test: they can work, they choose not to, and hence most Americans increasingly, and in Mead's view rightly, are fed up with them.

It ought to be clear why someone committed to this point of view would not find structural theories compelling, for such theories locate the cause of unemployment, and therefore poverty, in forces outside the control of individuals. To prove his point, Mead takes every single aspect of a structural theory of poverty and attempts to refute it. Are wages too low? There are certainly jobs that pay little, but, Mead asks, "why does one *quit* work when one cannot make ends meet? It is not a reaction that struggling middle-class Americans are likely to understand" (83). Are jobs available? "at least low-paid work is readily available, at least to those seeking work at a given time" (85). Does discrimination bar access to employment? "it is difficult to believe that many competent black workers are being denied opportunity" (114). Is childbirth an obstacle to employment? A hodgepodge child-care system "seems generally adequate for purposes of employment" (123), and "the difficulties that children pose for working mothers appear to be far more manageable than is often supposed" (119).

Mead, like Hacker and Jencks, documents his claims by citing statistical evidence. Some of those statistics are surprising and back Mead's case, such as survey data he cites to the effect that large numbers of poor people believe work to be available, even when they themselves do not have it. But in general Mead's analysis is similar to Hacker's, in that both authors want to make a case for a single cause of black poverty—white hostility in the one case, an unwillingness to accept jobs that do exist in the other—and interpret their data accordingly.

The mismatch thesis itself illustrates the overdetermined quality of Mead's argument. Wilson's point that jobs have left inner cities seems intuitively obvious to anyone who spends time in them; empty factories line the street, public transportation to suburban industrial parks does not exist, whatever jobs are available are for the very young at McDonald's, and, as a result, large numbers of black men stand around on street corners during the day. Intuitions can be wrong; careers are made in social science by demonstrating that they are. But to overcome a popular misconception—one founded on something that most people believe they can see with their eyes—statistical evidence must be more than just neutral between the intuitive understanding and the theory being offered by the social scientist.

Mead has no such convincing data. First, he argues that proponents of the mismatch theory "have failed to demonstrate a causal connection between economic restructuring and non-work" (100). This is a peculiar point; not only is causal determination impossible with statistics, but the burden is on Mead to undermine the theory, not on its proponents to nail its truth down beyond the possibility of attack. Next Mead himself uses numerous qualifiers. "The fall in employment *might* result from the population abandoning older cities, especially ghetto areas, rather than factories abandoning workers" (100). It might, and it might not, and it is not clear whether it matters. Then Mead says that the mismatch theory "may explain *part* of the inner-city non-work problem" (103), but only in places like Chicago, Newark, Philadelphia, Detroit, New York, and Cleveland— places which, he argues "do not typify American cities (103)," as if Phoenix or Seattle do. Finally, Mead's ultimate sentence on this topic, if analyzed carefully, says little or nothing: "Inability to reach jobs, therefore, *appears* to play only an incidental role in the problem of nonworking poverty considered nationally (103)." Given all these qualifications, no case is ever made that popular intuitions concerning job loss in the black ghetto are wrong.

The same kinds of problems exist with the remainder of Mead's points. Can poor mothers find affordable child-care so that they can work? The overwhelming answer from nearly every quarter is that they cannot. Mead argues that they can—or so it seems. He actually concludes that the difficulties are less difficult than usually proclaimed, which means that they can still be quite impossible in a practical sense. Moreover Mead

feels quite strongly that poor mothers *should* find work, an odd point of
view for him, since, as we shall see shortly, he believes in the need to inculcate moral character, which is usually done in families. (Women who
work have less time to teach discipline and instill moral maxims in their
children.) I came away from his book convinced that those who argue
that an obligation to work should never be part of the social contract over
welfare are myopic, if not disingenuous; many welfare mothers, Mead
documents carefully, do work. But knowing how hard it is for my own
middle-class family to find affordable and adequate child-care, I would
require far more evidence than Mead provides before I was prepared to
conclude that the lack of child-care is not an obstacle to female work
among the urban poor.

   The New Politics of Poverty, like Hacker's *Two Nations*, conflates the difference between the urban black poor and the urban black working class.
Jobs are available for the one, although recent cutbacks in government
are making them less available (Mead pays insufficient attention to the
fact that blacks, far more than whites, work in the public sector). But for
the other group, even a rapid infusion of low-paying jobs would make
little difference so long as the conditions bred by extreme poverty continue to exist. It is difficult to avoid the conclusion that Mead is so focused
on numbers that he fails to understand the actual, everyday conditions of
life among the urban poor. He should have learned something from
Christopher Jencks. "All . . . ideologies lead to bad social policy" (20),
Jencks writes in the introduction to *Rethinking Social Policy*, concluding
that "The ongoing quest for internal consistency that I see as the hallmark
of any successful ideology makes realism extremely difficult" (21). Mead
demonstrates, inadvertently to be sure, that realism can be as absent on
the right as it often is on the left; anyone who appreciates the realities of
balancing work and child-raising on a minimal income would know that
even working families can who obey all the right moral rules can remain
poor. Liberals like Hacker have no monopoly on ideological explanation.
In taking a direct look at poverty, Mead is in the realistic tradition of social criticism. But in pursuing his analysis in a relentlessly ideological
fashion, he undermines his realistic sensibility. His reader is forced to
ask: is this the reality or the ideology speaking? All too often the latter
seems to be winning.

   It is important for Lawrence Mead to demonstrate that people, even
among the urban poor, are potentially competent, for his aim is to rein-
troduce questions of character and moral behavior: the third of the explanations for black urban poverty being considered here. For Mead,
dependency has a "wider meaning" (210), one that literally demands "a
new tradition, even a new political theory" (211). For at least two centu-

ries a fundamental assumption of Western politics has been that people always exist in some kind of Newtonian motion that moves them up and down the economic scale. If people cannot move up, it is because some impediment is in place, and one task of liberal democratic politics is to remove those impediments. Such a tradition, rooted in assumptions of self-reliance, is becoming obsolete, Mead argues, because there are ever larger numbers of people who are not self-reliant. That is why "we need a new political language in which competence is the subject instead of the assumption. We need to know how and why the poor are deserving, or not, and what suasions might influence them" (239).

Mead's new language, however, is remarkably like our—and England's—old one. Most nineteenth-century discussions of poverty were in fact discussions of morality. Charles Booth, for one, would, in Gertrude Himmelfarb's words, "have rejected the antithesis between morality and science. . . . He would not have understood why it was scientific to regard low wages as a cause of poverty, but not intemperance or improvidence."[25] Mead is quite incorrect to stress the end of the Western tradition and the need for a new political theory; in current debates around poverty and moral character, we find ourselves right in the heart of the Western tradition. But if we look beyond Mead's occasionally apocalyptic remarks, he is quite right to argue for the importance of morality and character in politics. For all liberal societies are premised on a contract. (The terms of and parties to the contract are usually what is at stake in liberal debates, not the existence of the contract itself.) If one party violates those terms—or is even perceived to violate them—all hell breaks loose.

Contractual understandings of the social order require that the parties to the contract be understood as rational, in control of their passions, and responsible for the consequences of what they do. These are often stern requirements. To adhere to them, we expect people to rise above external temptation and internal weakness of will. Is it fair to have such expectations of the very poor, whose conditions of life seem so far removed from the traditions of Protestant rectitude out of which contractual liberalism grew? James Q. Wilson—whose Catholic upbringing in Southern California is also far removed from John Locke's England—believes that it is. Wilson is one of those rare social scientists willing to take on difficult questions of moral behavior; his book *The Moral Sense,* which I will discuss in Chapter 10, is a major effort to revive the moral principles associated with David Hume and Adam Smith. But Wilson has also published many of his essays—the earliest from 1967, the latest from 1991—devoted to the theme that "a modest American concern for good manners and personal decency seems the height of democratic sensibility."[26]

Wilson attributes many of the problems facing American society to "the working out of the logical consequences of the Enlightenment" (37). He argues that, especially in the universities and among leftist intellectuals, what had once been a liberal doctrine emphasizing self-control was turned into a doctrine emphasizing self-expression. There were sources of resistance to the emergence of cultural patterns emphasizing unrestrained freedom, especially in ethnic communities and in the Long Beach of his youth. There still are parents who know the right way to punish children. Some schools still teach values. But, overall, far too many Americans now lack character. And nowhere is this lack more seriously felt that among the urban black poor.

> The folk culture of urban blacks . . . was and is aggressive, individualistic, and admiring of semiritualistic insults, sly tricksters, and masculine display. This popular culture may have been a reaction against the repressive and emasculating aspects of slavery; whatever its origin, it was not a culture productive of a moral capital off which people could live when facing either adversity or affluence. (36)

This insistence that we look at people's moral character has touched off a war of words among social scientists. Whereas Mead thinks that we ought to develop a political vocabulary in which deservedness would occupy a central position, Herbert Gans argues that the concept of the undeserving poor is simply a "stereotype" which only turns attention away from "the more basic faults and social fault lines in America."[27] Or, as Michael Katz puts it, "most extreme poverty arises from economic and social forces, from sickness and disability, or from childhood and old age, but not from character. No sharp line divides the very poor from the rest of us; the distinction between the worthy and unworthy poor has always been a convenient but destructive fiction."[28] In more recent years, this debate has focused on the term "underclass." Gans proposes that it "is a code word that places some of the poor *under* society and implies that they are not or should not be *in* society."[29] Katz assembled a group of historians who "do not accept the word *underclass* as an appropriate description of the conditions about which they write."[30] For writers of this inclination, progress lies in drawing a line between the social scientific discussion of economic inequality and questions of morality. Honesty, discipline, sobriety—or criminality, licentiousness, and sinfulness—all such character traits are, in their view, randomly distributed throughout the population. To discuss poverty in the context of character is to return us to the hypocritical world of the poorhouse.

As is often the case with debates of this sort, the real issue is not whether we talk about the "underclass," or "the undeserving poor," but how we do so. Gans and Katz can be criticized because their point of view insufficiently appreciates the struggles on the part of the very poor who *do* have character; we ought to congratulate those who overcome extreme poverty rather than develop a language that cannot acknowledge their achievements. But this is not the major point. What is really at issue is whether some of us have any right to pass moral judgment on others. Some believe we do not; Andrew T. Miller, a contributor to Michael Katz's collection on the underclass, believes that white families are so pathological that they disallow any negative comments on black families.[31] But surely, so long as we all live in the same society, we have an obligation to judge each other. For no contract has only one party. The denial of the importance of morality and character, in not permitting us to make judgments about others, denies our ability to make judgments about ourselves.

If the real question is not whether we make judgments about others but how, James Q. Wilson also leads us in the wrong direction. Wilson, indeed, gives the Gans and Katz position a certain credibility, for he most certainly takes the moral values of one particular group in the population and extends them to everyone. It is refreshing, in this age of pious politeness toward the Other, to read an unabashedly frank defense of a world that kept people of color at a distance, denied women some fundamental venues of self-advancement, and brought up children to be clones of their parents, but such nostalgia ought not to be offered as part of a serious social theory touching on some of the most sensitive issues of the day.[32]

Wilson, in short, is right to be concerned with character. But he does so in a way that is far too limited. "Like multiplication and grammar," he writes, "morality is largely learned by rote" (35). Obedience, for sure, is learned by rote, but it is by no means clear that morality is. Strongly influenced by behaviorism, Wilson's psychology fails to grasp a veritable revolution in that discipline's understanding of the construction of the moral self. Increasingly, we are learning that an individual's moral character is formed by narrative and culture. Contracts between us are not enforced by laws or economic incentives; people adhere to social contracts when they feel that behind the contract lies a credible story of who they are and why their fates are linked to those of others.

Neither side in the debate over the underclass offers such a story. Those who occupy the "hard" position of insisting on obligation rightly appreciate morality but wrongly insist on obedience. Those on the "soft" side understand pernicious authority but are antagonistic to morality. We ought to carry forward the nineteenth-century concern with the deserving and undeserving poor, but we also ought to change the terms of what it means to "deserve." The extreme urban poor deserve our attention and care. But we deserve respect for life, law, and the rewards of individual achievement. If a new social contract is to be negotiated that will make it possible for Americans of all races and classes to live together in peace, it will have to see adherence on both sides. Jencks, as usual, has it right when he says:

> The unwritten moral contract between the poor and the rest of society is fragile at best. We usually treat the poor badly, they often treat us badly, and perhaps worst of all, they often treat each other badly. But the solution cannot be to tear up the moral contract or to deny that the poor are responsible for their own behavior. That approach must eventually lead to a Hobbesian war of all against all. The only viable solution is to ask more of both the poor and the larger society. (141)

Realism and Racism

Social science research about race seems to tell two stories simultaneously. One of them calls attention to the persistence of significant differences between the races in American life. Housing is the most conspicuous example. Whites may find themselves encountering more blacks in the workplace, but, given a suburban majority in the United States, residence remains the one area of American life in which classic patterns of segregation remain substantially unchanged.[33] In addition, there took place during the 1980s a slowdown in the rate at which black Americans were improving their economic lot.[34] The picture, in short, is anything but one of full equality between the races. Even among well-off blacks, stories of police harassment and everyday discrimination continue to be told.[35] America is certainly a long way from living with racial peace, equality, and harmony.

Yet social science has another story to tell as well. White Americans, when surveyed on these kinds of questions, indicate strong support for integration, support so strong that it cannot be simply written off as a subtle dismissal of a deeper underlying racism.[36] Affirmative action is deeply disliked, but this can reflect support for the historic ideal of a color-blind constitution as much as it can opposition to blacks.[37] Along these lines, Paul Sniderman and Thomas Piazza argue that white opposition to the black leadership's agenda does not represent racism but rather antagonism to liberal solutions which rely on expensive government programs.[38] However far America may be from solving its racial problems, it has come a long way since *Brown v. Board of Education.*

Has it come far enough for the realism of social science to replace the denunciation of classic social criticism? There is a danger in trying to move the conversation on race in a more realistic direction. Many writers who have long expressed skepticism about the possibility of equality, let alone racial equality, speak a language of realism; for example, the authors of *The Bell Curve* pepper their analysis of data with comments about how they, unlike liberal romantics, are able to look at reality face-to-face.[39] Realism with respect to race could turn into resignation: Look, the realist says, white people are just not going to put up with the pathologies which, rightly or wrongly, they associate with blacks. That's tough, but so is life.

In the face of that kind of realism, believers in racial equality often tend either to deny that any pathologies exist or to blame them on whites' attitudes toward blacks, Yet these reactions are not so different from the one they oppose. Romanticism is also a kind of resignation: the notion that the realities of inner-city life are so untoward that they cannot be discussed honestly strips from the inner-city poor their right to be treated exactly as they are. Groups which are sentimentalized are treated unequally; equality is not possible until faults can be acknowledged as well as virtues. The Herrnstein-Murray version of realism and the ideas of romantic multiculturalists are not that far apart on one issue: both, obsessed with race, imagine a world in which individuals are rarely treated as themselves, rather than as members of the groups to which they belong.

Realism must be a two-way street. Public policies guided by reciprocal realism would combine an insistence on behavioral change with the political leadership and financial means necessary to challenge white resistance. They would demand of the left that it take seriously white fears, while demanding of the right that it take seriously black despair. We will find such national solutions only when a Lincolnesque figure willing to heal our wounds emerges. In the meantime, social critics and social scientists can get the conversation started by speaking in the most honest way they can about a subject that has resisted honest conversation for as long as anyone can remember.

THINKING ABOUT GENDER

Theory and Description

Gender competes with race (and class) as one of the irresistible topics of contemporary social criticism. But although race, class, and gender are usually invoked as a trinity of concerns about injustice in America, they are rarely treated with equal emphasis or in the same manner. Class, for one thing, usually drops out of the picture.[1] In the real world, Marx's proletariat has little sympathy for the plight of women, gays, and blacks; yesterday's oppressed worker is today's angry white male. Nor are race and gender treated in similar ways. When social critics deal with race, the emphasis tends to be on empirical description, not theory. To be sure, there are efforts to theorize about what racism is and why it takes the form it does,[2] but racism, to most observers, is so transparent a wrong that relatively little attention is devoted to explaining why it exists. For all of its length and often ponderous prose, *An American Dilemma* established the model of social criticism that would flourish long after its publication: a contrast between what a racially just world would resemble and how America actually looked.

If the balance between description and theory in matters of race leans toward the former, in matters of gender it leans toward the latter. Many of the well-known descriptions of the inequalities faced by women— starting with the classic work of Betty Friedan—have been written by nonacademics.[3] Academic feminists, by contrast, spend far more time theorizing about patriarchy than most writers on race spend theorizing about racism. This is not universally the case; there are feminist social scientists who have done fine-grained ethnography, documenting the actual lives of women in the real world,[4] just as others have used quantitative methods to address some of the fundamental issues of American society, from comparable worth to gender discrimination in employment.[5] Moreover, the feminist contribution to historical studies has been an outstanding one; the entire field of American history has been revitalized by feminist historians.[6] Yet the bulk of feminist scholarship in the university, especially in the humanities, has been marked by its reliance on European, primarily French, theorists whose work is guided by philosophical speculation much more than by empirical analysis.

Strongly influenced by postmodernism, feminist theory has been speculative, imaginative, often audacious. But it has also adopted a romantic and utopian stance, which has produced a body of work that has an odd relationship with the tradition of social criticism. Critical this work surely is: it finds considerable flaws with a "gendered" society and offers a radical alternative to it. But both the criticism and the alternative, divorced from reality as they are, lack persuasiveness, as if the critic is writing only for the already convinced, not for those seeking to understand and to change gender relationships.

To criticize books written by humanists for their failure to take reality into account would hardly be fair; works of the imagination require criticism of the imagination. But the pervasiveness of theory in feminist studies has spilled over from the humanities into the social sciences, where its presence is more problematic. Social scientists gather data, conduct experiments, or analyze the data of others, but in all cases they have an obligation to understand the practices they are examining, even if—one could say especially if—their objective is to criticize them. Yet feminists have explicit political goals; they know that patriarchy is wrong and that women will be better off once it is abolished. How successful have feminist social scientists been in linking their empirical work to their normative concerns?

In this chapter I examine the work of three feminist social scientists: psychologists Sandra Bem and Helen Haste and sociologist Judith Lorber. Each of these writers has made important contributions to social science. But, influenced by their feminist sympathies, they have all chosen to write books seeking larger explanations of why men dominate women. In these books, theory takes over from research and romanticism takes over from realism; anxious to understand the persistence of patriarchy, all three writers go far beyond the evidence that they, or any other scholars, have assembled, leading then down the paths of inconsistency, speculation, and utopia-building. The result is a new genre of academic writing which is neither social science nor social criticism. When compared to the realistic and empirically grounded way in which Christopher Jencks and Elijah Anderson have dealt with race, scholarship dealing with gender in the social sciences all too often leaves reality behind in ways that cannot help, and could even harm, the women whose interests it presumes to serve.

Gender Means Everything/

Gender Means Nothing

Sandra Lipsitz Bem is a highly regarded experimental psychologist who questions whether differences between the genders are real. In the Bem Sex Role Inventory (BSRI), which she first developed in 1971, respondents were asked to rank on a seven-point scale the degree to which a number of attributes—assertive, tender, understanding, independent—applied to them.[7] By scoring the results in accord with conventional understandings of gender difference, the respondents could then be ranked according to their masculinity or femininity. The objective of the BSRI, in today's terms, was to "deconstruct" the concepts of male and female by demonstrating how many people were neither—or, with later refinements, both. One of the major conclusions of Bem's research was that androgyny was far more common than anyone who walked around with fixed images of male and female roles would believe.

In Bem's account, the BSRI served two goals simultaneously: science and therapy. On the one hand, scientific psychology had gotten gender wrong by assuming fixed categories. Gender roles were not, as many psychologists believed, inherent aspects of human personality; they were, as she puts it in *The Lens of Gender* (winner of the 1993 Best New Book in Psychology award from the Association of American Publishers) "cultural stereotypes to which people conformed at their own peril."[8] Because they were anything but fixed, moreover, strict gender roles were unnecessary for adequate mental health:

> whereas it had been assumed that mental health required men to be masculine and women to be feminine, now it was being suggested not only that everyone could be both masculine and feminine but, even more important, that standards of mental health should be genderless. (121)

If ideas about gender are not fixed in the personality, where do they come from? Bem argues that these roles are something we internalize as children and make our cognitive property, even if we never recognize what we are doing. Her book suggests that the ways in which institutions, cultures, and people deal with gender difference are filtered through three invisible assumptions which she hopes to make visible: *androcentrism,* the belief that male ideals are universals to which women should conform; *polarization,* the belief that men and women are so different that all aspects of society should be organized on different bases; and biological *essentialism,* the belief that these differences are rooted in anatomy or genetic factors. The bulk of her book is devoted to showing why all three lenses are myopic, although, from the start, Bem realizes that some criticisms of gender polarization are androcentric and that some forms of feminism are gender-polarizing.

In some prehistoric time biology may have played a role in originating gender difference, according to Bem, but that time is long past. Women are more likely to be care-givers, especially to infants, but this is due to centuries of socialization, not any particularities of women's bodies; any credible explanation of gender difference must rely on the contribution that culture makes to biology. Bem's account of androcentric ideas is somewhat different; she does not try to disprove them but to show how common they have been in Western culture, as she, in the best part of her book, traces them through the Bible, Aristotle's philosophy, Freud's writings, and U.S. Supreme Court decisions. Gender polarization, finally, is a problematic idea because, as her research convinces her, male and female are not distinct categories. Bem concludes that men and women learn their sex roles by internalizing the assumptions of androcentrism, polarization, and essentialism, no matter how false these assumptions may be.

Helen Haste has made important contributions to understanding the making of moral personalities.[9] Her most recent book, like Bem's, goes beyond her particular discipline to larger reflections on how a gendered world came to be.[10] For Haste, gender is not a lens but a metaphor. Gender oppression is pervasive and reproduces itself so effortlessly because it has been incorporated into our language and, in that way, into our thought. Each of us is a "lay theorist"; we make sense out of the world by thinking and acting on the basis of theories about how the world works. When we want to move between what we know and what we do not, we find metaphors seductively waiting to take us across the bridge into new realms of experience.

Consider, Haste invites us, the metaphor of Man the Hunter. Repeated enough times and in enough ways, the notion that at one time men hunted while women cooked what they caught becomes, not a story about reality, but reality itself. The power of this, or any other, metaphor, lies in its duality. In Western culture, Haste argues, we divide things into themselves and their opposites; hence we understand woman as the opposite of man, not as something in her own right. Dualistic metaphors protect us from the darkest fears we confront, such as losing our reason, being absorbed in the other, or raging out of control. To challenge the dichotomy between male and female is therefore to question everything; in searching for more authentic metaphors, feminists must take on reason itself.

Haste calls for a "cultural feminism" that goes well beyond the rationalistic prognosis of liberal and socialist versions, which seek only to replace one kind of order with another. Cultural feminism subverts gender categories by holding them up to ridicule, as, we are told, Madonna does in every performance. It asks women to fight, not only for equality of wages or access to power, but also for an *anti-logos*, a determined effort at "deconstructing and changing the fundamental principles on which we base lay social theory and folk modes of gender" (105). Even Sandra Bem's work is insufficient for this task, for although it "broke the metaphor of duality and polarity," it nonetheless "took for granted traditional descriptions of masculine and feminine traits" and "was closer to rationalist reconstruction than to finding new authenticity" (13). A substantial portion of Haste's book is devoted to a friendly critique of other feminisms for not digging deeply enough into culture, a realm that, in contrast to the economy or the polity, inevitably reaches the hearts of darkness upon which sexuality touches.

Judith Lorber's *The Paradox of Gender* is the most ambitious of these recent efforts to theorize about gender.[11] Lorber argues that gender is both a status assigned to individuals and a way of organizing social institutions. All aspects of society take on gendered properties, not only the division of labor, but also kinship, sexual scripts, personalities, forms of social control, ideologies, imagery, identity, beliefs, and techniques of symbolic display.

To demonstrate the ubiquity of gender, Lorber takes the reader on a tour of human culture since its invention. Her intent is to show that, historically speaking, there were alternatives to gender inequality, in the sense that women's status was relatively high in hunter-gatherer and horticultural societies, although even back then, people were still divided by sex into doing different tasks. The "major shift" (141) took place around five thousand years after the discovery of agriculture, when more intensive methods of farming began to be implemented. Once plows came into use and animals were domesticated by agricultural employment, men's work was no longer compatible with child-rearing. Out of the inequalities that began to emerge, property relations and patriarchy eventually developed.

We who are modern, Lorber continues, live in the shadow of the gender relations that were constructed with and after the rise of modern agriculture. Lorber's book is an encyclopedia of misery, a compendium of every conceivable way in which contemporary industrial society tries to assign women to second-class status. Reviewing a wide range of secondary sources and summarizing experiences from all over the world, Lorber finds gender discrimination in every nook and cranny of modern society, from the relative worth of boys and girls, to family structure, to the unequal rewards for domestic labor, to the glass ceiling, and, finally, to the structure of politics itself. The situation facing modern women could not be grimmer:

> Gender statuses today are inherently unequal, and the whole point of gendering is to produce gender inequality. Subordination of women is an intrinsic part of the modern social order. . . . The subordination of women persists because it produces a group that can be exploited as workers, sexual partners, childbearers, and emotional nurturers in the marketplace and in the household. (292–93)

The lesson taught by all three writers, then, is clear: male and female are not real categories. They reflect false assumptions about the human personality, serve as metaphors for unequal power relations, or are necessary for the smooth functioning of an arbitrary division of labor. Not only does each writer agree on the artificiality of gender categories, but all of them base their conclusions on social science findings: the notion that male and female are suspect categories is not just my opinion, each author claims, but an indisputable fact supported by the weight of experimental, historical, sociological, and anecdotal evidence.

Bem, Haste, and Lorber want to challenge a world in which men have kept women out of positions of privilege. For them, gender difference is the enemy and a vision of a genderless society the goal for which they are striving. But just as many African-Americans began to discover virtues in living, voting, and counting by race, many feminists began to argue that there was nothing wrong with gender difference. Women had different ways of knowing, different ways of caring, different ways of learning.[12] Often appealing to a younger generation of women, "difference" feminists began to question whether androgyny was a desirable ideal; Adrienne Rich published a poem celebrating androgyny in 1973, eliminated it from her collected poems in 1974, wrote a critique of the concept in 1976, and finally in 1978 wrote a new poem announcing that androgyny was one of two words that "I cannot choose again."[13] (The other one was "humanism.") The feminist critique of gender difference, like the black-awareness critique of racial integration, had turned itself inside out.

There is nothing wrong with any of this; political movements ought to reexamine first premises from time to time. But what about the social science that accompanied the earlier phase of feminism? Gender difference, we were told, had no basis in fact. But now women wanted to believe in gender difference. So which is true: are women and men essentially different or fundamentally the same? The question seems so crucial to every topic raised by considerations of gender that a definitive answer would appear to be unavoidable. Yet answering the question poses risks. If men and women are basically the same, feminist theory ought to seek such goals as equality and universality, even if, in doing so, it must refrain from attacking men and celebrating women. If they are different, feminist theory can point with pride to women's special contributions and characteristics, but only by undermining commitment to full equality.

Bem has thought long and hard about this dilemma, which may be why, despite the self-confidence of her early findings about gender arbitrariness, she now has difficulty providing an unambiguous resolution. As the feminist zeitgeist shifted in the 1970s away from sameness in favor of sexual difference, so did Bem. Having invested a considerable amount of intellectual energy in the notion that gender polarization is problematic, Bem knows that she cannot accept a celebration of feminist difference. But Bem cannot bring herself to engage in serious criticism of difference maximizers who stress the positive sides of women's experience. For one thing, celebrations of difference contribute to the breakdown of two of her three lenses: androcentrism and essentialism. In addition, she argues, we might understand difference theories not as empirical descriptions of actual differences but as poetic expressions of self-awareness.

Typical of the problems Bem has in resolving the question of difference is her discussion of androgyny. Her initial BSRI was motivated by a strong belief that both genders were fundamentally the same. In *The Lens of Gender*, Bem now acknowledges the criticisms of the concept that come from writers like Adrienne Rich and Carolyn Heilbron; not only does androgyny focus on individuals rather than social structure, she writes, it "reproduces—and thereby reifies—the very gender polarization it seeks to undercut" (124). Yet having pointed out the theoretical and practical limits to androgyny, she nonetheless is still sympathetic to her earlier endorsement of it: "I do not find any of the critiques so devastating as to justify the exclusion of *androgyny* from the feminist lexicon" (124). Bem believes that there is no such thing as male and female *and* that being female is a special and valuable experience. Here is her tortured conclusion: "Yes, androgyny has apparently had an androcentric history, but it need not be used androcentrically—and has not been used androcentrically—by modern feminists" (124). A sentence like this one makes it clear how far Bem has traveled, not only from her once-firm belief in androgyny, but also from any sense that social science can give us firm answers to such puzzling questions.

Yet this did not stop Bem from trying to redesign her social science experiments to account for an explanation of gender difference that would not be hostile to male/female difference. In the early 1980s she argued for what she called gender-schematicity.[14] In these experiments she gave subjects a number of words and asked them to repeat the words in any order they chose. Some of the words had male connotations and some female; some of them were male and female names; others had no gender associations. If people walk around with cognitive schemas in their minds linking otherwise diverse phenomena, she reasoned, there would be patterns in the order in which they recalled names. And so there were; male and female were mental constructs for recalling things, especially for people who were conventionally gendered. If at one time people's minds were blank slates upon which society wrote a gender script emphasizing differences between men and women, now the mind was hard-wired (by culture, not biology) to be either male or female. In her early work, Bem argued that gender was arbitrary; in her later work, she began to argue that it was necessary. Although experimental psychology prides itself on being a science—on its ability to demonstrate truths independent of the point of view of the scientist—Bem was using scientific technique to argue for truths that seemed to cancel each other out.

Bem's inability to make up her mind about male and female difference, as problematic as it may be for theory, is even more problematic for a theory about human personalities. Psychology is a special social science because, divided into experimental and clinical branches, it not only seeks to understand the mind but also to improve it. In her early research Bem reached the conclusion that mental health is significantly enhanced if people are genderless; one can only wonder what she thought about mental health as she became more sympathetic to feminist gender polarization. The picture one gets of gender-troubled children twisting in the winds of psychological fashion—today encouraged to be different than conventional gender roles, tomorrow urged to be in accord with them— does not give a very positive impression of the state of academic psychology. As Bem's work illustrates, when all is said and done—when the experiments are carried out, the reflections upon them reformulated, and the mental health recommendations proposed—we still do not know whether men and women are two variations of a common category or two completely different categories.

Similar problems arise from feminist efforts to claim that gender is a "socially constructed" phenomenon. All these writers, and indeed the great majority of feminist theorists, are "social constructionists." The dividing line in feminist theory is not between social construction and some other way of understanding gender, but between different understandings of how much of the world is constructed socially. One point of view holds that sex is biological but that gender is cultural. This notion has been challenged by a more radical position, usually identified with lesbian theorists, who argue that sex itself is a social construction.[15] Judith Lorber endorses this reading. Bem, although marginally more sympathetic to biological differences between men and women than Lorber, writes that biological differences "will depend, *in every single instance*, on the situational context in which men and women lead their lives" (38; my emphasis). In these formulations, the world is polymorphous until human beings write their social practices and ideas upon it.

Yet if these writers accept a radical interpretation of social constructionism, they do not want to confront its theoretical implications. There is a tension between the notion that something is constructed and that it is permanent. This tension is not necessarily a contradiction; we just might be able to change the genes with more ease than we can change society. But the ease with which these writers go from the assertion that gender is arbitrary to the notion that gender is deeply entrenched gives one pause, for the shift from one side of the argument to the other seems to have more to do with politics than with theoretical understanding, despite an oft-repeated tenet of feminism that theory and politics are the same thing.

When they talk politically, Bem and Lorber find in social constructionism a way of proclaiming the possibility of social change. Lorber's aim "is to challenge the validity, permanence, and necessity of gender" (5). She writes that "human beings have constructed and used gender—human beings can deconstruct and stop using gender" (297). Bem emphasizes her "own commitment to eradicating [gender] from both the culture and the psyche" (193). In this political voice, gender, because socially constructed, is like a cyst; if it bothers you, remove it.

But if gender is a transitory thing politically, it cannot be quite as deeply etched into the history, institutions, practices, and psyches of our society as Bem and Lorber, in their theoretical voices, proclaim. Culture, according to Bem, transforms itself into gender difference by utilizing "the institutional preprogramming of the individual's daily experience into the default options, or the historically precut 'grooves,' for that particular time and place" (139). This psychology is one that imagines human minds as hard-drives that receive software instructions from the culture. We are as capable of thinking for ourselves as our PCs are to reject WordPerfect in favor of Nota Bene.

By finding the ultimate cause of gender discrimination within the individual, psychology gives credence to how very radical the problem must be. It is no longer a question of "false consciousness," of digging beneath layers of rationalization to find real interests. It is rather that people themselves have come to live within their gender roles; the ultimate carrier of oppression is the psyche of the oppressed. The individual, in Bem's view, is "a deeply implicated—if unwitting—collaborator in the social reproduction of male power" (139). The stoic Kantian self, guarding its autonomy against passion and prejudice, becomes "a constructed self," composed of "a gendered personality, a gendered body, an androcentric heterosexuality, and the abhorrence of homosexuality" (152). If this is the case, one can only wonder how human beings who have no sense of an autonomous self can find the internal resources to challenge gender and render its oppressive powers irrelevant.

The same intellectual fatalism holds for Lorber, if in sociological, rather than psychological, form. Because gender reproduces the culture, gender is necessary; "Once gender is ascribed," she writes, "the social order constructs and holds individuals to strongly gendered norms and expectations" (25). Gender fulfills such important social functions that it is futile to challenge its overwhelming power; "social policies that ignore this structure of gender inequality and assume that remedies can take place on the individual level are doomed to failure" (298). Just as Bem relies on a cognitive psychology that ignores the ability of human minds to attribute meaning to the world around them, Lorber relies on a functional sociology which understands all existing institutions as reproducing social relations without people being able to exercise any power over their fate by themselves.

There is nothing inherently wrong with functionalism. Indeed, social criticism tempered by functionalism, as I will argue in the chapter which follows, by enabling the critic to understand why an institution continues to exist, can make the critic's denunciation of that institution that much more effective. But Lorber's functionalism strikes me as a different sort, one so relentless in its insistence that gender roles can never change that it effectively renders criticism irrelevant—no matter how radical the ideas of the critic. For if it is true that "in the micro-politics of everyday life and the macropolitics of laws and state policies, dominant men are so privileged that they continue to dominate without much conscious effort (298), why should one spend one's time criticizing male domination? Criticism tempered by functionalism enables the critic simultaneously to respect and attack social practices. But if the critical and the functional never blend, the only alternative to oppression is complete liberation. The final destination of criticism without functionalism must be utopia.

From Reality to Utopia

Gender, socially constructed on the one hand, is opaque to individuals on the other. Gender empowers; gender disempowers. It should not be surprising, consequently, that these theorists believe that gender never changes, but that gender will also wither away. All three authors proudly sketch an outline of the utopia they would like to see come into being. Having argued that gender in the here-and-now of contemporary America is everywhere, they turn and argue that gender need not in some imaginary world be anywhere.

Helen Haste's utopian fantasies are in some ways the most justifiable; since her entire book in an attack on reason, why not fantasize? Indeed Haste seems to like fantasists more than feminists; she has kind words for two bêtes noir of contemporary feminism, Camille Paglia and Robert Bly, because both of them are, and celebrate, mythic figures. Haste's cure for the dualistic thinking that oppresses women is to offer them mythology. She likes ancient myths and woolly-minded ecological speculation, since they "are self-consciously challenging the dominant metaphors of the culture" (197). In a passage that ought to make a (quasi) difference minimizer such as Sandra Bem cringe, Haste writes: "When the women at Greenham Common weave webs on the wire, or use flowers and toys as symbols of protest, they are affirming feminine symbols to challenge the masculine hierarchy expressed in the power metaphors of war, but they are also offering an alternative way of looking at the world" (197).

Sandra Bem, however, has a utopia of her own to offer, even if it is less colorful than Haste's. She envisions a world in which

the totality of human experience would no longer be divided into cultural categories on the basis of gender, so people of different sexes would no longer be culturally identified with different clothes, different social roles, different personalities, or different sexual and affectional partners any more than people with different-colored eyes or different-sized feet are now. (192)

Haste's utopia smashes dualities by transforming them into multi-plicities; Bem's seeks the same end by transforming dualities into singularities. In Bem's utopia, genderlessness finally wins out over gender difference; we will all be one. It is a matter of individual taste whether a genderless world is attractive, but there can be little question that a world without gender markings, even if more egalitarian, would also be sociologically impoverished, stripping from human beings their capacities to judge others by the signals that people like to transmit about their identities.

The most surprising of these utopian visions is Judith Lorber's, for of all these books, hers is the most relentlessly down-to-earth in its single-minded insistence that gender rules everything. True to form, Lorber brings utopia closer to the world we know but, precisely for this reason, she offers, at least to this reader, the most nightmarish utopia of all:

In a world of scrupulous gender equality, equal numbers of girls and boys would be educated and trained for the liberal arts and for the sciences, for clerical and manual labor, and for all the professions. Among those with equal credentials, women and men would be hired in an alternating fashion for the same type of jobs—or only men would be hired to do women's types of jobs and only women would be hired to do men's types of jobs until half of every workplace was made up of half men and half women. (298)

It would take an active government to police society to achieve such results, but we could ensure that responsible officials were also gender neutral by insisting that two men could run against each other followed by two women, so that the seats would be evenly split. Art museums would ensure that half of all paintings were done by women; book publishers would be required to publish an equal number of books by each. Sports, pornography—Lorber has thought of it all. Give her this much; she is relentless in her pursuit of gender inequality and equally as determined to see it eradicated in every way.

It may well be the utopian urge in their writings that leads these authors to celebrate any unconventional sexual or gender category. Gender nonconformists—"gay men, lesbians, bisexuals, transsexuals, transvestites, and 'gender-disordered' children" (167)—fascinate Bem, for they challenge the gender polarization of our culture. Similarly, Haste understands homosexuality as undermining man-woman dualism, while Lorber, in her encyclopedic way, lists five sexes on the basis of genitalia; three sexual orientations based on object choice; five gender displays; six types of emotional bonds; ten to fourteen kinds of sexual identifications; and an uncountable number of sexual practices. The notion of a third—or even a fourth or fifth—sex is as important to feminist theory as a celebration of Madonna.[16]

Feminist theory, having made its leap into romanticism, prefers the anthropological to the sociological; the taste for the strange is far more powerful than an appreciation of the familiar. But a most peculiar anthropology this is, for, in its zeal to make sweeping statements about all gender relations at all times, feminist theory loses the enthnographic method of anthropology even while adopting its taste for the exotic. The result is a backhand acknowledgment of the durability of the world around them they find so troubling, for if one has to travel to life at the margins in order to find the truth about gender, then life at the center, while not particularly exotic, is also not particularly problematic. The fact that there may be many genders at the extreme reenforces the point that there are only two in the here-and-now. Gender exotica serves as one more triumph of romanticism over realism in feminist theory. The unknown out there is always preferable to the known closer to home, as if the truth of the conventional is too uncomfortable to deserve close attention.

Nor is it clear that the exotic necessarily exposes the artificiality of the conventional. For these writers, gender-benders are performing a useful service for feminism by demonstrating the artificiality of gender categories. But, let us recall, there is also within feminism a strong preference for gender categories. Just as individuals of multiracial background may object to affirmative action on the grounds that it perpetuates categories of black and white that do not apply to them, cross-dressers and transvestites can be as subversive of female difference as they are of female stereotyping. Bem, Lorber, and Haste all are aware that lesbians can, on occasion, take masculine identity more seriously than many men, just as male homosexuals can do the reverse. And male homosexuals are men—there is no reason why their interests will always be the same as heterosexual white women. Gender-bending reenforces and challenges gender stereotypes but, in both cases, there is no clear link with a feminist agenda.

Finally, this insistence that nonconventional gender roles tell us more about the truth of gender than conventional ones undermines the autobiographical voice that is a defining feature of a good deal of feminist scholarship. Typical is Sandra Bem, who announces in her preface that although she has lived monogamously with one man for twenty-seven years, she does not consider herself heterosexual. (Nor, it comes as no surprise, does she consider herself lesbian or bisexual.) Yet by celebrating the nonconventional, it is as if these writers, for all the personal tone, find their actual circumstances—their heterosexuality, their academic careers, their bookishness—prosaic. Bem is the only one who knows she is on difficult ground here for, having celebrated the unconventional, she goes on to praise

> feminists, both male and female, who actively oppose the gender scripts of the culture, and even the relatively traditional women and men who become gender nonconformists merely by reversing some critical aspect of the male or female script—by choosing, if they are women, to sacrifice marriage and children for an ambitious full-time career, and by choosing, if they are men, to do the reverse. (167)

The tenured academic, it would seem, is really a rebel against gender stereotyping.

Despite their fascination with exotic genders, two of these authors are not really talking about polymorphousness; their desire is not to want sexuality spread around but rather to have sexuality abolished. Lorber and Bem choose to end their books with such a suggestion. In a perfectly gender-neutral world, Lorber hopes, we might lose our humanity, transforming ourselves into cyborgs who move back and forth from the human to the technological with ease. And Bem wants us to

> view our sex as so completely given by nature, so capable of exerting its influence automatically, and so limited in its sphere of influence to those domains where it really does matter biologically, that it could be safely tucked away in the backs of our minds and left to its own devices. In other words, biological sex would no longer be at the core of individual identity and sexuality. (196)

Gender—and, in Bem's formulation, sex—is not to be bent, but broken. If both gender and sex are abolished, the problem of deciding between miminizers and maximizers of male-female difference is overcome. Feminism wins by eliminating the feminine.

The taste for utopia which marks these books suggests that dualistic thinking, contrary to Helen Haste, is not a monopoly of masculine reason. All these writers are dualistic in the sense that they make a sharp distinction between this world and some other. But whereas a comparison to the historical past might lead to the conclusion that the situation of women, still unequal, has nonetheless improved, a comparison to an unknown future allows any conclusion one wishes, irrespective of any real-world checkpoint. The attraction of utopia for science-fiction writers is understandable; most feminists like the novels of Ursula LeGuin, even as they are uncomfortable with the more sharp-edged dystopias of Margaret Atwood. For social scientists, however, the construction of utopia is self-defeating, announcing a resignation from any effort to come to an understanding of the world in which, for better or worse, we happen to live. For these feminist writers, if in varying degrees, utopian speculations serve as a substitute for their missing social science. Each world of the duality they create lacks the texture of real life, the one we have now because it is so relentlessly unable to change, the one we hope to come into existence because it is so contrary to everything that has come before.

Is Feminist Theory Necessary?

The question remains why a political movement such as feminism, which has made so many excellent studies of the concrete, has such difficulty with the abstract. At least one answer may be in order. Looking reality in the face means developing a finely tuned sense of how oppression and discrimination by gender have been persistent features of human societies since their beginning. But it also means developing the ability to recognize change, even change for the better, when it occurs. Feminist theories, if the three writers I have been discussing are any indication, have yet to find the balance.

There is every reason why the feminist as social critic would want to emphasize the persistence of women's oppression: rallying the troops to the cause requires the telling and retelling of the evils that motivate the cause, even if reality is distorted in the process. But feminists who are also social scientists have to test their theories against the real world, however uncomfortable such tests may be for their political commitments. Advancing the interests of women and understanding the role that gender plays in subordinating women are not identical tasks. One requires reconciling differences and expressing solidarity, the other tough-minded thinking and a willingness to choose one position when it contradicts another. One appeals primarily to other women, but the other must reach out and be persuasive to anyone. One wants to imagine a new world, the other insists that we first must understand the present world.

Although the role of social critic and the role of social scientist are different, they can be combined in the same person. Interestingly enough, examples of trying to balance the one with the other are more likely to come not from academic feminists but from political ones. There are feminist writers such as Susan Faludi who maintain a posture of "nothing has ever changed" militance,[17] but a number of other feminist writers who are attracted to a political agenda—such as Naomi Wolf or Betty Friedan—have begun to be openly critical of some of the more utopian and impractical aspects of feminist thought.[18] They have been joined others, primarily nonacademics, who have begun to question feminist assumptions about date rape and pornography.[19] A rebellion against the pieties of feminist studies programs has even taken place among academic writers.[20] The real world has most definitely intruded on feminist political concerns. Power is there to be obtained; a surprising amount has been obtained; strategies should therefore be tailored to obtain more.

At the same time, academic feminists—who in theory are obligated to accept or reject ideas based on evidence, logic, and reason—stress the permanence of gender discrimination and downplay the change. The more the situation of women improves, the more radical becomes the critique of female inequality. It is as if the theorizing about gender conducted in the American academy has been excused from the necessity to bring theory and real world events into any relationship with one another. "It is only now, in the 1990s, that a full-fledged analysis of gender as wholly constructed, symbolically loaded, and ideologically enforced is taking place in American feminism" (5), Judith Lorber writes. Yet it is only now, in the 1990s, that those committed to improving the situation of women in the real world are discovering how irrelevant Lorber's theory would be to them. Feminist theory surely is necessary; it is also unlikely to come from feminist theorists.

Unwilling to recognize that power relations between men and women have changed, feminist theorists sacrifice their social science to preserve their political commitments. At the same time, they also sacrifice their social criticism for the sake of theory. As social criticism, the books produced by academic feminist theorists, like the products of cultural studies, are curiously lacking in critical indignation. They are both more scholarly in appearance and yet less rigorous in argument than the social criticism of the "golden age." On the one hand, their books look like academic books: they are published by top-of-the-line university presses; every effort is made to mimic the colorless prose that generally passes for scholarship; footnotes abound; and theoretical understanding is proclaimed the objective. In that sense, they are books meant to appeal not to those who read Betty Friedan or Naomi Wolf but to those who write other works of feminist theory.

But if these books are academic in form, they are sloppier in their reasoning, less careful in their analysis of data, and simply not as persuasive as many of the books written for general audiences. Without any reality check, all too many feminist academics cite each other's work in self-referential fashion, develop nonfalsifiable arguments, rely on first-person anecdotes, dismiss the possibility of real-world truth, ignore or interpret away evidence contrary to their speculations, and inevitably end their books with utopian fantasies. Determined to hold on to the notion that gender oppression is as deeply structured and pernicious as it has ever been, feminist theorists seek political objectives that override all other commitments, even as political feminists develop respect for evidence and the discomforting properties of ideas. By ignoring real-world complexities in favor of single-minded interpretations, these books fail to establish the sense of credibility and intellectual honesty required of first-rate social criticism.

Many of the problems revealed by these efforts to create a theory of gender have a common cause: the world of feminist theory remains a narrow one, confined to academics of similar political and intellectual dispositions. This is a situation that need not, and should not, persist. There is every reason to want to see an ambitious effort to understand why women have not achieved the full equality and respect as persons they ought to have. If women, despite the dramatic gains they have made, are still unequal, one can understand a certain reluctance not to look the real world in the face. Yet neither change nor understanding will come until those who deal with gender develop theoretical respect for the very realities for which they have political contempt.

CRITICISM BEYOND IDEOLOGY

The New Criticism

Social criticism has become more complicated not only because, on some key issues of the day, left and right have switched sides but also because, on others, there are no coherent sides to switch. Positions which once were morally certain increasingly seem filled with complicated traps. Free speech is a good thing, but should it be used as a defense of "words that wound"?[1] The war in Vietnam was an example of American imperialism, but America's slowness to intervene in Bosnia is an example of moral indifference. The military, denounced uniformly by the left a generation ago, is touted as a success story for racial integration. An ecological consciousness is vital, but a zero-growth economy creates few new jobs and has little need for immigrants. The right to privacy of everyone should be respected, especially those such as gays who are stigmatized by the majority, but to control AIDS we also need public health measures that can sometimes override an absolute right to privacy. On issues such as these, terms such as right and left lose all meaning.

Ideological complexity creates serious problems for the social critic. The critics of the golden age knew they were on the left, but if no one knows what being on the left means, where does the critic stand? Social critics generally think of themselves as truth-tellers, playing the heroic role of informing society of unpleasant realities it does not want to hear, but if what people hear are the complicated, morally puzzling, ideologically ambiguous positions associated with so many contemporary issues, what happens to the social critic as hero? Social critics generally find themselves comfortable with a polemical style, driving home what to them are obvious truths in the face of even more obvious lies, yet if the truth of so many issues is unclear, can polemic be the appropriate disposition of the critic? And if not, what can replace it?

In this chapter I examine questions such as these by focusing on two policy issues which, because they are morally complicated and impossible to reduce to simple right and wrong positions, have upset categories of right and left. Pornography—which confronts a belief in freedom of expression with a commitment to equality for women—has split the left badly, breaking up friendships, disrupting alliances, and causing painful misunderstanding, due, in no small part, to the fact that the protection of women from violence and a skepticism toward censorship are both goals that liberals ought to support. In a similar way, immigration has driven a wedge on the right between those who believe in open markets (and with them, open borders) and those who want to regulate who is allowed to enter the country. Like pornography, immigration often divides well-intentioned people; there is a strong case for open borders, but no country can open its doors to everyone who might want to come.

One response to issues such as these is to keep alive the spirit of 1960s social criticism—even to redouble its zeal. This is certainly true of the pornography wars. Andrea Dworkin is implacable in her denunciation of pornography; like many critics certain of their views, she cannot help but compare what she detests with the Holocaust, except, for her, what men do to women in pornography is *worse* than what Nazis did to Jews in concentration camps: "The Jews didn't do it to themselves and they didn't orgasm. . . . No one, not even Goebbels, said that the Jews liked it."[2] In the debate over immigration, one also hears such ideologically sure opinions; Peter Brimelow, for one, warns that the Immigration Act of 1965 will destroy American democracy as we have always known it by admitting a disproportionate number of people of color, who will reproduce themselves faster than whites.[3]

In taking an extreme position on one side or the other of a complex issue, the critic can keep alive a heroic stance; the rest of the world, indeed some of my once closest allies, such a critic believes, may be fooled by sweet reason, but not me. I will continue my voice of principled dissent, no matter how lonely I become. (Actually, such critics rarely become too lonely; Dworkin's position is quite popular among younger feminists, and the Buchanan wing of the Republican Party shares Brimelow's perspective on immigration.) For critics of this persuasion, ideological and moral complexity, rather than being grounds for moderating polemic, becomes the rationale for intensifying disagreement and conflict.

Yet because they are irreducible to simple moral positions on either side, issues such as pornography and immigration reveal many of the limitations of heroic social criticism. I will argue in this chapter that issues of this sort require a new criticism, one that proceeds step-by-step, not down from a preconceived idea of how the world should work, but up from the realities of dirty movies or immigrant experience. Critics dealing with such issues should be as prepared to learn as they are to proclaim. The best they can offer is not a legal brief for an already determined position but a willingness to use social science as a way of discovering why the realities they detest nonetheless persist. A criticism which aims to explain rather to declaim is most necessary when its plot is least obvious. If a social critic believes that the emergence of issues which conform to no particular ideological position is not just a coincidence, but reflects an understanding that the social world is more complex than critics once believed, the only plausible stance for him is one that tries to find truths on all sides rather than Truth on one.

Denouncing Pornography

Pornography exists where sex and politics meet. Sex is, or at least is supposed to be, intimate, caring, invisible to others—the very definition of private. Politics is, or is supposed to be, open, debatable, a spectacle—the essence of public. A world in which sex and its representations were of no concern to others could not, by force of definition, contain pornography. A world in which politics regulated all sexual activities and their representation could not, by force of police, contain pornography either. To discuss pornography at all is always to discuss a matter of balance.

Our politics—the way we balance public and private things—is the politics of liberal democracy. As Richard Randall stresses, both liberalism and democracy are intimately linked to the pornographic inclination, even if that link is troubling and contradictory.[4] Liberalism respects a private sphere within which government—that is, other people—ought not to find itself. Although the founders of liberal political theory might be unable to imagine their arguments for freedom of expression used in defense of the prurient, pornography could not exist without the two most fundamental props of the liberal world order: a market responding to supply and demand efficiently, with little concern for the morality of what is traded; and a legal system placing a premium on individual rights.

Yet if liberalism is inclined to protect the pornographic, democracy is inclined to forbid it. Randall is correct to emphasize that it is the elite which seeks to defend the right of pornographic expression and the majority which seeks to curtail it. Politicians never run for office by being in favor of pornography. Unmoved by appeals to artistic expression, little concerned for constitutional subtleties, worried about the vulnerability of their children, Americans would gladly give up this one liberal right if they could be guaranteed that in return they would be rid of unwanted ugliness. Legislatures and city councils, responsive to democratic demands, regularly try to control pornography; courts, undemocratic in principle and liberal in practice, try to stop such efforts.

In the past twenty years, liberalism and democracy have both expanded in scope. Pornographers have shared, surely disproportionately, in the expansion of liberal rights that define American judicial practices since the Warren Court. The rise of the Moral Majority and other censorial movements, on the other hand, is one of the by-products of increasingly plebiscitary democratic urges, as is, in its own way, the concern with pornography arising out of feminist movements. Three additional developments since around 1970 have set the stage for new ways of thinking about the pornographic.

First, the form of pornography has changed beyond recognition. Any images men may have in their heads about stag films—left over from memories of fraternity bashes of the 1950s—have nothing to do with what pornography represents now. The sex, for one thing, is far more explicit; today's hard core is tomorrow's R-rated movie, or, putting it another way, yesterday's illegality is today's television commercial. In addition, the quality has improved. As Linda Williams points out, plots have been added, full-length feature status is now the norm, and efforts at some credibility have been introduced.[5] The symbol of these changes is the video revolution; most people now watch pornography at home in living color, not in grungy inner-city arcades.

Second, nearly all legal efforts used by local communities to control pornography in recent years failed to do so. The Supreme Court's decision in *Roth v. United States*—despite its famous language banning material which "appeals to the prurient interest"—effectively opened to the door to previously forbidden sexual expression. (Thirty-one obscenity convictions were reversed between 1967 and 1973.) The ability of pornographers to use courts and the First Amendment to their advantage— Donald Downs notes that in Minneapolis, the Minnesota Civil Liberties Union offices were in a building owned by one of the MCLU's major clients, a leading producer of pornography, presumably rent-free—led local police to give up even trying to win convictions.[6] Even a town as conservative as Indianapolis was able to initiate only two obscenity cases between 1979 and 1985.[7] During the 1970s and early 1980s, in short, pornography grew increasingly available as the ability to regulate it declined proportionately.

Third, our awareness that pornography involves violence against women has increased. Of the three developments this is the most controversial, because there is no absolute proof—nor will there ever be—that pornography *definitely* results in harm to women. Still, the images contained in pornography, while brutal toward all, are most brutal toward women. Pornography is primarily a feminist issue. If the old politics of pornography posed freedom of expression against community norms and morals, the new politics of pornography is a conflict between the First Amendment and the right to women to be free of harassment and violence. The new politics of pornography crested with the 1986 Meese Commission, which concluded that pornography (including the violent kind) had increased to the point of being out of control.[8] What was most striking about the Meese Commission was not its conclusions but the way it reached them. For the commission focused specifically on the insult and injury to women involved in pornography. Robin Morgan's fighting words—"pornography is the theory; rape is the practice"—were accepted far beyond the circle of radical feminists to whom they were once written.[9] The feminist critique of pornography had arrived. That critique was the product of the meeting of two minds: legal theorist Catharine MacKinnon and essayist Andrea Dworkin.

Although MacKinnon is better known, Dworkin's position, because more rhetorical, is also more illustrative of a politics of denunciation. In Dworkin's view, sex is power, nothing else, and all the power belongs to the man. Every man is a beast; every women an innocent and passive victim. Pornography, like heterosexual sex in general, is merely an extreme form by which men exercise power over women. The philosophy in Dworkin's bedroom is that of Hobbes. Dworkin, in that sense, is really not all that interested in pornography itself; the chapter of that name in her book *Pornography: Men Possessing Women* is four pages long, whereas the one called "force" is seventy. Let Dworkin herself speak:

> In the male system, women are sex; sex is the whore. The whore is pornē, the lowest whore, the whore who belongs to *all* male citizens: the slut, the cunt. Buying her is buying pornography. Having her is having pornography. Seeing her is seeing pornography. Seeing her sex, especially her genitals, is seeing pornography. Seeing her in sex is seeing the whore in sex. Using her is using pornography. Wanting her means wanting pornography. Being her means being pornography. (202)

Dworkin does Robin Morgan one better: sex is the theory and extermination the practice. Pornography is the ultimate expression of "male sexual domination," which itself is "a material system with an ideology and a metaphysics" (203). There is, Dworkin concludes, "no way out" (223), although, in a 1989 preface to her original 1981 book, she did offer women this advice: "know the bastard on top of you" (xxxviii).

This kind of analysis would hardly seem the stuff of local ordinances—especially in the American Midwest. But in 1983 MacKinnon invited Dworkin to teach a class with her at the University of Minnesota School of Law. Two essential conclusions were quickly reached in the seminar: pornography is not a question of free speech, because women cannot speak; and, because pornography harms women, it violates civil rights, not civil liberties. MacKinnon, an effective politician, lobbied for a new ordinance based on these principles; the resulting Minnesota ordinance was a first in American law. Pornography—not, as in most judicial decisions since *Roth*, the narrower notion of obscenity—was defined as discrimination against women. Finding herself depicted in what she believed to be pornographic fashion by any image—nine definitions of such depictions were given in the ordinance—any woman could lodge a complaint with the local Civil Rights Commission and, after a series of steps were followed, could win the right to a hearing. The Minnesota ordinance was eventually declared unconstitutional.[10] Still, the case for censorship on feminist grounds has not receded. We will be wrestling for some time with the difficult question of whether the harm to women represented in pornography is so great that we are justified in using our democratic powers to stop it.

The first reaction to the rise of a feminist movement for censorship was to argue that the attack on pornography can give aid and comfort to those who would roll back the sexual revolutions of recent years, which have been by and large good for women.[11] That was followed by another: a frank, in some cases graphic, account of why pornography is a good thing, pleasurable and enjoyable, to women as well as men.[12] While in a narrow sense accurate, these points missed the point. When a political position has as much popularity as the position to control pornography, we ought to give those who hold it credit for their views, not dismiss them as know-nothing, anti-intellectual philistines. When the rage of women is so eloquent and dramatic, we ought not let Andrea Dworkin's angry rhetoric lead us to deny that pornography is demeaning and that women are its primary targets. Although we cannot prove that pornography causes violence, it certainly offends the sensibility of some very engaged citizens.

Even more unsatisfactory as a response to the feminist case against pornography was a civil libertarian emphasis on rights. Harm is concrete, sensate, unambiguous. Rights are abstract and intellectualized, at least one remove away from immediate experience. Balance the two, and the argument against harm will win, at least to the popular majorities that decide these things. In an age of AIDS, moreover, it is difficult to make the case that sexuality is a purely private affair of no concern to a community's morality; so long as tax monies are used to save lives, there *is* a public interest in private sex. The state may not be the best regulator, the regulation itself can often misfire, but a community cannot take a position of moral neutrality toward the libido. Most people recognize, in short, that your sexuality is at least in part my concern. Some sexual freedom is clearly necessary to discover the self. Some regulation is clearly necessary to protect the society without which there can be no selves.

Feminists critics are right, therefore, to argue that pornography has no redeeming social value. By artistic criteria, it is close to worthless. Attempts to defend the pornographic imagination by Angela Carter and Simone de Beauvoir (in the case of Sade) or Susan Sontag (in the case of Georges Bataille and Pauline Reage) deal with a rarified aspect of the genre that has little to do with the predictability and sheer mediocrity of much of contemporary pornographic expression. By criteria of psychological development, secondly, pornography fails again. It infantilizes people, mostly men, locking them into a stage in which limits do not exist, all desires can be satisfied, and every complexity is avoided. By the Kantian criterion of respect for persons, furthermore, pornography fails a third time, treating women as things available for the whimsical pleasures of men; pornography in that sense is also without redeeming moral value. By civic criteria, finally, pornography flunks most severely. Although free speech gives much to pornography, pornography gives almost nothing to free speech. It does not enhance our capacity to act as citizens—rather the reverse. It does not cause us to reflect on rights and responsibilities. It does not encourage participation in the life of the community. Pornographers are free riders on the liberties of everyone else. If a human activity with so little value is balanced against even a slight possibility that it may cause rape and mayhem, the feminist case for censorship would seem to win.

Yet for all that, there is one missing ingredient in the feminist case against pornography: a satisfactory explanation of why, despite its lack of value and over and above the harm it does to women, it nonetheless continues to exist. Because it does, the social critic's condemnation must at some point give way to the social scientist's effort to understand. Why pornography? No one knows the full answer, but two reasons touch on matters of social psychology: human beings have a need to make sense out of multiple realities and a need to be aware of the dark side of sexuality.

Those who would censor pornography have complete epistemological confidence that they know exactly what it is. "The word pornography does not have any other meaning than . . . the graphic description of the lowest whores," Dworkin writes. "The pornographic system is objective and real and central to the male sexual system. . . . The force depicted in pornography is objective and real because force is so used against women. The debasing of women depicted in pornography and intrinsic to it is objective and real in that women are so debased" (200–201). Catharine MacKinnon goes further:

> To say that pornography is categorically or functionally representation rather than sex simply creates a distanced world we can say is not the real world, a world that mixes reality with unreality, art and literature with everything else, as if life does not do the same thing. The effect is to license whatever is done there, creating a special aura of privilege and demarcating a sphere of protected freedom, no matter who is hurt.[13]

In this passage, MacKinnon claims for herself the label of realist. Those who argue that pornography has meanings above and beyond violence to women, she claims, are the romantics. This will not do for MacKinnon, who is determined to keep her eye on the real thing and not be taken in by such counterfactual claims. So intent is MacKinnon to speak in the name of realism that she even claims, at one point, that pornography is "more sexually real than reality" (20).

There are many ways not to consider the world as it is; arguing that it is not as real as its pictures may well be one of them. For there is another reality to pornography beyond its existence: its popularity. Why do people—primarily men, but also women—watch it? Realistic when it comes to portraying pornography, neither Dworkin nor MacKinnon are realistic when it comes to understanding pornography's persistence. In insisting that pornography is only one thing, feminist critics fail to understand that, for its viewers, pornography is anything but what it appears to be for its censors.

What actually happens when people look at pornography? Linda Williams, whose book *Hard Core* argues against the position that pornography represents one thing only, believes that they look for meanings, multiple meanings, in the images around them. Williams urges that we take pornography seriously, which does not mean that we must like it or believe it is art. Remarkably nonjudgmental in her description of pornographic films—only once does she pass a negative judgment: on the quality of the music in *Deep Throat*—Williams wants us to learn the rules of the pornographic genre. All forms of representation have genre rules, including musical comedies, which, like hard-core porno films, regularly break narrative to introduce numbers. The rules of the pornographic genre are defined by one fundamental contradiction: if a man enjoys pleasure inside a women, generally viewed by men as the most satisfying way to experience sexual pleasure, the physical evidence of his pleasure is invisible. The conventions of pornography follow from efforts to capture what the trade calls a "money shot": proving visibly that the man has satisfied himself.

Pornography cannot mean one thing, and one thing only, because genre conventions, instead of confining all reality within preestablished frames, enable multiple interpretations of reality to exist simultaneously. That is why pornography is not, as Dworkin claims, *only* about men brutalizing women. It may equally be the case that what men want to see in pornographic movies is not the naked woman, since most men, in the course of their lives, get to see that with some frequency, but the image of another man enjoying himself visibly, which most men never get to see. We do not, of course, know whether this interpretation is correct. But Williams's subtle and fascinating explications suggest that, in not knowing, we are best off allowing pornographic representations to exist.

If the feminist censor's conviction that an unambiguous map of reality is reflected in pornography is naive, so is her conviction that, knowing the single-minded evil it represents, we can abolish it by force of law. Richard Randall makes a convincing case that such an optimistic view of the powers of law is not justified. It is, in his view, the dark side of pornography that makes it important. Humans are the "pornographic" animal, fascinated and appalled by their sexuality. The pornography we see out there is a reflection of the pornographic deep within ourselves. Since pornography is part of what we are, we harm only ourselves by regulating it too severely. At the same time, however, since "complete sexual freedom is a contradiction of the human condition" (3), we will need to control our sexual impulses in some way. Neither censors nor civil libertarians, Randall argues, understands that "we cannot be characteristically human without both the pornographic and the impulse to control it" (6).

The recognition that pornography speaks to needs within the self—both its need to interpret as well its need to express itself sexually—provides a much firmer base for one of the balance points in the new politics of pornography than the purely libertarian notion of individual freedom. For one thing, the issue is not the abstract right of shady businessmen to sell dirty pictures or the equally abstract right of sexual pleasure-seekers to purchase them—rights that in both cases apply to minorities. Pornography is important, rather, because, in speaking to the self, it is speaking to a universal: we all have an interest in the many ways in which fundamental human conflicts are represented in print and film.

A case against censorship ought to be based, not on the fact that we can discover some redeeming virtue in pornographic expression, but because we cannot. Liberals interested in not being cruel need to be reminded that cruelty is omnipresent. Pornography does that. (So did great novelists like Conrad and great sociologists like Goffman.) Imperfect creatures growing to adulthood with sexual conflicts unresolved, many of us—surprisingly many, by most sociological accounts—need outlets for our imaginations, relying on our power to give meaning to representations of fantasies buried deep within the self, even if the pictorial representations of those fantasies involve, on the surface, harm to others. The good pornography serves is a bad. As long as pornography exists around us, we will have a hard time believing in human perfectibility, a better assumption upon which to build a liberal political order than the notion that humans will always be inherently good.

The feminist case against pornography is powerful and eloquent. But the elements upon which it builds its case—rhetorical overkill, gender stereotyping, absolutism—at some point become ill-suited to the debate. If we try instead to understand why there has always been a pornographic inclination, we inevitably lose a sense of critical indignation, but we may also come closer to the truth of what, to condemn, we first have to understand. The feminist case against pornography has been dominated by lawyers, as has the civil libertarian case against censorship. The next phase of the debate will be better informed if it includes at least some recognition of sociological realism: a sense that things which exist, no matter how detestable, must have a reason for existing which it behooves the critic to investigate.

Sentimentalizing Immigration

The issue of immigration is also one that arouses passionate opinion which overlaps little, if at all, with conventional political categories. It too is generally discussed in the form of an "old" and "new" politics; the former involved primarily with white people who came from Europe, the latter primarily with people of color who came from all over the world. In 1980, 6.2 percent of the American population was foreign-born, nowhere near the 13.2 percent of 1930, but far higher than it had been in any of the previous thirty years. The bulk of this new immigration came from Third World countries, especially Mexico, the Dominican Republic, India, China, Iran, Cuba, and Vietnam. Because this development was unexpected, immigration gives rise to the same kinds of passions as pornography.

Alarmed by the prospect of people of color constituting the majority of the American population in his son's lifetime, Peter Brimelow warns against American immigration policy in language as emotion-laden as Dworkin's tirade against the prurient: continued arrivals of people from Third World countries will create public health hazards, increase welfare costs, worsen the conditions of blacks, weaken the natural environment, shrink educational institutions, and undermine the very concept of an American nation.[14] On the other side of the issue, immigration has its passionate defenders. Alejandro Portes and Ruben Rumbaut—who are far more careful in their use of data and far more nuanced in their interpretations than Brimelow—nonetheless have few doubts: anticipating the emergence of someone like Brimelow, they write that "restrictionists' gloomy rhetoric concerning all present immigration is likely to prove as groundless as in the past."[15]

How should we talk about immigration? Questions involving belonging are at the emotional heart of any society; it would be foolish to expect that issues involving national identity—let alone the financial question of who pays for the costs and who receives the benefits of newcomers—will be discussed in the cool and clinical language of social science. Yet precisely because so much heat is generated by the question of immigration, this is also an arena which calls for sociological realism: Why has America been receptive to immigration? What can previous efforts teach us about present ones? Fortunately, there are first-rate books by sociologists dealing with the experiences of earlier immigrants which constitute the obvious place to begin a sociologically informed discussion of the newer ones.

The grandchildren of the first and second waves of immigration from Poland, Italy, and other European countries are now our elderly. What happens to immigrants after four generations in this country? Do they retain a strong ethnic identity that affects how they live? Or have they become so assimilated, intermarried, and influenced by commodity culture that their ethnicity, for all intents and purposes, is nonexistent? Mary C. Waters and Richard Alba have explored these questions.[16] Alba studied a random sample of the residents of the Albany, New York, region, while Waters identified thirty residents of two suburbs, one outside San Jose, California, and the other outside Philadelphia. Their books make it possible to answer with certainty who won the war between the culture of the old country and the lifestyle of the new.

The new won, hands down. According to Alba's survey, ethnicity barely exists among white ethnics. Only 2 percent of the ethnics he identified ever had help from in business from others within their "clan"; 4 percent experienced discrimination because of their ethnicity; 1 percent claimed to eat ethnic foods daily; almost none were fluent in the language of their ethnic group; 9 percent were curious about the ethnic background of others; about 10 percent claimed to have made a visit to their ethnic homelands within the previous five years; 2 percent were members of ethnic lodges or social clubs; and 11 percent lived in neighborhoods that had any significant concentration of similar ethnics. The great majority of ethnic Americans are intermarried, participate rarely in the culture of their inherited ethnicity, do not pass on their ethnic heritage to their children, and consider themselves, in actual behavior if not always in nostalgic reminiscence, fully American.

Ethnicity, in an influential formulation by Herbert Gans, has more of a symbolic than a real meaning for most Americans.[17] But if Alba is correct, we are dealing with a symbol twice removed, for the way Americans treat ethnicity has been separated from the particular symbols of specific ethnic cultures. Americans eat Chinese food at Oktoberfest and stay away from parochial school on Yom Kippur. Ethnicity, which had once been understood as exclusive—if you are Jewish you cannot be Irish Catholic —is now an inclusive phenomenon. Alba's main discovery is the existence of a new group called "European Americans." It no longer matters where your ancestors came from in Europe. What matters is that your roots somewhere at sometime were in Europe. If there really are "European Americans," then a fundamental change has taken place in the way white Americans think about their roots. They are emphasizing universality, not particularity. Ethnicity, which once implied difference, is increasingly suggesting sameness.

The discovery of "European Americans" also means, of course, that whiteness is crucial to identity. Alba has no doubts that the discovery a few years back of a new ethnic consciousness among European Americans had more to do with a reaction against the civil rights movement than it did with a sudden discovery of the wonders of being Polish. In the face of the threat they perceive from blacks, all whites increasingly perceive themselves as similar. This, needless to say, contributes to the feeling on the part of many black Americans that America's romanticization of ethnicity shuts them out. Hence the term "African American," which is meant to suggest that blacks, too, are immigrants like everyone else.

Although she used a different methodology, Waters's findings are remarkably similar to Alba's. Her respondents also knew almost nothing of foreign languages, rarely attended ethnic events, and were unable to explain, except in the most cliché-ridden terms, what ethnicity meant to them. Waters's respondents are "into" being Irish rather than simply Irish (141). When one of her subjects was asked about her husband's ethnicity, she replied thusly:

> He would have answered Russian Jew and English and Scottish on the census form. He really likes his Russian Jew part. We have a mezuzah on the front door. He converted to Catholicism when he married me. He grew up with his mother and she was Baptist, so he was kind of raised in that tradition. But he likes his Russian Jew part more, he feels close to being Catholic and that part goes together more. They are kind of similar. (91–92)

Responses like these, and Waters's book is full of them, confirm Alba's conclusion that Americans have general, not specific, ethnic identities. Indeed in a surprising number of cases they are not even sure what ethnic identity they have, changing their stories in response to different questions. In her most interesting finding, Waters discovered that a variety of different ethnic groups all claimed to be special because they placed particular importance on patriotism, the family, and education. The same ethnic qualities seemed to exist divorced from whatever ethnic label one happened to attach to them.

Ethnicity, it would seem, has become a commodity: we can shop for it, like we do for cars, changing our models to fit our station in life. If so, one would assume that ethnicity would go the way of all commodities: mass production, cheaper prices, lower quality, eventual sameness. From the empirical data presented in both Alba's and Waters's books, ethnicity in America seems as thin as beer. (There is a direct relationship between the decline of ethnicity and the decline of beer.) Americans are about as loyal to their ethnicity as they are to their political parties, identifying with one, but switching to another for not especially compelling reasons. (The relationship between the decline of ethnicity and the decline of the political parties is also, of course, direct).

Are Americans, free to choose, therefore able to choose their ethnic heritage as well? Waters thinks they are. Although it is in the first instance determined by genes, ethnicity is not completely without social choice. Following up that insight, Waters tries to show how sixty ethnic Americans construct their own ethnic identities. For example, if O'Toole marries Schwartz the child will be half Irish and half Jewish. But if O'Toole is the father and Schwartz the mother, the child will grow up with an Irish name, be perceived by others as Irish, and would therefore be more likely to choose an Irish identity. Genetically speaking, the child would have an identical ethnic heritage if the mother were O'Toole and the father Schwartz, but the socially constructed identity would differ. *Ethnic Options* is a title meant to raise an eyebrow.

And yet what makes ethnicity important is precisely that it is not an option. In stressing the fluidity of ethnic choice—if Italian is a more positive ethnic identity than Scottish, more people will choose Italian as their ethnic identity—Waters enters into debates about the nature of modernity. For what distinguishes the modern from the traditional is that instead of being born with our fates determined by our parents' place in a fixed structure, we are increasingly able to choose where and how we want to live. Communitarians who deplore the alienation of modernity lament the hegemony of choice, while liberals and modernists praise it. But both tend to agree that the single most important premodern legacy that survives in the modern world is ethnicity: our ethnic status remains ascribed, not achieved. Ethnic identity is understood to be the one thing we cannot alter.

Because she stresses that "ethnicity is increasingly a personal choice of whether to be ethnic at all, and, for an increasing majority of people, of which ethnicity to be" (3), Waters would appear to be a modernist, documenting the decreasing importance of ethnic identity. This is confirmed by her discussion of the functions which symbolic ethnicity performs for Americans, allowing them to belong without making excessive demands on them as the price of belonging. All of this makes sense, but Waters also asserts at one point that Americans hold on to their ethnicity "tenaciously" (147), a formulation that is unsupported by the actual data she so painstakingly collected. It seems that Waters confuses two quite different things: the choice of whether to be ethnic at all and the choice of which ethnic identity to be.

It is perfectly reasonable for people to decide that they would rather not be ethnic, at least not in any way that constrains their freedom of action and belief. But Waters argues that people can pick and choose from a template of various ethnic characteristics: "With a symbolic ethnic identity an individual can choose to celebrate an ethnic holiday and refuse to perpetuate a sexist tradition that values boys over girls or that channels girls into domestic roles without their consent" (168). To do so, however, is not to construct a new ethnic identity but to reject ethnicity altogether. Ethnicity with freedom of choice is no longer ethnicity. Waters's claim that we can take the best in our ethnic traditions while leaving behind the worst reveals a lack of realism. Ethnicity is a package deal; when you are ethnic, you take the good with the bad. It is the unstable combination between being tied to a clan and wanting to free of the clan that defines what it means to be ethnic. Waters's sensitive and revealing portraits of sixty American lives strikes me as true to life. But what she has shown is not that people have ethnic options, only that they have opted not to be ethnic.

There may well be good reasons for Americans to have made that decision. If everything is choice, the individual is not ethnic. But if everything is clan, the individual is not modern. Americans have chosen to be modern. To be sure, America is a less interesting place after assimilation has run its course—its food more bland, its symbols less rich, its language increasingly homogeneous. But interesting places have a way in which their people, when not killing each other over roots, retreat into that special kind of narrowness and superstition that ethnicity alone can legitimate. Mary Waters is not alone in celebrating America for the wrong thing. We should be proud that ethnicity means so little to us, that we have transcended tribal needs. But all too many writers on ethnicity do the opposite: they comb the country for every sign of ethnic consciousness, to praise *it*, rather than the assimilation that renders it harmless.

There are two losses which follow when we sentimentalize ethnicity. The first is to the immigrants themselves. To make it in this country required transitions of such difficulty that people often sacrificed their entire lives so that their children would feel at home. Only when the work was done—the language mastered, the parochialism put aside, the passage assured—could they, or their children, then afford the token gestures toward their origins that passes for ethnic consciousness in America. Celebrating people for what they tried to escape demeans the importance of what they wanted to become. Ethnicity became so easy only because the transition from ethnicity was so hard.

Ethnic sentimentalism also demeans those who already were here. Americanism, not ethnicity, is the truly socially constructed identity. Those who made it have every right to insist that their identity as Americans be taken seriously, even if it is an identity rooted in white bread and suburban tract-housing. Americanism is a continually evolving identity that changes with each new group that arrives but only by insisting that all new groups share in its prerequisites. In many sentimentalist accounts, although not in Alba's or Waters's, long-term residents of this country who insist on English and the shedding of customs of origin are portrayed as nativist and ignorant. They are more realistically viewed as descendants of those who struggled to become American, their insistence embodying a memory of that struggle that ought not to be extinguished.

The original immigration from Europe, it would thus seem, turned out to be neither as the nativists nor as the pluralists would have it. Contrary to what the Peter Brimelows of an earlier period believed, nearly all the original immigrants wanted to be as American as fast as possible. They have, along the way, not diluted American culture but enriched it enormously. But if Brimelow sentimentalizes an America that was never as uniform as the one of his imagination, pluralistic enthusiasts sentimentalize an ethnicity that previous immigrants could not wait to shed. America did not find a balance between difference and sameness. We solved the problem of ethnicity by transcending it. Groups do not live in peace with each other in the United States; individuals do. The only reason we are not Lebanon—or Canada—is because language, theology, and culture have so little meaning to us. Americans, who are among the most religious people in the world but also among the least theological, talk about ethnicity so much only because they have so little of it. Ethnic Americans reinvented Americanism, not ethnicity.

If this conclusion is true, there are significant lessons are to be learned with respect to the wave of immigration that has swelled in America since 1965. On the one hand, reborn nativists like Brimelow are wrong to believe that immigrants will produce an alien nation; they will rather rejuvenate the meaning of America at a time when WASP elites are more cautious celebrating their country than newly arrived Latinos and Asians. On the other hand, enthusiasts for the new immigrants such as Portes and Rumbaut cannot proclaim the benefits to America from immigration *and* call sentimentally for the preservation of the languages and customs of the areas from which the immigrants came. The old will have to give way if the new is to flourish.

Language is the primary process by which this takes place. One thing the old immigrants did to participate in the civic culture was either to learn English or to insure that their children did. There is substantial evidence that the new immigrants share the same desire. The heyday of bilingualism is over; even its defenders argue that its purpose is to help make the transition to English. But Portes and Rumbaut, convinced that the attack on bilingualism is an attack on immigrants, seem to want to render linguistic ability as barrier-free, rather than viewing barriers as necessary for achievement and growth—a crucial *rite de passage* that makes a new identity worth having.

"Unlike in several European nations, which are tolerant of linguistic diversity," they write, "in the United States the acquisition of non-accented English and the dropping of foreign languages represents the litmus test of Americanization" (182). Yet no country is more chauvinist toward language than France; the Scandinavians insist on linguistic competence to participate in the welfare state; German Swiss rarely learn Italian Swiss; and the Belgians are even more divided than them. The truth of the matter is that Americans insist on English for reasons that have little to do with language. If language had some kind of transcendent meaning for us, we would take pride in the teaching of English, which we clearly do not. If we cared more about English, we might learn to respect Spanish. And there is no such thing as non-accented English, or, for that matter, Spanish.

Portes and Rumbaut rightly fear a movement that would prevent immigrants from speaking their own language at home. But if there is such a movement in the United States, they fail to find it. Groups like U.S. English, efforts like Proposition 63 in California (which preceded the more immigrant-hostile, and more successful, Proposition 187), or repeated attempts to pass an English-language amendment to the Constitution want the *official* language of the United States to be English: such movements may indeed be using their official position as a smoke screen for a larger agenda designed to drive out all other languages in private, but Portes and Rumbaut do not make that case. There is good reason not to support such movements, since they fail to recognize the tremendously positive contributions made by recent immigrants to American life. Yet Portes and Rumbaut consistently confuse the issue by arguing as if opposition to bilingualism were an opposition to the Spanish language, when, in fact, many of those who oppose a rigid insistence on bilingualism in the schools, such as Rosalie Pedalino Porter, are not only fluent in Spanish but have great respect for languages other than English.[18]

The fact is that all immigrants will learn English, as Portes and Rumbaut themselves point out. Why then insist on the official recognition of more than one language? The answer is that some immigrants lose their original language slower than others; "Asian immigrants," Portes and Rumbaut write, "appear consistently more inclined to shed their native tongue than those from Latin America" (204). But this difference in linguistic assimilation is just as much an argument against official bilingualism as for it. For not only would an insistence on English tie new immigrants and resident Americans together, it would also tie the new immigrants themselves together. Pakistanis and Peruvians, if they are to have anything in common, will have to talk to each other in a language foreign to both of them. The story of immigration cannot be told unless there is a language in which it can be told, and that language, in this country, will be English. Of course one can respond, as some Mexican-American activists do, that immigrants from Mexico, in coming to Texas or California, are simply coming home, but that argument, carried to its logical conclusion, suggests that Spanish-speaking immigrants ought to be held to different linguistic standards than all other immigrants. It would be a tragic conclusion to this wave of immigration if those coming from Spanish-speaking countries were not to be held to the same standards of membership as those from other countries. An insistence on bilingualism could drive a wedge between Latino and other immigrants if the latter were to perceive the former as more interested in the preservation of Hispanocentrism than in the actual lived realities of immigrant life in American cities.

The battle over bilingualism tends to take place over the heads of the immigrants themselves, who in general only want to learn English as fast as they can. Interest groups (and intellectuals) with a stake in politics and policy, on the other hand, make the issue of bilingualism into an ideological litmus test: those on the left are presumed to be in favor of cultural diversity, while those on the right insist on one standard for all. But right and left have little to do with immigration, and the attempt to find correct positions on the issue—for either side—can only lead to trouble.[19]

Portes and Rumbaut provide a further illustration of why it makes little sense to reduce the question of immigration to a matter of left and right. A hallmark of being on the left is to sympathize with those who are poor and oppressed. But who, in matters of immigration, is poor and oppressed? Obviously there are immigrants who would seem to qualify: Chinese working in New York sweatshops, Mexicans tilling the California fields without access to toilets, Vietnamese struggling to make a living in an alien environment. Yet such a picture is superficial. For one thing, many new immigrants are relatively well-off, as Portes and Rumbaut insist. For another, immigrants sometimes leap over people who are already poorer than them and have been here longer; blacks in Miami are not wrong to perceive Cubans as a favored group.

Moreover, even relatively poor immigrants to our shores tend to be better off than those who stay behind. Because they are so sensitive to the immigrants who come here, Portes and Rumbaut are remarkably insensitive to the "brain drain" consequences for the countries of origin. They note the problem, especially for island economies like Jamaica's, but develop no convincing arguments against those who hope that more Indian doctors would prefer Calcutta to Scarsdale. And even if we focus more on farm workers than physicians, the uncomfortable fact is that immigrants come here to sell their labor, which American capitalists are overjoyed to buy. To defend unrestricted immigration is to defend pure capitalism—and of the nineteenth-century variety. Portes and Rumbaut are anything but sympathetic to unrestricted capitalism, but their desire to make the strongest possible political case for the new immigrants forces them into a defense of markets that sits uneasily with their other political perspectives.

The new immigration ought to make all Americans proud, both of ourselves and of those who have overcome so many obstacles to come here. But if we are to be made proud, it will not be by welcoming immigrants with no strings attached. Neither the immigrants themselves nor those who already live here can feel good about a process that refuses to set conditions. For all the passion that questions of immigration and diversity generate, a fairly well understood compromise has been worked out between residents and newcomers. You are welcome here, the residents say to the arriving. But there are costs: you have to learn our language and accept our customs, overcoming the same obstacles that our ancestors overcame. We accept your offer, respond the new arrivals, the great majority of whom are nonpolitical, hardworking, determined to learn English, and avid believers in the importance of belonging. Passing tests of language and culture become for them confirmation that the risks they took in exposing themselves to statelessness paid off in new statehood.

Not everyone accepts this compromise fully, and battles over the terms of the compromise still take place. For that reason alone, the arena of ethnicity and immigration will generate more than its share of ideological heat. But the fact that a compromise is possible suggests something else: despite the passions of the sentimentalists, most Americans understand what social scientists and historians know about the experiences of previous generations: we are a nation that defines our identity through immigration but simultaneously requires of immigrants that they give up the old world for the new. That is probably as sensible an approach as one can take.

Criticism Tempered by Functionalism

Pornography and immigration, because they arouse the passions they do, illustrate a cycle of denunciation and sentimentalization. Certain that the evil she confronts is unspeakable, the critic writes to denounce. A long tradition of the jeremiad comes to her aid; Catharine MacKinnon has many resources in an earlier version of Puritanism to revive a language of condemnation for its current manifestation. The temptation to preach becomes almost irresistible to social critics, which may be why some examples of contemporary social criticism have close affinities with the sociology of religion.[20] Denunciation is a genre of its own; to call it preaching to the already converted gets it only partially right. In recounting the debates over the Minneapolis ordinance against pornography, Donald Downs describes the electric, religious experience of hearing Dworkin's and MacKinnon's rhetoric.[21] Although Dworkin's denunciation includes Norman O. Brown,[22] she shares with him an apocalyptic tone of complete rejection. This is not a style that makes for liberal compromise.

Perhaps in reaction to the denunciation of so much social criticism, a contrasting style often emerges which, on its face, seems the exact opposite. Sentimentalists praise what the jeremiad condemns. If nativists denounce the foreign habits of immigrants, sentimentalists praise ethnicity, find positive things to say about their religion and language, and celebrate an America that has room for many different cultures. The sentimentalist criticizes the critics and absolves those under criticism from blame. Only a sentimentalist urge can explain why Portes and Rumbaut, both excellent sociologists, can argue that immigrants want to learn English as fast as possible but should have their Spanish recognized as an official language. The point is to defend those against whom the enemy is poised to attack.

Sentimentalism and denunciation may be opposite styles, but they also significantly overlap. Both belong closer to the romantic tradition in social criticism than the realist does. Neither takes the world as given. Neither wants its picture complicated by evidence. Both are defensive. No wonder that they can easily exist as part of the same mentality. There are many on the left who sentimentalize the single-parent families of the inner city even as they denounce the stable nuclear families of the suburbs. There are many on the right who idealize the market even as they condemn the violence (and pornography) produced by the market.

Ideologically complicated issues call for a social criticism that avoids pictures which are either too negative or too positive to be real. One way to avoid these traps is to temper criticism by what Robert K. Merton—C. Wright Mills's colleague at Columbia University during the golden age—called "functionalism."[23] Borrowed from biology, functionalism defined an approach through which the sociologist tried to understand a phenomenon by focussing on the functions it performed for society as a whole. Mills denounced functionalism as a conservative apology for the status quo,[24] a charge that Merton deflected by pointing out how many of Marx's key ideas, such as the notion of a reserve army of the proletariat, served the function of reproducing capitalism.[25]

Functionalism is "conservative" in the sense that it forces one to recognize that even the most hateful things must have some utility or they would not exist—and therefore not be available to be hated. A critic tempered by functionalism will invariably be less ideological, less polemical, less heroic, less passionate, less zealous than one who is not. After all, a feminist trying to understand the persistence of the nuclear family may find herself coming to respect what she wanted to denounce. If her politics are made uncomfortable from what she learns as a social scientist, perhaps it helps to know that the conservative faces the same problem: if you want to know why teenagers get pregnant or why they use drugs, you may learn things that fit uneasily into your conservative sermon.

Criticism tempered by functionalism will be better criticism. One does not have to like pornography to understand its ubiquity. Recognizing the integrative aspects of weak ethnic identity does not mean that weak identities are always good things. The functions that immigrants perform in renewing the American ideal need not correspond with a political position on the Immigration Act of 1965. All these examples indicate why social science and social criticism are not necessarily at odds. Given the fury of the debate between C. Wright Mills and his critics, it is striking how, in retrospect, each had something to offer the other.

WHAT GENERATIONS OWE TO EACH OTHER

Bashing Through Praise

Although pornography and immigration are topics which arouse the deepest passions, their capacity to tear American society apart, however significant, pales in comparison to relations between the generations. An emerging generational civil war, in which the young fear that they have no future and the old lament a lack of respect for their past, not only has serious fiscal and political implications, it also conveys a tragic moral sensibility. What could be worse, for those who believe that bonds between human beings are important, than weakening connections between one generation and the next? A society incapable of strengthening the ties between generations is literally one that can be said to have no moral fiber.

How we address the question of aging in American society has changed dramatically since the postwar high point of social criticism and social science. In those more optimistic days, social critics made their mark by deploring the ways in which America treated the elderly. Everyone, it was believed, was entitled to live not only as long as they could but also as well as they could. Aging was a category which fit relatively easily into the heroic mode of social criticism: confronting age discrimination, scandalous nursing-home conditions, and society's emphasis on youth and beauty, critics tended to paint a fairly black-and-white portrait, designed to demonstrate that no one, least of all the aged, deserved the fate of obsolescence in the eyes of everyone else.[1]

Such an approach would no longer ring true. In part because of the response to earlier calls for action, old age and poverty are no longer synonymous (although there remain large numbers of elderly individuals who live in poverty). Because of the political power manifested by organizations representing the elderly, no one could seriously claim that the elderly are discriminated against in public provision compared to, say, the very young. Medical advances have increased longevity to an extent barely contemplated by previous generations. With these developments, the burden of criticism shifts. Now we hear statements by politicians and medical ethicists about rationing medical care for the elderly and generational selfishness.[2] Once again an odd role reversal takes place: those speaking for the elderly tend to defend the status quo, while those who call themselves critics find themselves accused of heartless cruelty.

The question I address in this chapter is whether it is possible to enter the contemporary debate over aging in ways that try to dampen the fires of intergenerational conflict. It may not be; aging is one of those issues in which people give little quarter to their opponents. Still a critical sensibility, attuned to the truths of both sides in the debate, could at least try to find out whether there is a way to account for our obligations to those who preceded us without short-changing those who come after us.

One place to begin is with history. As the historian Thomas Cole reminds us, being old in a young country was never very easy.[3] Nineteenth-century America—forward-looking, pressed for time, anxious for efficiency, always mobile—had little patience with the frail. Homage may have been paid to their wisdom, but contempt defined their treatment. The old, Cole demonstrates, constituted an implicit rebuke to Victorian morality. Albert Barnes, a New School Presbyterian, said it best: "One task alone remained for the old man: to tread his solitary way, already more than half forgotten, to the grave. He has had his day, and the world has nothing more to give him or to hope from him" (89).

Such harsh images of sinful decay were ultimately moderated by a Romantic view of aging, in which, as Cole writes, "death was fast becoming a kindly nurse who put old people to bed when their life's work was done" (138). Closely linked to ideals about personal hygiene, the active life, and good character, visions of innocent senescence and sweet death may have sounded pleasant, but they were, if anything, more contemptuous of the elderly than the Revivalist messages they replaced. Now the old, like everyone else in a market society, were responsible for their own fate. And as the idea percolated through society that good health and long life were available to all, their approaching death seemed that much more an offense to the living.

Aging is one biological process which is unquestionably "socially constructed." Cole's fascinating journey through sermons, self-help manuals, paintings, autobiographies, and other cultural artifacts reveals a society never able to make up its mind about the elderly. We have, Cole argues, created a "psychologically primitive" (230) dichotomy of good and bad aging, shifting back and forth from its horrors to its potentialities. He is right to emphasize the duality, but it is also true that no society has ever quite figured out what to do with people who are dependent and experienced at the same time.

If nineteenth-century Americans worried about being old in a young society, today we fear being young in an old one. Preoccupied with economic stagnation, environmental damage, and the costs of social security, we could, according to Cole, learn about the reality of limits from the inevitability of death. Instead, denying what is most obvious about the elderly—their physical decline and need for others—we either praise them for being just like everyone else or condemn them for their greed. A spate of recent books foreshadows a new round of elderly bashing disguised as admiration for our seniors. In them we do not hear the Revivalist message that the old are a useless drain on the energies of the young. The attack instead takes the Romantic form, insisting that the elderly are just like everyone else—perhaps better.

The new *zeitgeist* was first sniffed, as so many are, by Betty Friedan, whose 1993 book *The Fountain of Age* found many of the nation's elderly living vibrant, creative lives, indifferent to biological and gerontological wisdom about their inevitable decline.[4] Friedan, exposing our collective "denial" of aging, denounced the American obsession with youth and beauty on the one hand and praised the search of the elderly for lives of dignity on the other. Guided through the issues by Robert Butler, former head of the National Institute of Aging (and the man who introduced the concept of "ageism" into our language),[5] Friedan concluded that the elderly had every right to retain their "autonomy, independence, and real opportunity to continue to participate fully in life" (542). For her this meant not only defending and expanding all aspects of the welfare state which seek to help the old, but also calling for recognition from the rest of us that aging can be as much about adventure and discovery as about death and decline.

But no one has taken up the task of dooming the elderly through excessive praise with more gusto than Gail Sheehy.[6] "Surprise!," she gushes, "The second half of life is *not* the stagnant, depressing downward slide we have always assumed it to be" (xii). Those unhappy forty-year-olds who once confessed their despair of midlife have turned into productive, energetic sixty-year-olds. A revolution in the life cycle has created something no generation has ever before experienced: second adulthood. Just when we think we are being put out to pasture, we discover the real person buried inside us. Ahead lies not Alzheimer's or poverty but the passage to the age of integrity, after which we can experience the Serene Sixties, the Sage Seventies, the Uninhibited Eighties, the Nobility of the Nineties, and even Celebratory Centenarians.

Men and women enjoy their second adulthood in different ways,

Sheehy writes, but both are wonderful because in them each sex becomes more like the other. Men, the silent gender, learn how to talk. They express their anger and emotions. Reflecting on their careers, they begin to live by what is right, not by what others expect. Warlike politicians become peacemakers. Hard-nosed businessmen melt into pussycats. Men in their sixties rekindle old romances or imitate Clint Eastwood and have late babies. Their impotence disappears. They can even recover from cancer spontaneously when given up for lost.

But none of this is as impressive as the second adulthood of women. Women in their sixties and seventies lived before the feminist revolution, but now they are its biggest beneficiaries. They start new careers. They become the strong partner. Released from the only man they ever slept with, they seduce a series of (mostly younger) men and learn the joys of uninhibited sexual pleasure. They are, Sheehy writes, the wisewomen. "I have thirty years of total freedom *ahead* of me now, to make all sorts of choices," a women named Elise tells Sheehy. "The idea of putting limits on myself, when for the first time I'm without limits, is abhorrent to me" (403).

"Let's don't even call it aging anymore," Sheehy exclaims. "The word carries pejorative baggage. Let's refer to successful aging as *saging*—the process by which men and women accumulate wisdom and grow into the culture's sages" (420). Sheehy says these things as if she is doing the elderly a favor. Her naiveté, if that is what it is, is astounding. Growing old is hard enough. To grow old feeling that you are not one of the beautiful people is devastating. "Will your personal life story in Second Adulthood be conceived as a progress story or a decline story? To a large degree, *you* have the power of mind to make that choice" (172). This is Faust with neither the tragedy nor the poetry.

Sheehy seems unaware that, if you have the choice, you pay the price. No one has to take care of the elderly if they are taking care of themselves; by imagining the elderly as independent, she undercuts the case for interdependence. What happens when the elderly discover that their sense of mastery was an illusion, that they need the support and love of those they spurned in their quest to make themselves over? A younger generation wanting to renounce its obligations to its parents could devise no better strategy than to picture them as leading lives of bliss. Armed with her treatise, we need never again think of them as in need of our support.

Liberalism has not handled well the less than self-reliant. But rarely was this a problem, at least for too long. The young, after all, would reach maturity; all we had to do was wait. And the old, at least in the days when liberalism was young, would die off before their dependency became a cause for concern. But now our political system is caught between the fears of the young and the needs of the old. As the desire of the one to expand government weakens, the reliance of the other on government expands. This clash, the most serious we face, is nowhere more on a collision course than in the relations between generations; the current controversy over Medicare is just the beginning. No one knows how to avoid it. But one thing that will increase the damage is preaching a gospel of unvarnished selfishness. Calling it self-discovery doesn't change that.

Rational Aging

Which brings us to Richard Posner, for whom selfishness, or at least self-interest, is the key to everything. Posner tries to reduce all behavior to economic calculation while expanding economic calculation to include all behavior. One never knows whether to be awed by his ambition or angered by his narrow-mindedness.

Posner is in constant search after universals, practices so ubiquitous that they can only be explained by one thing. Sex, the subject of one of his previous books,[7] was a step in that direction, but not everyone has sex. Perhaps inspired by last year's best-seller, which was about how we die,[8] Posner may have realized that, while all of us are not yet dead, all of us some day will be. If economic tools can help us understand how we age— the one thing, other than birth, we all have in common—they can presumably help us understand anything.

And so Posner sets out to persuade us that "economics can provide a *unifying* perspective in which to view *the whole range* of social problems concerning the elderly."[9] This statement, anything but modest, actually does not begin to capture Posner's ambition, for, in the course of his new book, he rarely stops with mere "social" problems; he applies economic analysis to the psychology of aging, the politics of aging, and even, at times, the biology and neuroscience of aging. For him, economics is crucial to both positive and normative analysis. On the one hand, it can explain phenomena which no other approach even notices. On the other, it gives us a standard—the maximization of individual freedom—against which legal rules can be fashioned and public policies judged.

There is no question that economics is a valuable tool in explaining some "noneconomic" behaviors. In yet another book that Posner wrote (together with Tomas Philipson), he made a thoroughly convincing case that calculations of self-interest do more to explain the epidemiology of AIDS than any other available theory.[10] In contrast even to Jeremy Bentham, who argued that in situations where the stakes are frightfully high utilitarian calculations can break down,[11] Philipson and Posner showed that nothing makes one calculate self-interest more powerfully than the possibility of death. Although I found the normative aspects of their analysis unpersuasive, the evidence they presented was irrefutable: in choosing partners and what we do with them, we factor in estimates of the stakes involved in doing it.

If economic analysis applies to AIDS, can it also apply to aging? Can it even—an irresistible challenge to the economic theorist—apply to a process which has little voluntary choice associated with it?Members of the Chicago school of economics, with which Posner has long been associated, believe that economic analysis can be used to shatter our notions that relying on the market always makes things worse. When applied to aging, Posner continues, such a perspective not only sheds light on how people act as they grow older, but also counters the "the Chicken Littles of this world" (12), who believe that the gradual aging of the American population is a serious public policy problem, that the elderly have become dependent on the young, or that Social Security faces a crisis.

Posner, a federal judge, is the most prolific social scientist of our time and well on his way to becoming one of the most influential. If we take an economic approach to aging, we would conclude that the elderly ought to be treated like everyone else because, rational beings, they are like everyone else. Posner's social science thus points in the same direction as Sheehy's stories of personal fulfillment. If the world operated the way Posner thinks it does (and should), there would be no need to develop strong accounts of our obligations to the dependent for two reasons: we have no such obligations and there is no such dependence. We therefore ought to pay some attention to Posner's arguments, for if they turn out to be valid, the problem of how to treat the aging will have been solved.

Judge Posner's book tackles everything you wanted to know about getting older but were afraid to ask. Economic analysis, he claims, can help us understand behavioral correlates of aging, such as why the crime rate goes down as age goes up. It can teach us why we respect age among leaders but not among mathematicians or physicists. It counsels against damning the old for their selfishness. It can help us understand the costs and benefits of tenure without mandatory retirement for academics (and judges). And it tells us whether or not we should abolish laws against age discrimination. (We should.)

Economic theory can do all these things only if the traditional tools, especially human capital theory, are modified to take account of the discounted time-horizon which aging implies, according to Posner. Human capital theory is the notion that just as we invest in plant and equipment, we also invest in human capacities. Education and job experience are two economic decisions in which individuals or firms spend now to receive benefits later. In a simple human capital model, calculations of costs and benefits are independent of the age of the calculator. But this is clearly wrong. If we have to decide whether attending medical school will return appropriate benefits later on, the "later on" will be influenced by how old we are when we make the calculation. Very few sixty-year-olds ever think about going to medical school. And this is not only because the expected future benefits are lower; the present costs are also higher, for young people usually learn new things easier than old people do. That's why the elderly are usually nostalgic for the past; they incur far too many costs in trying to keep up with what is au courant.

Posner adds two wrinkles to human capital theory to make it relevant to problems of aging. The first involves the "last-period" problem, a term strikingly reminiscent of "The Fixed Period," William Osler's 1905 valedictory address to the Johns Hopkins Medical School which rued a situation of "professors growing old at the same time."[12] In economic theory, people behave in a certain way because they assume that such behavior will improve their prospects. But suppose, Posner asks, they have no prospects? It would be wrong to conclude, he argues, that just because there is no future, there is also no strategic calculation. This is because of what Posner calls "posthumous utility." Why does a dying academic struggle to her last breath to finish a book? Because we care about our reputation after we die, which means that we are willing to burden ourselves with costs now for utilities that will be realized by posterity. Rationality lives after we no longer do.

The second concept Posner explores at some length is the notion of "multiple-selves." It is widely known that twenty-five year-olds will resist being taxed to support seventy-five-year olds in their retirement. But what if the seventy-five-year old to be supported is the twenty-five year-old fifty years from now? Well, it turns out, the reluctance is still there, an anomaly that can be explained by rational choice theory, so long as it applies to two selves, not one. Why should we assume, Posner asks, that "a person is a single economic decision-maker throughout his lifetime"? (84). After all, "aging brings about such large changes in the individual that there may well come a point at which it is more illuminating to think of two or more persons 'time-sharing' the same identity than of one person having different preferences, let alone one person having the same preferences over the entire life cycle" (86).

Posner introduces these wrinkles on economic theorizing because, in his opinion, they both help us understand the world and can serve as grounding points for normative debate. I do not find his normative arguments convincing, as one example may demonstrate. Free-market advocates of strict persuasion do not like Social Security, for it substitutes the paternalistic judgment of the state for individual choice. If a young person is so myopic that he won't save for his retirement, he deserves the penury he will face in old age, such a point of view seems to suggest. This is too harsh, even for Posner. Instead, he suggests that if we think of the person as having a young and an old self, "a compulsory pension system, like a prohibition against enforceable contracts of assisted suicide, imposes a limited fiduciary duty on the young self" (263). In this way, "the multiple-selves argument for compulsory social security, unlike the paternalistic argument, does not depend on any notion that people are ignorant or that government knows best" (263).

The problem, as any strict advocate of laissez-faire would agree, is that in any system of social security, government *is* making a judgment that the young need to be protected against their hedonism. Posner may find that the concept of multiple-selves enables him to justify social security to himself, but most writers have been content with other normative reasons. Governments tax the young to support them in their future because we know from experience that, without such programs, the end-period of life, already difficult enough, can become unbearable. There is something called human dignity. For nearly everyone save rational choice theorists, securing it in old age is sufficient justification for a program of social security, even if a certain paternalism has to be tolerated to achieve it.

So unhelpful are the normative features of "multiple-selves" that Posner himself abandons the concept. He is, for one thing, aware that the concept would wreak havoc in criminal law. As the Menendez brothers might have said, we did not kill our parents, our other selves did. The whole concept borders on the notion of multiple personalities, the clinical diagnosis often alleged to be found among those who consider themselves victims of Satanic ritual abuse.[13] And if it the notion is problematic for criminal law, think of what it would do to constitutional law. Rights inhere in persons. Which person's rights ought to be upheld, then, the free-speech right of the self which seeks pornographic pleasure or the community-order right of the self which, ashamed at what its other self is doing, seeks to censor pornography? Is mandatory testing for AIDS justified because the self who wants to know is more important than the self who does not? Is the fetus a separate self or a multiple of the mother in whose womb it lies? Some believe we have too many rights as it is; giving each us more selves expands even a constant number of rights to infinity.

Once the concept of multiple selves is introduced, the prospects for judges are endless.

If Posner's concepts are not very helpful in normative argument, perhaps they can serve more strictly social-scientific purposes, such as clarifying theoretical issues or helping to predict human behavior. A moment's reflection, however, ought to indicate that neither the concept of posthumous utility nor the notion of multiple-selves can be of much explanatory use, at least in an empirical sense: how can one determine what our posthumous benefits are (were?) or which of our selves is making which economic decision? Both concepts border on the mystical, as if the economist wants to understand the self-interest of the soul. Posner is not (at least I hope he is not) claiming that we actually expect to complete our posthumous transactions or that each of our selves has a physical existence and behaves in quantifiable ways.

Clearly, Posner introduces concepts such as these for other than reasons of description and prediction. These are meant to be heuristic devices—fictions which nonetheless enable us to explain aspects of reality which would otherwise be obscure without them. Posner likes mind puzzles. He approaches theory playfully, as if the role of the social scientist is to take an idea and stretch it this way or that to see if it sheds new light on old issues. But as much fun as it may be to watch Posner engaged in his stretching exercises, there is about them a deep sense of futility. For rational-choice theory to work, all people, young and old, have to be motivated by the same incentives. But if the young and the old are as different as the notions of posthumous utility and multiple selves suggest, why insist on a unified theory capable of subsuming their divergent behaviors?

Posner is fully aware that the elderly are different. "Anyone who doubts that there are palpable, substantial, systematic, measurable, demoralizing, and in the present state of biological and medical knowledge inevitable declines in physical and mental functioning even for the 'normal' or 'healthy' aged in this the world's most medically pampered society . . . is out of touch with reality" (24), he writes. But he then insists that the significance of age-related characteristics can be exaggerated and argues that "there is scope for rational debate over when decline sets in" (24). Because the elderly both resemble and are different from the young, the social scientist must decide whether those differences are so minimal that a unified theory of human behavior can still be salvaged or so major that such a theory would have to be rejected.[14] I suspect that the only reason for Posner to introduce the truly bizarre notion of individuals "timesharing" the same body is to save his theory, not to advance our understanding of reality.

There is one way to test whether my suspicion is correct. If rational-choice theory, even when modified, does make accurate predictions about human behavior, then Posner is right to rely upon it. Certainly Posner thinks it does; his book is filled with empirical claims. Let me illustrate one of them by following his reasoning through the question of whether the elderly ought to be allowed, with the help of a physician, to take their own lives.

An argument against the idea of physician-assisted suicide is that by making suicide easier, we make it more acceptable. This can even be expressed in economic terms: lower costs for suicide will increase demand. But, Posner argues in typically counter-intuitive fashion, "cheaper suicide will result in less suicide"(248). For although terminal illness is awful, the question is not whether the utility of living is negative, but whether it is negative (or positive) compared to something else. There are two alternatives. One would be a regime in which physician-assisted suicide is illegal; the other, one in which it is permitted.

In the former case, an individual facing pain, suffering, and eventual death can commit suicide now. "He will experience neither positive nor expected utility from living," Posner writes, "because he will be dead, but he will incur the cost of getting from the state of being alive to the state of being dead" (246). If, on the other hand, he postpones his suicide, he avoids those costs, but he cannot be certain about the utility of staying alive. He will therefore commit suicide "if the expected utility of death now, which is to say the disutility averted by death now, exceeds the expected utility of life plus the cost of suicide" (246).

Next, assume that the same individual can commit suicide now or commit it later, given constant cost, with the help of a physician. As the individual waits, the unknown aspects of the expected utility of life begin to become clearer; a new drug may be discovered (or not discovered), the pain is found to be as real (or less real) as anticipated, the dignity of being terminally ill more or less than imagined, and so on. By committing suicide now, an individual forecloses the information that would become available if he waited. Not all of that information would result in a decision to avoid suicide, for some of the information could be worse than expected. But some will also be better. It follows that introducing physician-assisted suicide will reduce the number of suicides by just that number of people who are mistaken about expecting the worst from their terminal condition. Thus those who believe that making suicide "easier" will increase its frequency are simply wrong.

Posner's reasoning—presented with numerous algebraic formulae which I have left out—may strike some as far-fetched; after all, potentially suicidal individuals could still postpone their decision, even if physician-assisted suicide were never introduced. At this point, we are best off leaving theory and turning to actual data. Yet as soon as the possibility of a reality test is posed, Posner's analysis enters into a strange world in which simple hypothesis testing never resolves anything. Oregon is the first state to have authorized physician-assisted suicide, but, delayed by legal challenges, its law has not at the time of this writing gone into effect. No evidence there. Posner then demonstrates that states with lower per capita income and lower percentages of minorities have higher suicide rates. This is an interesting finding, but not relevant to his main point. Moreover the finding itself could be "spurious": poor states, often more religious, may have taboos against classifying suicides as suicides; states with high minority populations may witness more members of minority groups dying before suicide becomes an option.

There is one variable that might shed some light on the question that interests Posner. While physician-assisted suicide is not given official approval in any American state except Oregon, it is defined as criminal behavior in some states and not in others. Posner shows that states which criminalize physician-assisted suicide have higher suicide rates than those which do not, although the relationship is not statistically significant. Yet once again even that weak relationship has to be qualified. First, the number of cases—fifty, given the number of states—is small. Second, Posner does not repeat the test over a number of years but confines himself to 1991. Third, his procedure compares a rate, which can vary from 0 to 100 percent, with a binary state: either there is a law criminalizing the behavior (in which case Posner assigns a value of 1) or there is not (in which case it is classified as 0). This is an acceptable statistical procedure, but not one upon which strong confidence can be built, as it bears an uncomfortable similarity to coin-flipping. Fourth, as Posner recognizes, states which do criminalize physician-assisted suicide rarely enforce the law. If the law is on the books but is generally ignored, we cannot say much about the actual practice of physician-assisted suicide. These are statistical relationships meant for the trash can, not the text.

And if these were not problems enough, the evidence from the one place in the world where such an experiment has been tried is even more ambiguous. It turns out that there has been a dramatic drop in suicides in Holland after the legalization of euthanasia. Deaths attributed to euthanasia are not counted as suicides in Holland, however, with the result that even Posner concedes that the Dutch data are useless for his purpose. But the always curious Posner should have noticed something else from this example. Sociologists have long argued that suicide rates measure, not the behavior of those who take their lives, but the behavior of the coroners who decide which deaths constitute a suicide and which do not.[15]

Suicide rates, like crime rates, tell us more about the culture in which individuals live than about how individuals behave.

If there is no proof either way, we ought to reject the hypothesis that physician-assisted suicide would bring down the number of suicides. This is the one thing that Posner will not do. Here is one summary of his findings: "the fear that . . . physicians will hustle their patients to a premature and undesired death seems greatly exaggerated; indeed, the suicide rate might actually fall if physician-assisted suicide were permitted in the subset of cases that I have described" (260). This is a rather outrageous statement: Posner has never demonstrated that potentially suicidal people, including the elderly, think about life and death as rational calculators. Yet he is prepared to advocate that doctors should be permitted to help people take their own lives, fully confident that the world will be a better place if they do. I do not know where his confidence comes from. It certainly does not come from any data presented in his book.

Aging and Old Age promises a radically new approach, one which cautions against exaggerating any problem we might identify with increased longevity. Yet without a strong normative, conceptual, or empirical base for his arguments, can we trust Posner's recommendations on such serious issues? It turns out that not even Posner can; if anything, he gives credence to the "chicken littles" who worry about these things. The elderly, Posner points out, have more time on their hands, so the costs of investing in politics is lower for them, giving them disproportionate political power. They form a natural alliance with the near-elderly. The first generation under Social Security received a windfall—retirement benefits for which they did not pay taxes—an anomaly that, by Posner's estimate, did not fully disappear until those born in 1960 came into the world. All Posner can offer against all this is the notion that the elderly are conservative and do not like to tamper (although three pages earlier he noted that they disproportionately supported Hitler) and that Social Security relieves the private costs of caretaking which the young would have to provide for the old. Posner's conclusion about our current programs for the elderly is therefore anything but counter-intuitive: "it would be reckless to suggest that the programs approach optimality or to deny the possibility that they may involve a large and perhaps unconscionable transfer of wealth from young to old" (296).

Posner—always in a hurry, impatient to get to the next argument or problem—has written a deeply flawed book. "I admit that the analysis might be too static" (296), he says of one (too static) analysis. "The empirical results in this chapter," he says at another place, "are merely suggestive" (218). His analysis of relations between the generations is "conjectured as well as proven" (294). After suggesting that "a dollar spent on fighting women's diseases is likely to buy more longevity than a dollar spent on fighting men's diseases" (275), Posner says that redirecting medical funds from one gender to the other would require "plugging numbers into the variables in my equations, something I have not attempted to do" (278).

Maybe he should have. In the long run, if such a thing can be said to an economist, Posner's contribution to our legal, political, and social-scientific life would be greater if he tried to write one tightly argued and well-documented book rather than a series of brilliant, thought-provoking, but sloppy and, for all their length, incomplete ones. Posner's appetite is voracious, his inquiries free-ranging, his reading extensive, his courage inspiring. The trouble is that, when he writes about some of the most contentious issues we face, there is not necessarily any truth in anything he says.

At the Body's Limits

"It would be quite inadmissible to reduce the phenomenon of aging and being old . . . to a few fundamental problems of social structure and of market and profit economics," wrote Jean Améry in 1968.[16] "Améry" was an Austrian named Hanns Mayer, who escaped from the Nazis to Belgium, became active in the Resistance, was captured and sent to Auschwitz, survived, settled in Belgium, scrambled the last letters of his name, and published, in 1976, *At the Mind's Limits*. What did "we"—the non-believing intellectual—lose in Auschwitz? Améry asked. "We lost a good deal of arrogance, of metaphysical conceit, but also quite a bit of our naive joy in the intellect and what we falsely imagined was the sense of life."[17]

On Aging, published two years later than *At the Mind's Limits*, but only recently translated into English (from the German) by John D. Barlow, applies the same nonsentimental, unadorned sense of realism to the problem of getting older which would later mark Améry's attempts to get at the truth of the concentration camp. Améry was fifty-five when he wrote his book, the same age as Posner when he wrote *Aging and Old Age*. "For the aging," Améry wrote, "the autumn of life is the last autumn and therefore not an autumn at all" (17). Time loses its cyclical sense as the person becomes older. Every moment, even those of great joy, counts against us, for it is one more tick off a clock that cannot be reversed. Aging, in this one sense, is like the camps; it mocks our intellectuality, our sense that we can make rational meaning out of life.

People comfort the aging by telling them that it is a normal condition. But there is no norm to which the aging person returns. One can overcome an illness, but never to the point of "normality" before one became sick. We are better off treating aging as an incurable disease, Améry writes, recognizing thereby that the enemy against whom we are fighting is going to win. And we generally do this—but not until just before the end. In the meantime there is a transitional state: aging, as opposed to death. In this limbo, we act very much like Posner's multiple selves—alienated from our own aging body, as if we could preserve the ego of the nonaging self even as we watch a tooth here and a heart there deteriorate. We discover our body as we begin to lose it, only to realize that we will soon experience its negation. "When we have crossed the top of the mountain and begin to go down the other side and it quickly becomes steeper and steeper, faster and faster, it is no longer our place to think in a way appropriate to the conquest of the world, feeling compelled to demonstrate for ourselves an image of the world in logic" (51). Inevitably, "alienation from oneself becomes alienation from being, no matter how faithfully we still attend to the day." (52).

We also age in the eyes of others. "All at once we realize that the world no longer concedes us credit for our future, it no longer wants to entertain seeing us in terms of what we *could* be" (55). Rebel as we might, we are as without recourse in the battle against social age as we are against physical age. Even if we try to make declarations about the nature of the world, we discover that it no longer belongs to us. The young steal from us our sense that we can say something important; they not only no longer read the books we write, they do not even read the books we read. That may be why the once modern conductor Ernst Ansermet can write a diatribe against serialism or Oskar Kokoschka can denounce modern painting. The culture conspires against the aging person, designing roads for which he has no maps. "For him the logical question whether the acceleration should be called progress is not even under discussion" (96). The aging understand a world which no longer exists and the world which does exist no longer makes sense to them.

All that is left for the aging is to think about death. But this takes no special abilities, for the genius and the imbecile, unequal in everything else, are equal in this: neither knows what extinction will be like. It is better to contemplate dying than death, for one takes place in the present and can be understood, while the other has no time, present or future, and is literally unknowable. We cannot ignore our approaching death nor can we welcome it. All we can do is to live with a "bad compromise" (123), the lies we tell us ourselves to get through the moment. "In aging, finally, we have to live with dying, a scandalous imposition, a humiliation without compare, that we put up with, not in humility, but as the humiliated" (128).

Améry, whose book *By One's Own Hand: A Discourse on Voluntary Death* appeared in 1976, put his theory into practice a year later.[18] Shortly before his suicide, he wrote: "Today as much as yesterday I think that society has to undertake everything to relieve old and aging persons of their unpleasant destiny" (*On Aging*. p. xvix). I, for one, do not share his bleakness, let alone his rationale for euthanasia. His relentlessly unhappy vision of what happens to us as we lose our mental and physical powers is so colored by his experiences with human evil that they surely are as unreliable a guide to public policy as the cheery optimism of Sheehy or Posner. But if his pessimism disparages life, his humanism affirms it. By the sheer act of trying to make sense about our existence, Améry reminds us of why human life is so precious. That is why his recognition that there are limits to our capacities is a welcome contribution to the American debate over intergenerational obligations.

That debate has been marked by a reluctance to acknowledge that differences between people are possible without such differences necessarily being invidious.[19] The elderly have been subjected to their own form of "mainstreaming." Just as educators shy away from tracking students by ability or advocate incorporating disturbed students into the regular classroom, we treat the elderly as if there was nothing special about their condition. But there is. They are facing death. It is tragic that in an age of AIDS so many young people have the same experience, but not all young people have dying on their minds. All old people do.

At the very least, the way we think about aging ought to be colored by the reality of what aging means. Even Posner, so optimistic about so many things, knows that aging is hardly hunky-dory: "I am not a Pollyanna," he insists. "I dread old age as much as the next person. I suggest merely that it may be a more serious personal problem than it is a social, an economic, or a political one" (50). Yet how can a personal problem shared so by so many not be a social one as well? After all, the next couple of decades will witness, as public policy problem number one, the aging of one of the largest birth cohorts this country has ever produced. A group of people given to selfish introspection can only become even more narcissistic when persuaded that limits are as unnatural as they are unnecessary. I shudder at the thought of my generation reaching old age, not because our there may be little in the till to bail us out, but because we have not done well with good fortune and are likely to do far worse with bad.

Toward Compassionate Realism

No society in the entire scope of human history has ever had to think about how to support a significant part of its population for three or more decades after they have stopped working. Dealing with the challenge of this irreversible demographic fact cries out for what can only be called compassionate realism.

"Deliver me from compassion" (26), Betty Friedan thought, as she listened to experts discuss problems faced by the elderly; there are fewer words more out of place among the new celebrants of the last years as "gratitude," "caring," and "indebtedness." But a society which forbids the young from expressing their thanks to the old is a cold society indeed. They created the world in which we were raised; as much as we might be tempted to blame them for its imperfections, we are indebted to them for its existence. If they want to work past sixty-five we ought to recognize the amazingly large number of years they have left and let them do so. They are entitled to a regular income and decent medical care, and it matters not a whit that they have not quite paid their full share, even if they believe they have. The notion that our obligation to provide future generations balanced budgets overrides our debt to those who suffered through a depression and won a world war has little credible moral backing.

It is precisely because we have such strong obligations to the elderly that we owe them realism as well as compassion. We cannot accept their claim that any acknowledgment of their declining powers is a form of "ageism." (On this point I agree with Posner.) While recognizing that there are always new wonders to experience and capacities to develop, we must discourage the elderly from pursuing an illusory course of individual self-reliance foolish even for the most active and productive among the young. And, most important of all, we are right to resist their efforts to use their political power to protect their group advantages, because a game of playing one generation off against another is one that every generation will eventually lose. For better or worse, the elderly are as dependent on us for their future as we are on them for their past.

We are a long way from having the appropriate language for strength-ening interdependence across the life cycle. Sheehy's retreat to the power of positive thinking, Posner's torturous efforts to deny that dependency is real (let alone his surreal use of economics to describe matters so close to the human heart), and Thomas Cole's suggestion that we are experienc-ing "the emergence of a postmodern course of life, in which individual needs and abilities are no longer entirely subordinated to chronological boundaries and bureaucratic mechanisms" (240) are the wrong ways to go. We do not owe our elders a narcissistic reflection of ourselves. We owe them the courage to acknowledge their dependence on us. Only then will we be able, when we are like them, to ask for help.

VIII

SOCIAL CRITICISM AND SOCIAL INSTITUTIONS

Institutional Ambivalence

A hallmark of classic social criticism was the way it took institutions seriously. C. Wright Mills made a major point of this: the trouble with "grand theory"—Mills's term for the hypertheoretical work of Talcott Parsons—was that it "delivers the sociologist from any concern with . . . political and economic institutions" and "deals much more with what have been traditionally called 'legitimations' than with institutions of any sort."[1] Whatever one thinks of Mills as a social critic, his sociology was characterized by in-depth treatments of business organizations, the military, and labor unions—the last of these scrutinized in what may have been Mills's best book.[2] Mills had been a student of American pragmatism,[3] and at least one of the pragmatists, John Dewey, brought to philosophy the same concern with social institutions—in particular, the schools—that Mills brought to sociology.

But Dewey's legacy was also problematic for the way social critics treated social institutions. For all its influence upon schools, Dewey's educational philosophy had little respect for actually existing institutions; "his understanding of how religious life would operate in the absence of what we currently call churches," Alan Ryan writes, "was much like his understanding of how education would proceed in the absence of what we now call schools."[4] Nor did Dewey give all institutions equal weight: he wrote relatively little about the family, even though this institution has played an important role in political philosophy from Aristotle to the present. Dewey was, in fact, ambivalent about institutions, an ambivalence that was shared by most of the social critics of the golden age: on the one hand, he wanted his ideas to be grounded in reality; on the other hand, he did not like reality. As a result, Dewey's criticism of real-life institutions often failed to appreciate why they existed in the form they did.

The social critics of the golden age not only followed Dewey in their institutional ambivalence, they also paid particular attention to education. As was true for Dewey, schools for them were a metaphor for society; the real problem was the conformist inclinations of the latter, which the schools, as mirrors of society, facilitated. Schools were indicted for their lack of imagination, their failure to challenge complacency, and their inability to relate to the natural rebelliousness of youth. Social critics in the 1950s generally held a Rousseauian view of the relationship between innocence and society: adolescents—a term that had come into widespread use—were "growing up absurd" because the institutions directed to their needs were failing them.[5] The culture had almost nothing positive to say about the schools: films depicted them as little better than prisons; novels like *One Flew Over the Cuckoo's Nest* were read as parables of the educational experience; and critics such as Edgar Z. Friedenberg or John Holt wrote angry polemics about the inability of schools to educate.[6] Although these critics did discuss matters of pedagogy and curriculum, they would also have agreed with one of the most biting of their number, Jules Henry, who wrote that "the high school is not only a place where children spend five or more hours each day for three or four years, but it is an institution run by adults *for the entire community* and, because of this, expresses the demands of the community and the idiosyncrasies of the adults who run the high school."[7]

Little has changed in this regard in recent years. As with so many of the topics I am treating in this book, the politics of education have shifted. In part because of Dewey's influence, schools changed from places emphasizing discipline and rote learning to places emphasizing inclusion and accommodation, with the inevitable consequence that criticism would more likely come from the right than from the left.[8] But what has not changed is the fact that both right and left treat schooling as a substitute for their larger political complaints. When conservatives criticize the schools, they blame them not just for failing to educate, but for a decline in American morality and manners as well. The only difference with their adversaries on the left is that the latter blame the schools for different social ills, such as the inequalities of race and gender: Jonathan Kozol's indictment of the contemporary school, written in the style of classic social criticism, concentrates on the income disparities between wealthy white experience and poor black experience,[9] while schools have also been criticized for paying more attention to the needs of boys and, in the process, shortchanging girls.[10] The tendency to treat the schools as byproducts of larger social forces has, if anything, increased since the 1950s.

There are reasons for this, of course. From the Scopes trial to air-raid drills, schools have always been places over which adults have fought out their political differences. Today it is impossible to discuss schooling without touching on all the other issues dividing Americans: sex, morality, character, taxation, multiculturalism, gender, technology, religion, AIDS, race, immigration, and violence. Any conversation about an institution like the school is really about America, and any argument about America cannot fail to include the school. Yet because we cannot talk about the school without discussing the larger society, we have lost the ability to talk about institutions as things in themselves: Why discuss schools if your real topic is the decline of morals or the inequities of race and gender? And since most critics would prefer to address larger political questions than delve into the mysteries of how young people actually learn, we seem to know less about education the more we write books about it. As tempting as it may be for the social critic to use the schools to teach lessons about the society in which schools are embedded, it is a temptation that critics might well resist if they are to have anything interesting to say about education.

The Politicization of the School

Why have American schools become such inviting political targets for both the right and left? The short answer is that schools have inevitably become political institutions. De Toqueville once said that in America all political issues eventually become judicial ones. Now every political issue eventually faces a school board—or, more precisely, a school board in New York City. Although New York City is anything but representative of the United States as a whole, its experience illustrates in the extreme what can happen when the boundary between politics and education collapses.

An entire period can be dated by how New York governs its schools. This period begins with Ocean-Hill Brownsville in 1968, when black parents, supported by the Ford Foundation and a number of political activists, sought the removal from their schools of existing teachers, many of them Jewish, in favor of hiring new teachers, many of them black. Two defining events of contemporary American politics can be traced to that confrontation: the widening split between blacks and Jews and the support of liberal foundations for what would eventually be called multiculturalism.

This period ended with another issue of school governance: the inability of New York City to keep superintendents for any length of time. To run a school system as large as New York's, a superintendent must be both an educator and a politician, and all too often the skills necessary for the one come into conflict with those required of the other. None of New York's recent chancellors, from Joseph Fernandez to Ramon C. Cortines, have been able to walk this line. The experiences of Fernandez are particularly interesting, at least in part because he wrote a book about his life and his educational philosophy.[11]

Fernandez is best known for his April 1992 support of a set of curricular materials which mandated that "classes should include references to lesbians and gays in all curricular areas," called for the treatment of "lesbians/gays as real people to be respected and appreciated," and instructed schools to begin such lessons in first grade. One of the school districts in the city, District 24 in Queens, objected to the inclusion of materials dealing with homosexuality in the classroom, with the consequence that, for the only time in his three years as chancellor, Fernandez suspended a board and took over its powers. Justifying his actions, Fernandez told the *New York Times* that "Our schools are the single most important front in the battle against discrimination." Defending hers, the head of District 24, Mary A. Cummins, said, "I will not demean our legitimate minorities, such as blacks, Hispanics, and Asians, by lumping them together with homosexuals in the curriculum."[12] But Fernandez did not ultimately win the fight. The city's school board did not renew his contract, and the process of searching for new school chiefs every year or so continued.

The bitterness of this conflict indicates how deeply entwined American schools have become with politics. But unlike the "real" politics of city councils and state legislatures, where bargaining and deal-striking is common, no compromise was possible between the supporters and defenders of the gay and lesbian curricular initiative. Although few can doubt that Mary Cummins was a demagogue—her authoritarian style did not include consultation with the parents in her district—Fernandez also wanted a fight. The incident suggests that something in America's system of public education insists that we destroy it. It is worth trying to figure out what this might be.

Fernandez' autobiography gives us a clue. His book shows exactly what public schools can and should do. Growing up in Harlem, Fernandez dropped out of school, played with drugs, and seemed determined to wind up one more victim of poverty and discrimination. His life was turned around by two institutions rarely appreciated by those who want to see poverty and discrimination ended: the Catholic Church and the U.S. Air Force. Because respect and strong discipline saved his life, Fernandez is tough-minded on issues of school security. Graffiti and disorder drive him wild. He wants to educate inner-city kids, not make them feel good. The school year ought to be expanded well into the summer, he believes. Fernandez supports national testing and general national standards. In the world of professional education, Fernandez is as realistic as they come. But that, alas, does not tell the whole story.

No one works his way up in the urban school bureaucracies without becoming a master of the pragmatic maneuver, a specialty in which Fernandez excelled. Why, if Fernandez was a pragmatic manager, did he force a political confrontation in Queens? If his main concerns were with management, why did he get so deeply involved with the no-win issue of homosexuality in the curriculum? What explains how a man whose life was saved by the Catholic Church could be so determined to override the beliefs of ordinary Catholics? There are no doubt answers to these questions known only to Fernandez. But an answer is also contained in the way he thinks about the boundary between education and the rest of society. America's public schools have less to do with education and more to do with trying to resolve the social ills that America's welfare state cannot handle. Managerialism and discipline may work as a bureaucratic strategy to run school systems, but Fernandez wanted to speak to the larger social issues as well, which demand a different kind of response.

Fernandez knows that public schools have assumed functions well beyond education. "The frustrating part, the thing that kills you in inner-city schools, is the amount of time you have to spend doing things that aren't directly related to school" (103). "We have overwhelmed our classrooms with sociological indoctrination," he laments. "The scholastic consequences have been disastrous" (2). Education is a mess because society, unwilling to take on problems of poverty, teenage pregnancy, drug addiction, and other ills directly, passes them on to hapless teachers. When schools, in his words, are required to "run the gamut from safe driving to safe sex" (2), it may well be the case that "we expect too much" from them (3).

Faced with a situation in which schools are no longer teaching, we might expect educators to insist that they begin to do so once more. But this is conspicuously what Fernandez does not do. "I'm not saying our schools should retreat from these issues" (3), he writes. If society demands it, the schools must respond. It was not Fernandez' job, as he saw it, to use his position to be an advocate for learning. When the New York City Board of Education split down the middle on a plan to provide condoms to school children, Fernandez approached the issue as a policymaker, not an educator. "Somebody had to take a position of leadership," when so many children were dying of AIDS. "So why not the schools?" (245). Fernandez was willing to consider anything that might work. He wanted higher standards but was willing to try gradeless schools. Integration was important to him, but he supported the notion of an all-black and all-male academy. He was for parental involvement but rejected the notion of a parental "opt out" clause for the condom availability plan. Fernandez is a can-do guy; give him a problem, and he will set out to find a solution. So what went wrong? Although it may seem obvious that schools ought to be used to combat the larger problems of society, there are at least four dangers involved.

First, education and policy-making are not the same. Policy-making works best when a consensus already exists about the course we ought to take. When such a consensus does not exist—as it clearly does not on issues involving sexuality—public policy cannot, and probably should not, try to do too much. Education, by contrast, does not presuppose a consensus; one of its main functions is to mold ideas, not to represent them. When we mix these realms, we reverse the assumptions that make each of them work, assuming a consensus in the educational realm (where one should not exist) because we realize that no consensus exists in the policy realm (where one should). The consequence is not only to ask too much of the schools but to ask too little of the state.

Using the schools to teach about morality because we assume that families and churches no longer do so causes similar problems. There are obvious reasons why, if families have failed, we expect schools to pick up the slack. But so long as schools do, there is no reason for families to do what they ought to. This is a vicious dilemma, one of the most serious we face, but it is a dilemma. Those who urge the schools to provide the sex education, moral training, and general upbringing once provided by families and churches ought to realize that, even if they solve one problem, they cause another. Schools are simultaneously too rigid to substitute for families and too fragile to substitute for government. They treat the intimate realm abstractly while responding to universal needs with particularism. Last to form a welfare state, Americans were the first to establish public schooling. We still do not have much of the former. By using schools the way we do, we may now be ruining the latter as well. Collapsing the boundary between school and family can destroy both.

Third, a reliance on schools to do what other institutions more properly ought to do works to make all schools inner-city schools. No one can doubt that the conditions of public schools in America's worst-off neighborhoods are scandalous. Those who witness on a daily basis what family disintegration, poverty, and violence can do to small children can hardly be blamed for wanting the schools to do whatever they can to help. But because public schools are public, there is always the temptation to apply a program that may help an inner-city school directly to schools in other neighborhoods which do not want the program. We sometimes forget that not all public schools are inner-city schools. By insisting that schools do social work rather than education, however many young people are helped are more than matched by others who are deprived of the teaching of basics they need and want.

A fourth and final reason for worrying about the collapsing boundary between schools and politics is that, if the schools do take on functions over which people disagree, then the same passions and ideologies unleashed in the political realm will be unleashed in the educational realm as well. When schools, in Fernandez' term, do not "retreat" from active involvement in bitter political controversies, they put themselves in the line of fire for all those armed to fight for their political beliefs. These days a furious war is taking place over education, as conservatives and liberals attack each other's ideas with accusations of bad faith and assertions of ideological certainty. Educators such as Joseph Fernandez are symptoms, not causes, of this ideological warfare, but there is also little doubt that, in helping break down the barrier between educating and trying to solve society's problems, they open the door to ideological conflict.

That conflict can be illustrated by looking at the charges made by conservatives like Thomas Sowell and William Kilpatrick. In *Inside American Education*, Sowell sees decline and deception everywhere. He begins, as do most critics, with test scores. Between 1963 and 1990, the average combined SAT scores in this country declined by 80 points. Thirty percent of American seventeen-year-olds cannot find Great Britain on a map. Korean schoolchildren do nearly twice as well at abstract reasoning than their American counterparts. Insofar as these things can be quantified, American students, like their textbooks, have been "dumbed down." "It is not merely that Johnny can't read, or even that Johnny can't think," Sowell argues, "Johnny doesn't know what thinking is" (4).

Johnny also feels good about it, and therein, according to Sowell, hangs a tale. Asked if they think they are good at math, Americans tend to answer yes when they are not, while Koreans answer no when they are. The reigning ideology in American education, Sowell insists, is therapeutic. All should be taught to appreciate themselves, even if they don't know a thing. Our schools have been captured by psycho-babbling products of a professional education establishment that cannot tell a fact from a feeling. Educators are good at protecting their jobs but little else. They inflate grades so that unprepared children are simply advanced through the system. They fail to understand that self-respect is something you earn, not something handed to you merely because you tried.

One of the more striking ways in which Sowell illustrates his charge deals with "death education." Some schools, it seems, ask students to write suicide notes, discuss death in their families, make coffins, imagine what it is like to be buried, and listen to funeral music. Rather than reading *The Death of Ivan Ilyich,* students are taken to a morgue and asked to reflect on their feelings. In short, Sowell concludes that our schools use their power over young minds to inculcate dubious, if not cultist, notions, rather than to teach the young how to think. The whole process works on the basis of emotions, not intellect. In the name of multiculturalism, bilingualism, sensitivity, relevance, the whole child, and globalization, students are introduced to half-baked nostrums and ill-designed thought experiments. Right and wrong, true and false, good and bad—all are dismissed out of hand. Anything that can displace learning will displace learning.

William Kilpatrick, who teaches education at Boston College, in his contribution to these debates, *Why Johnny Can't Tell Right from Wrong,* treats sex and drugs roughly the way Sowell treats death. A revolution in sex education has taken place in this country, he asserts. *Changing Bodies, Changing Lives,* a text recommended by the *School Library Journal,* contains graphic descriptions of the pleasures of gay sex and cunnilingus. Students in a junior high school in Montana receive condoms in their valentine cards. A video produced by the Massachusetts Department of Public Health discusses the advantages and disadvantages of Nonoxynol-9. A brochure used in the eighth grade in western New York discusses fisting, rimming, vibrators, watersports, and phone sex ("100 percent safe"). A homework assignment, again in Massachusetts, is to go to your room and masturbate. The schools, in Kilpatrick's view, are dominated by individuals who want to deromanticize love, undermine marriage and the family, and promote sexual pleasure without responsibility. Contemporary educators claim to be approaching sex nonjudgmentally, but, Kilpatrick argues, they are encouraging students to sleep around. They provide information, but they fail to encourage discretion. They say they are freeing students to be themselves, but they really want their students to be controlled by them. If charged with promoting a particular lifestyle, they would deny it, but they view abstinence as a false choice.

Kilpatrick's picture of how our schools teach about drugs is equally alarming. Under the influence of humanistic psychologists, schools try, as much as possible, to avoid anything that smacks of preaching or distinguishing right from wrong. But what seems an interesting approach is actually quite dangerous. Parents are no match for drug therapists trained in the nondirective, esteem-enhancing methods of Carl Rogers. After all, parents spent a considerable amount of time saying no. To their children, they are familiar, even predictable, in their responses. The drug counselors, by contrast, are forgiving, charismatic, hip. They may be ostensibly warning against the use of drugs, but they are surrounded by the aura of the forbidden and exotic. Kilpatrick concludes that drug education consistently increases drug use, just as, according to Sowell, death education increases death.

Kilpatrick's most serious charge is that our schools promote "moral illiteracy" (112–28). They fail to teach character by ignoring the moral lessons so central to religion, myth, music, and literature. Addicted to abstract moral dilemmas and value clarification, they undermine the virtues—including honesty, heroism, and loyalty—that a good society requires. To put them on the right track again, Kilpatrick offers a guide to great books for children—a rather sensible guide, actually, and certainly one worth having.

Kilpatrick seems to speak directly for those, like Mary Cummins, who dislike the secular humanism so commonly taught in public schools. If so, then Jane Roland Martin, who teaches philosophy at the University of Massachusetts in Boston, speaks on behalf of all those professional educators who would use the schools to promote their own desired vision of social change. Martin argues that because families are changing, schools must as well. She imagines the creation of a Schoolhome—"a new kind of school" to which "youngsters of all ages, many of them dragging a parent along, have come to make sure their needs are met."[13] The bulk of her book is a picture of what will take place inside this new institution. Gone would be competitiveness, mastery, conflict, anger, fear, discipline, brutality, selfishness, and stereotyping—in short, reality, whatever one thinks of it. In their place would stand what Martin calls the three Cs of caring, concern, and connectedness.

Martin is the kind of educator who would turn *Moby Dick* into a parable to save the whales. She frowns on chess or cheerleading, is skeptical of photography, and likes theater, farming, and animal care. Every moment of the day presents an opportunity for didacticism: "I want litter in the halls and chaos in the lunchroom to be perceived by everyone as fruitful opportunities for moral education" (168). Because "keeping the atmosphere loving is everybody's business," any expressions of anger would be followed by everyone saying in unison "peace, love, and respect for everyone" (105). One of the functions of the Schoolhome is to prevent "mothers from feeling guilty about leaving home each morning" (154). All children will be given daily instruction in racism, sexism, and gender, even if, to do so, blacks always, in Martin's world, speak only for blacks, women for women, and immigrants for immigrants. More advanced students would be asked to ponder whether Thoreau could not have channeled his ideas into more positive activities, like volunteering in an AIDS hospice. Science would be engaged in politics, especially environmental politics, since "modern science's distance and disinterest mask Western man's desire for mastery and control" (199).

In principle, the idea of asking schools to assume functions once performed by the family is not flawed; schools have been doing this since the nineteenth century. There are even occasions when we might want the schools to intervene somewhat heavy-handedly into the domestic realm, although the best reason I can think of—the desire of recent immigrants to have their children learn a language and culture unfamiliar to them— is never mentioned by Martin. But Martin has another objective in mind than helping parents raise their children. She thinks the Schoolhome "can remap the public world" (162). Her book illustrates how some 1960s radicals, unable to win their agenda anywhere else, eye the schools as their last best hope. Martin is not shy about her desire to use the schools to bring about radical social change. Echoing the concerns of the feminist theorists discussed in Chapter 5, she would, like the early Sandra Bem, use the schools to break down gender roles:

> Should the Schoolhome be encouraging . . . 'gender crossing'? Does it place boys at risk? The case is quite the opposite. . . . Given that the ability to take the point of view of another is a basic element of morality itself, it is unconscionable—I would say positively immoral—to deprive them of the opportunity of identifying with the other half of humanity.(76)

The ideas of Judith Ronald Martin, if read by enough parents, would turn Sowell and Kilpatrick into best-selling authors, but neither offers much of an alternative. In part this is because both authors exaggerate their claims. Sowell views his antagonists not as misguided idealists but as evil enemies: "We need to face the harsh reality of the kind of people we are dealing with, the kind of bitter fight we can expect from them if we try to disturb their turf and perks—and the bleak future for our children if we don't" (296). He laces his account by making a quite false analogy between often naive educators and totalitarians, relying on words like brainwashing, cultural gauleiters, Newspeak, and storm-trooper tactics.

Kilpatrick is also not always judicious. His chapter on drug education is organized around the experiences of Dr. William Coulson, who was once a figure in the human potential movement but who has gone over to the other side. Unfortunately Coulson is something of a kook. As Joan DelFattore relates, Coulson has testified as an expert witness in textbook censorship cases on behalf of fundamentalist parents. In those cases, he came out against home economics textbooks on the grounds that they encourage students to choose their own careers. Parents, in Coulson's view, have been chosen by God to guide the fate of their children, and the only proper role for the schools is to teach students blind obedience to their parents' wishes.[14]

For all their differences with reformers like Jane Roland Martin, conservative critics like Sowell and Kilpatrick agree with her that schools have vast power over children's minds. None of these writers really wants to educate children; all of them want to use the schools for a larger political purpose. Public schools will always be political institutions, for they are paid for by taxpayers and run by government. Moreover, we have certainly learned from our recent political wars that curricula must change as societies do. Yet those who believe that education and politics are the same understand neither. When the schools take on so many functions other than the transmission of knowledge, they inevitably become battlegrounds in ideological wars. All those who fight in these wars, irrespective of the side they take, have a panacea, not a well-thought-out solution to the educational crisis in America.

In the Absence of Education

To the degree that schools become mired in political controversies, they have less time for education. So intent are the parties that fight over the schools to make points for their particular political vision of the world that they ignore such basic matters as what children need to know. Lost in the political shuffle, in short, is the idea that there exists a realm of knowledge which most people ought to acquire—knowledge which does not add up to an ideology but which is essential if a person is ever going to form a view of the world.

As if to demonstrate the point that schools, having become political footballs, are no longer in the business of educating, the idea that schools should do something other than transmit knowledge is the latest wisdom among a wide variety of educational critics. It is not just those with a political agenda who find the schools tempting places for trying out their ideas. America is awash in as many dubious psychological theories as it is in political ones. Edward de Bono, for example, argues that "academic thinking," which has been concerned "with analysis, with critical thinking, with argument, with scholarship," needs to be supplemented by an emphasis on emotions, feelings, perception, and design.[15] He offers the reassuring news that intellectual ability is only one aspect of thinking, and a minor one at that; practical intelligence—de Bono calls it "operancy"—is available to anyone.

The invention of the computer strongly reenforces the arguments of those who downplay the acquisition of knowledge and the development of analytic skills as the major goals of education. According to Lewis Perelman, the human brain is remarkably inefficient as an information storage mechanism. Everything the average person might ever want to know—"all the books, manuals, magazine and newspaper articles, letters, memos, reports, greeting cards, notebooks, diaries, ledgers, bills, pamphlets, brochures, photographs, paintings, posters, movies, TV shows, videos, radio programs, audio records, concerts, lectures, phone calls, whatever"—will be stored in a device no bigger than a book within the lifetime of the very young among us.[16] Because machines are intelligent, it is not important whether people are. No longer involved in the transmission of knowledge from one generation to another, schools should be thrown out. We will miss the whole expensive, space-intensive, and cognitively backward thing as little as we now miss the horse and buggy.

Once we get rid of the schools we can begin to address the need for what Perelman calls "hyperlearning" (23). What distinguishes learning from schooling is that the former is process, not content. As Perelman envisions it, all of us will be linked together by our machines, interacting with them—and hence with each other—to solve problems through trial-and-error reasoning. Hyperlearning does not require school buildings, libraries, tests, teachers, counselors, credentials, or culture. You don't have to worry about integration if there are no schools to integrate. The age-old difficulty of separating church and state is solved by disestablishing both. The tax revolt will disappear overnight. All you need is a modem.

Perelman is a "gee whiz" writer, fully within the tradition of those who offer futuristic, technological fixes to contemporary problems. Yet his ideas about interactive technology overlap with those of Harvard's Howard Gardner, one of the country's most distinguished educational theorists. In a recent collection of essays and interviews, Gardner proposes, not that we abolish the schools, merely that we get them out of the business of making judgments about who is smarter than whom.[17] His most famous notion is the theory of multiple intelligences (MI). Those we generally view as smart possess logical-mathematical intelligence, he argues, but this is not the only way to be intelligent. At least six other forms of intelligence can be added to the usual one: linguistic, spatial, musical, bodily, interpersonal, and intrapersonal.

There is a kind of pluralism that says that there should be many ways to reach a common goal. Gardner's pluralism stresses that there should be many ways to reach many goals. He seeks schools that are "intelligence-fair," that is, schools which do not discriminate against those whose intelligence is, say, intrapersonal, in favor of those whose intelligence is mathematical or linguistic. If schools followed his ideas, "the notion of general brightness will disappear or become attenuated" (10). Schools will try to assess the kind of intelligence each student possesses and nurture it, rather than force all students to conform to a mode of intelligence that may be alien to their biological or neurological givens. Computers, a la Perelman, can help us here by allowing students to proceed at their own pace. So can apprenticeship programs or the imaginative use of children's museums.

In his book, Gardner offers a clear synopsis of MI theory, responds to criticisms made of it, and demonstrates how it has been applied in an entire school (the Key School in Indianapolis) as well as in special programs (Arts PROPEL). If the reader remains uncertain how practical his ideas are, so is Gardner. At one point he writes that his ideas "might even be called utopian" (11). Yet another point he "unequivocally" rejects is the notion "that individual-centered education is utopian" (78). Whether or not we can move away from the idea that there is a "univocal" phenomenon called intelligence to which all students ought to aspire, should we? I have my doubts. America has an anti-intellectual enough culture. If schools are increasingly teaching less and doing other things more, they will likely respond to any notion, especially one as democratic and inspiring as Gardner's, that lets them avoid the difficult, disciplined, and time-consuming process called learning.

The ideas of writers like de Bono, Perelman, and Gardner raise the intriguing question of how much actual learning takes place in American schools. If one listens to conservative critics, the answer would be very little. Much the same conclusion is reached by reading leftist writers, since their objective is not to advance learning but to propagate their particular vision of the world. A better source for answering the question of what actually takes place in schools is to turn to the cheerleaders for American education. Despite the doom and gloom of most accounts, they do exist. Some of them are publicizing their own efforts to escape the rigidities of school bureaucracies, such as the attempt by RJR Nabisco to invest $30 million in forty-three schools around the country.[18] Others are education specialists and journalists simply looking for a more positive story to tell about "schools that work."[19]

Larry Martz's account is one of the better of these efforts.[20] Martz examines twelve schools around the country in which teachers, parents, or administrators have led small-scale efforts at educational reform. These case studies cut across racial, class, gender, and geographic lines. Latino teenagers in San Antonio are used as student aids in elementary schools. A peer-group system deals with addiction in Moorhead, Minnesota. Lawrence Kohlberg's emphasis on moral decision-making is applied in the South Bronx, while college preparation is stressed in inner-city Cleveland.

Martz's stories, however, are only tangentially about learning. Many of them deal with programs that, however necessary, could be carried out by agencies other than schools, such as day care or addiction centers. Others have, even by Martz's own account, uncertain futures. Some dubious—or at least hotly contested—notions lie behind others, including codependency rhetoric, nonjudgmentalism, and moral relativism. One of them, in particular, strikes me as troublesome. Martz praises the unorthodox organizing ability of a suburban Los Angeles teacher who has his students engaged in all kinds of undoubtedly exciting projects, but ones whose educational value is uncertain. An eighth-grade class, for example, organizes a stop-and-search party to see whether drivers are wearing their seat belts. What do students learn from this? "The kids have learned about buckling up, for openers," Martz writes. They have also, according to their teacher, learned what it means to "Make a Difference" (124). They might have learned some math or history instead. If Martz, in short, is describing schools that work, our educational crisis is real indeed, for what they are successful at doing only indirectly involves young people using their minds. One can only shudder at the thought of what goes on in schools that do not work.

Educational writers with an interest in cognitive psychology have little in common with those who approach schools as political battlegrounds. Yet for all their differences, both contribute to an atmosphere in which the transmission of knowledge and the acquisition of analytic skills get shortchanged. Political writers—even those, like Thomas Sowell, who insists that his critique is motivated by a desire to improve learning, not to promote conservative ideas—all too often begin with a view of society and deduce from that what is wrong with education and what can be done to make it better. Psychological writers, even the best of them, have simply given up on schools. Advocating the position that students would be better off going to museums than sitting in school, Howard Gardner writes that "Attendance in most schools today does risk ruining the children."[21] One of the most radical of an earlier generation of social critics,

Ivan Illich, proposed the idea of abolishing schools completely.[22] That advice, once radical, seems to have become the position of choice for most contemporary writers on education.

What Do Parents Want?

Schools compete with parents for the attention of children. For writers like Jane Roland Martin, the Schoolhome is a frontal assault on the notion that parents know what is best for their own children. Not surprisingly, therefore, conservatives believe that greater parental involvement in education would undermine the authority of professional educators and would, as a result, be bound to improve the quality of education. One especially powerful form this argument takes, no longer limited to conservatives, is that the proper road to reform is to give parents more choices for their children. As John E. Chubb and Terry Moe put it: "The fundamental point to be made about parents and students is not that they are politically weak, but that, even in a perfectly functioning democratic system, the public schools are *not meant* to be theirs to control and are literally *not supposed* to provide them with the kind of education they might want."[23] So axiomatic has this idea become that a larger point has been lost: parents may not be in the best position to know what kind of education their children should receive.

There certainly will be times when parental control over the education of their children ought to be welcomed. Urban schools, for one thing, have become so rigid that greater parental choice would surely improve them, as has happened in East Harlem.[24] So long as there are educators as decidedly hostile to parents as Jane Roland Martin, moreover, parents will have an interest in protecting themselves, and their children, from those who would impose their own values upon them. But there are limits to every good idea, and nowhere are the limits to parental control better illustrated than in the extreme cases: parents who educate their own children at home and parents who insist that the schools teach their children the same religious and moral beliefs that the parents hold.

Home schooling—the exact opposite of Jane Roland Martin's Schoolhome—is based on one of the few hard facts we have about education. First in 1966, and then many times since, James Coleman demonstrated that parental background was the most important variable in explaining school success.[25] If education begins at home, David Guterson therefore asks, why not end it there as well?[26] No one, after all, knows the individual child as well as the parent. If our goal is to educate children, schools are fine. But if our objective is to educate Amanda or Brian, can we really expect harassed teachers and indifferent administrators to do the job? Only parents have an interest in really hearing what their children are saying and carefully watching what they do. No wonder that children educated at home schools consistently score higher on standardized tests. By now it is no longer news when a home- schooled child enters Harvard. (This trend was actually started by a radical sociologist, David Colfax, who was denied tenure in a bitter fight which eventually led to the closing of the sociology department at Washington University). If Howard Gardner is right that there are many kinds of intelligence, home schooling makes sense, for those closest to the child may be in the best position to know the kind of intelligence their children possess.

Guterson presents his case with anything but a zealot's certainty. He does not think that home schooling is for everyone—he himself was a high school teacher before writing a best-selling novel. All he wants is a kind of local option. People who feel as he does should have more than the right to keep their children at home. Schools should make a place for them during part of the day, as they do in the Twin Ridges Elementary School District in North San Juan, California. After all, home schoolers are saving the taxpayers money. They are taking Tocquevillian principles of voluntarism seriously. They sacrifice at least one parent's income. (Jane Roland Martin would no doubt be quick to point out which parent.) And they are in the mainstream of American tradition, or at least the tradition that existed before we had common schools (and cities).

The overwhelming majority of home schoolers, by all accounts, are the children of deeply religious parents who do not trust the secular institutions of modern society. (A smaller number are offspring of cultural radicals who might once have considered "free schools.") The challenge such parents present is illustrated by the experience of those parents who, disturbed by the very same kinds of textbooks and practices condemned by Kilpatrick and Sowell, brought suit against their school districts in the name of their fundamentalist beliefs. These parents were upset by far more than sex, drugs, and moral relativism. They challenged the portrayal of extraterrestrial creatures, the use of words such as "noble idea," and Anne Frank's advice to "just believe in something"—all on the grounds that exposure to such words would interfere with their children's free exercise of their religious beliefs.

It is possible to be sympathetic to these parents, who, after all, are not only powerless but genuinely concerned with bringing some kind of order to a world that, for them, is wildly out of control. One writer, Stephen Bates, has written an extremely moving account of Vicki Frost's battle to prevent her children from being exposed to what she considered Satanistic influences in their textbooks.[27] After reading his account, it is impossible to dismiss the Tennessee textbooks controversies as "Scopes II"—a clash between the forces of enlightened wisdom and reactionary backwardness. Yet for all that, Vicki Frost was wrong to believe, as Joan DelFattore summarizes her view, that "school officials were required to conform absolutely, without argument or explanation, to whatever parents wanted for their children" (19). This is parental control run wild.

The fundamentalist parents whose story Bates and DelFattore tell objected so much to what their children were asked to read that they did not, at first, even consider home schooling. Nor were they interested in organizing their local communities through the political process to change what they did not like. Not for them the give-and-take of living in a pluralist society. These parents willingly encouraged the arrest of their own children to make a point. They believed it their duty to try and prevent school officials from carrying out their legal responsibilities. Yet the prospect of an education paid for by everyone else was difficult for them to forego. At one point, these parents proposed a compromise in which they would come to school and teach reading to their own children outside the class, a proposal the principal rightly rejected out of hand. It is hard not to conclude that the parents wanted it both ways: the state should pay for the education of their children but should have no claims on those for whom it was paying. Only after their tactics failed did many of these parents remove their children from the public school and discover the virtues of home schooling.

I read these excellent books on home schooling and school censorship wars as warnings against the notion that parents necessarily know what is best for their own children. If we follow these accounts closely, we ought not to make home schooling an easily available option. Children can be captives of the religious and ideological beliefs of their parents and ought to have exposure to the claims of strangers. The state does have an interest in children, and the desires of the parents, which always have to be taken into account, can never be the final word, so long as we enjoy benefits that come from being members of a larger community. Limiting home schooling and resisting parental demands for textbook censorship are like insisting on motorcycle helmets, things we do to prevent people from harming themselves in the name of liberty.

Obviously home schooling and fundamentalism do not resolve the question of whether parents ought to get what they want from the schools, for both represent extreme positions. Yet for this very reason they also highlight an issue that can be easily overlooked. Fundamentalists and home-schoolers see a direct connection between the schools and their political or religious beliefs. There is no tension in their view, no obstacle that stands between them and their desires. Yet tension is at the heart of education. Schools work best when they take what is and transform it into something else, a process that introduces children to ideas, concepts, and methods that coexist uneasily with their preconceived ideas about how the world works (or even how it should).

Schooling ought never, in short, to be "easy," yet it is remarkable how many of the educational nostrums I have discussed in this chapter want to make it easier. Technology creates instant feedback, which returns to the student what he or she puts in. Multiple intelligence theory allows us to find the right kind of intelligence for any particular student's talents. Conservatives want schools to emphasize conservative themes to already conservative youngsters, while radicals and feminists assume that their views accord with the ideas students really have, if only they are exposed to them. Vouchers will enable parents to choose those schools the parents most want to choose. Home-schoolers want to protect their children so much that they are reluctant to expose them to the claims of strangers. Fundamentalists parents imagine schools as teaching revealed truth. There is, when one comes right down to it, no difference between the fundamentalists on the right and the multiculturalists on the left on this issue; Stephen Bates points out that the demands of Vicki Frost for separate religious instruction for her children in the public schools is little different than bilingual education or special classes for the handicapped, both of which are often defended by liberals.[28] The justification in all cases, he writes, is that keeping children with many different beliefs in the same school promotes "diversity" (316). If true, he is right, but it is equally as plausible that all sides will want a little piece of the public school to promote their private agendas.

All these ideas, so radically different, have one other thing in common: they imagine schools as places that work with what they are presented, rather than as places that want to transform what is into something else. Perhaps the single most important reason why politics and education are not the same is that democracy—let alone the kind of direct and immediately responsive democracy envisioned by so many of these writers—is appropriate for the one but not for the other. Schools that give people what they want are unlikely to be the kinds of places demanding enough to have much of an impact on the lives of students.

Public Education's Delicate Balance

Perhaps this excursion into contemporary educational theory and practice sheds light on why the controversy over District 24 in Queens became a powerful symbol of the changes taking place in American life. In the contempt he showed for ordinary people and their deepest moral beliefs, Joseph Fernandez embodied all those forces that seem anonymous, distant, and judgmental. If this is what modernity requires of us, many Queens parents responded, no thanks—we would rather rely on nuns.

But the Queens parents also misunderstood education. Like so many others these days, they imagined the schools as little more than a conveyor belt for teaching the values they already possessed. Surely the schools have an obligation to convey ideas that make people uncomfortable by challenging their received wisdom. Populism is as bad for the schools as it is for the political system, if not far worse.

Public education, in short, requires a delicate balance between maintaining popular support and confronting popular beliefs. If it leans too much in the former direction, it fails to educate. If it leans too much in the latter direction, it undermines its legitimacy, weakens its tax base, and stimulates a growth industry in private schooling. The controversy in Queens represents both horns of the dilemma. As long as school officials and parents clash like this, the vicious cycle that has sent American schools hurtling toward self-destruction can only continue.

If this cycle is ever to be stopped, we will need to rethink what we want schools to do. Obviously schools will do things that go beyond the mere transmission of knowledge. American schools have never been purely educational institutions. They have also acted as vehicles of assimilation, social mobility, public health, job training, day care, and psychological adjustment. They will continue to find new functions, including some efforts to teach about sex, drugs, and morality. (Perhaps we can dispense with death.) Given the realities of contemporary American life—the devastation of the inner cities, economically squeezed families, and the arrival here of children who will learn a different language than their parents—schools will inevitably be used, as they always have been, to smooth out the rough edges of raw social transformation.

Even though schools in America's past routinely took children away from their parents and introduced them to alien ideas, they also had the support of those very parents. For all the turmoil of what Diane Ravitch has called "the great school wars,"[29] many parents struggled to put their children into the schools, rather than, as today, finding ingenious ways to take them out. Those parents knew that although the schools were to some degree social welfare agencies, they also taught something. Such parents had a contract with the system. Distrustful and fearful of alien authority, they nonetheless understood that access to a new language, history, and culture, the learning of basic skills, and the opportunities provided by the mastery of ideas were things beyond their ability to provide for their children. The contract never worked on trust; it was self-interest on all sides.

No such contract currently exists. Public schools not only fail to teach the ideas necessary to get ahead, they seem to want to substitute in their place questionable psychology and irreverent morality. Knowing a bad bargain when they see one, parents either take their children out of the schools or demand that the schools do what they want, both of which cripple the ability of the public schools to do what they have to do. To make America's public schools work again, we have to convince parents to send their children to them. But we will never do that unless we insure that, whatever other purposes the schools have to serve, the transmission of knowledge is the essential thing they do.

Social critics who concern themselves with institutions can help in this process. Looking back on educational criticism since John Dewey, one is left with the impression that radical social critics have consistently misdiagnosed the problem because they had so little respect for educational institutions. Schools are obviously part of the larger society, but they are also unique institutions which do different things than families, neighborhoods, and governments. One may not like hierarchy and authority in politics, but in education they are essential—even for a politics that would challenge hierarchy and authority. The end result of fifty years of undermining education are now clear; the poorest in American society have fewer chances to grab onto education as a way of pulling themselves out of poverty, while the well-off do everything they can to avoid public education altogether. If that is what educational reform leads to, who needs educational reform?

But social critics on the right push agendas of their own, and not all of them are designed to improve schooling. Some want to prove the superiority of the market; for them, the boundary between economics and education should be breached, just as for many on the left the boundary between politics and education has to be overcome. Others argue for what would become, in practice, a bastardized pluralism: fundamentalists will be taught their own beliefs in the South and, in return, will support the notion of black males learning black male identity in the North. Yet others will give up on schools entirely; on the right as well on the left, one can expect, in a mood of antigovernment hostility, more parents determined to keep their kids at home, certain that being on the "net" will teach them as much as sitting in boring classrooms.

Social critics ought to recognize that criticizing schools is, in a way, much too easy. Because the schools have taken on so many tasks, they are bound to fail at most of them. The job of the critic is not only to point out the failures; it is also to remember that if schools did less, they might also do more. Critics love to argue that the boundary between the school and everything else is porous. Yet respect for an institution like the school demands that a certain boundary be in place. Having devoted half a century to tearing the boundary down, perhaps social critics can take on the task of building it up.

SOCIAL SCIENCE AND SOCIAL CRITICISM

The Uneasy Marriage of Social Criticism

and Social Science

Social science and social criticism live together uneasily. Even if the social critic is not by training a social scientist, the task of holding a society and its institutions up to judgment requires a grounding in empirical knowledge. The critic offers opinions, to be sure, and these are by their very nature subjective and controversial; not for the social critic a devoted adherence to the fact-value distinction. But for a work of social criticism to rise above the opinionated, it must also persuade through fact. Although rhetorical skills are essential for that task, a convincing case will require familiarity with methodological conundrums, the ability to draw conclusions from imperfect data, and an appreciation of the ways in which even the most passionate of beliefs must be modified when evidence contradicts them.

If social science is an essential component of social criticism, the reverse is also true. Few topics investigated by social scientists do not touch on matters of policy, public controversy, and moral belief; there is little or no innocent social knowledge. During the golden age of social criticism, C. Wright Mills was marginalized in the Columbia University sociology department because his public stance on the controversial issues of the day violated principles of objectivity that were central to the scientific ambitions of sociology. Yet two of Mills's colleagues, Paul Lazarsfeld and Robert K. Merton, signed a brief to the Supreme Court in 1954 pointing out the harmful effects of racial segregation in schools—surely an act, for its time, of social criticism.[1] A graduate student in the department at that time, James Coleman, went on to make a distinguished career as a social scientist,[2] but his career also involved him deeply in issues of public controversy; Coleman was a far better social scientist than Mills (and his politics were anything but Millsian), but he too could be understood as a social critic as well as a social scientist.

There is a distinction between social criticism and social science, then, but it is not always easy to find. In the 1960s, the war on poverty found attractive the hypothesis, formulated by social scientists (and social critics) Lloyd Ohlin and Richard Cloward, that delinquency was the result of blocked opportunities.[3] When that approach failed, the reason, according to Daniel Moynihan—another social scientist qua social critic, and also a policy-maker—was that it adopted the unworkable notion of "maximum feasible participation of the poor."[4] Sociological ideas may be less popular in the 1990s than they were in the 1960s, but Americans still use social knowledge to argue over some of their deepest differences—such as whether children should be bussed to school to further racial integration, teenage pregnancy perpetuates poverty, authority should be exercised in prisons, or knowledge of sexual behavior can help prevent the spread of AIDS.[5] So long as social scientists study human beings, and so long as human beings disagree with each other about the nature of the good life, it would be foolish to expect that social science and social criticism will remain completely distinct activities.

Throughout this book I have addressed the relationship between social criticism and social science through the eyes of the former. How, I have repeatedly asked, does the social critic deal with social realities which, by their very persistence and intractability, undermine the utopian worlds the critic would rather envision? A similar question, if in reverse, can be asked of the social scientist: How, one wants to know, can your readers be certain you have discovered a truth when your readers know that you also have strong opinions and beliefs?

In this chapter I address this question by discussing a major work in social science: Theda Skocpol's analysis of how the modern welfare state came into being.[6] Rarely has a book won as many academic prizes as Skocpol's.[7] The reasons are not hard to find. If institutions are crucial to an understanding of society, Skocpol focuses on the most important institution of all: the state. She does this, moreover, historically: "Lessons about the past," she writes in another book, "are not merely of antiquarian interest. They speak to issues that continue to animate U.S. social policy debates today."[8] Finally, Skocpol is an exhaustive scholar; her book is long, comprehensive, well-researched—an obvious effort to make definitive claims about the topics it investigates.

Yet Skocpol is not only a social scientist respectful of evidence; she also has pronounced views on the subjects she wants to understand. She is an effective and influential advocate for the welfare state, having written in favor of policies such as child support, parental leave, child-care assistance, job training, relocation assistance for displaced workers, and health insurance—policies embodying an "opening" for the principle of providing "extra benefits and services that disproportionately help less privileged people without stigmatizing them."[9] In addition, Skocpol writes as a feminist, if of a particular sort; the welfare state she wants to defend is "women friendly," for universality in provision guarantees that women, even women who do not work, will have access to public benefits. Finally, Skocpol also believes that America's welfare state is less extensive than those in Europe because we lack comparable administrative capacity; program design and intellectual groundwork by scholars, therefore, can help policy elites formulate more workable programs.[10]

Because she is both a scholar of and an advocate for what she studies, Skocpol's treatment of the development of the American welfare state is illustrative of the dilemmas faced by social scientists as they venture into the relatively unfamiliar territory of social criticism. Assuming that there are many possible interpretations of reality, how does the scholar balance what she uncovers as a social scientist with her normative and political convictions as a participant in present controversies? Assuming, further, that one of the tasks of social science is to help develop a theory of how the world works, what happens to such theories on those occasions when evidence points one way and political beliefs point another? If the social scientist is not forthcoming about such potential conflicts, can we trust the knowledge she offers? But if she is forthcoming, are we obliged to accept the normative judgments she makes? When a subject as controversial as the welfare state is addressed by a scholar as important as Theda Skocpol, the result is a test case that illustrates the ways in which social science and social criticism interact.

On the Origins of the Welfare State

The welfare state came into existence because workers needed the protection that government could offer in order to limit the insecurities of the capitalist market. Compared to Western Europe, America has a welfare state that developed late, never achieved a firm footing in the political culture, and is therefore constantly vulnerable. The exceptionalism of

America's welfare state is due to the political weakness of America's working class, which was never able to assume political power.

That, at least, is the way the American welfare state is usually understood, but, according to Skocpol, this view is mistaken. To be sure, American workers have not fared well by the standards of Europe. Our labor unions actually opposed legislation to regulate hours and wages. The courts in the United States went out of their way, until 1937, to strike down laws that gave workers a leg to stand on in their struggles with capitalists. Consequently the American working class was unable to lead the battle for benefits that would redound to the universal advantage of all, such as old-age pensions, social insurance, and government-financed health care. But the inability of workers to grasp hold of government and use it to their advantage did not mean that government was inactive. Soldiers and mothers demonstrated what a well-organized political campaign and administrative leadership could accomplish. They were able to bring about significant changes in the relationship between government and citizen, changes that still reverberate.

The story starts with soldiers. At least since the early nineteenth century, governments have not asked young men to risk their lives without promising them, implicitly or explicitly, that their needs—or those of their widows—will be met. Pensions were granted to all American war veterans in 1832, and four years later at least some widows started receiving them, too. But it was the Civil War that transformed soldiers' pensions and widows' pensions into "a kind of precocious social security system for those U.S. citizens of a certain generation and region who were deemed morally worthy of enjoying generous and honorable public aid" (102–3).

The amount of federal dollars spent on Civil War pensions increased dramatically between 1870 and 1910, as the veterans aged. The statistics culled by Skocpol are impressive. By 1893, 41.5 percent of the federal government's income was being spent on Civil War pensions. Approximately 28.5 percent of all elderly men, and 8 percent of all elderly women, were receiving such benefits in 1910. Ninety-three percent of all veterans were enrolled in the system by 1915. Some number of Americans, by all accounts not an insignificant number, enjoyed the government's largesse even at the height of the American worship of laissez-faire.

Ultimately it proved impossible, despite the best efforts of farsighted reformers, to transform the Civil War pensions into a system of old-age insurance or workingmen's insurance. The system died when the veterans did. But that did not have to happen, argues Skocpol: elite organizations such as the American Association for Labor Legislation pushed for social insurance, but a variety of factors—the reluctance of labor, fears of corruption, the AALL's rigid structure, a conservative political environment—proved fatal. Had such groups been able to build on the model of the war pensions, America would have had the same kind of paternalistic welfare state as England or Germany.

Still, the defeat of this system did have one potentially positive consequence. A maternalist welfare state succeeded when the paternalistic welfare state failed. What men could not accomplish, women achieved. Progressive social reform took place in America due to "the heights of social organization, ideological self-consciousness, and political mobilization achieved by American middle-class women around the turn of the twentieth century" (318). These women took the rhetoric of the household and extended it to the polity as a whole. If women were understood to have the special moral responsibility of caring for others, and if others were taken to mean not just the immediate family but also the larger community, the language for justifying an activist state had been found. Skocpol is fond of quoting Rheta Childe Dorr's book of 1910, *What Eight Million Women Want:* "Woman's place is in the home. This is a platitude which no woman will ever dissent from. . . . But Home is not contained within the four walls of an individual home. Home is the community. The city full of people is the Family. The public school is the real Nursery. And so badly do the Home and the Family and the Nursery need their mother" (21, 331).

Skocpol means three things by a maternalist welfare state. The first is protective legislation for women workers. Between 1900 and World War I, thirty-nine states passed or improved laws regulating the maximum hours that women could work. The Supreme Court ruled that maximum hours were unconstitutional in *Lochner v. New York* (1905), after *Dred Scott,* the most infamous case in its history. But three years later, in *Muller v. Oregon,* the Court indicated its willingness to uphold a law that regulated hours for women. The Court was to some degree moved by Louis Brandeis's historic brief, which focused on the real conditions faced by women in the workforce, though it also opined that the physical differences between the sexes required different levels of constitutional scrutiny. Skocpol interprets the successful campaigns for hours regulation as a victory for progress led by women. It is a debatable point, to which I shall return.

The second element of the maternalist welfare state was mothers' pensions. Before 1920, forty American states passed laws enabling local governments to give poor mothers cash help in raising their children.

Upper-class women reformers took the lead in agitating in support of the needy. They waged an effective public relations campaign, utilizing women's magazines and enlisting the help of prominent men. The result was a victory for women's activism over the opposition of charitable organizations (which did not want their monopoly broken) and labor reformers.

The third and most important feature of the maternalist welfare state is what Skocpol calls "statebuilding for mothers and babies" (480–524). The Child's Bureau, created by Congress in 1912, stands for Skocpol as a model of how political activists can carve out a niche in public consciousness and then organize around the state to keep attention focused on a social problem. The story of the Child's Bureau is quite remarkable. Before women won the right to vote, Julia Lathrop, soon to be head of the Child's Bureau, became an effective practitioner of lobbying at one end and using government at the other. Lathrop carefully studied the Department of Agriculture as a model for the politics of constituency-building, organizing public interest in the health of children as a way of putting pressure on the government to respond to the needs of children. Her crowning success was the passage of the Sheppard-Towner Bill in 1921, which provided federal funding for maternal and infant health programs. For Skocpol, activities such as these constituted an early lesson in the art and the science of using government to make the world a little better. So it was that American women understood the potentialities inherent in government long before the New Deal even came into being.

The maternalist welfare state, however, was not a long-term success. None of the three innovations discussed by Skocpol survived the 1930s. Widows' and mothers' pensions were funded inadequately, and became little more than "poor relief," offered only to the worst-off after demeaning entitlement tests were put in place. Maximum hours laws were upheld by the Supreme Court, but minimum wage laws for women were not. Sheppard-Towner was killed by Congress in 1929. And even the Child's Bureau, the greatest success in this story, was superseded by the Social Security Act of 1935. Still, Skocpol wishes to avoid a "downbeat" (536) conclusion, because contemporary feminists and welfare state advocates can learn much from the story. It should teach them to respect the ability of women to create "encompassing and geographically far-flung women's organizations" (538). The solidarity between rich women and poor women shown by these activists is worth emulating. True, "the United States is never going to have a European-style welfare state. . . . But the possibility remains that America might develop strong, universal social programs designed to help working single-parent and two-parent families live well and raise their children" (538).

Beyond the Traditional Interpretation

If Skocpol's analysis is correct, historians and social theorists have clearly misunderstood the path taken by the modern state. If she is right, we will have to rethink the problem of which social groups are the "carriers" of progress and substitute women for workers. We will have to conclude that protective legislation for women is not paternalism but progress. We will have to give a new date to the birth of an active state, a date at least half a century earlier, and discover its origins not in Progressivism, but in the system of Civil War pensions. We will have to reject the notion that political rights, especially the right to vote, are the basis of political progress. And we will have some basis for believing that a generous welfare state, even as late as the 1990s, is still possible, since precedents for it will have been found to exist.

All this, again, if Skocpol is right. But is she right? We might begin to answer the question by contrasting her interpretation of the events described in her book with the way they have been treated by others. There is no single interpretation that stands in contrast to Skocpol's, but something like one can be assembled from a wide variety of accounts.

The Bureau of Pensions, for example, was, in Morton Keller's words, "the most uncompromisingly political branch of the late nineteenth century federal bureaucracy."[11] A great deal of federal money was spent on Civil War pensions, but this was a product of the fact that so many members of Congress were themselves veterans—and Republicans as well. So long as tariff revenues were high, pensions absorbed the resulting budget surpluses; when pressures for free trade and harder economic times reduced the surplus, pension expenditures declined.[12] Even when pension expenditures were high, moreover, they were anything but universal (as Skocpol acknowledges). Those who lived in the states of the former Confederacy were denied pensions. Immigrants who came after 1865 need not have applied, which excluded a vast portion of the *fin de siècle* working class. Blacks experienced the usual discrimination in these matters, particularly veterans of the Union Army who had been former slaves. And despite widows' pensions, men benefited far more than women. If our objective is to discover precursors of universalistic, nonstigmatizing public policies, Civil War pensions would hardly seem to fill the bill. Indeed, it was precisely the widespread perception of Civil War pensions as virtual graft that stood in the way of creating a system of social insurance in turn-of-the-century America, as Skocpol also acknowledges. Far from being a shadow version of the welfare state, Civil War pensions were a major obstacle. Opponents of social insurance and workingmen's insurance could point to the Civil War system as proof that government benefits fuel only public corruption, not public virtue.

Alternative interpretations of the maternalist welfare state view it far less positively than Skocpol's. Protective legislation for women is understood by many historians as an important break in an otherwise relentless adherence to laissez-faire, but it also was premised on the acceptance of essential differences between and women.[13] It therefore accepted the nineteenth-century ideology of separate spheres, which held that women belonged in the home while men properly inhabited the larger public world of politics and economics.[14] From such a perspective, to extend the separate sphere of the home to the community as a whole is still to accept a separate sphere. Protective legislation came to an end in 1969 when it was held contrary to the principles of the Civil Rights Act of 1964 by the Equal Employment Opportunities Commission.[15] Most feminists were not unhappy with that outcome.

Only the ease with which men could accept the idea of women as different and in need of protection explains why protective legislation was passed to regulate hours but was forbidden when it came to wages. That women would work fewer hours would not only keep them at home more, it would also take them out of competition for jobs held by men.[16] It is no wonder that many states passed laws regulating how many hours women could work, but only fifteen states passed laws regulating wages. Skocpol writes that "given the obstacles, it is testimony to the efficacy of women's politics that minimum wage laws made as much headway as they did" (404). It would be more precise to say that it was testimony to the very unprogressive ideology of separate spheres.

For one thing, as Skocpol is the first to suggest, women's organizations did not lobby for minimum wage laws for all workers, men included. By restricting themselves to women, they strongly endorsed the concept of the family wage, according to which men should earn enough to support the entire family, which is anathema to many contemporary feminists. In addition, in many states the campaign for a woman's minimum wage was endorsed by state labor federations, whatever the opposition of the national AFL-CIO. What success they had, therefore, must be attributed not to female workers but to male workers. And there is also economic evidence that the passage of minimum wage laws acts as a bias against new entrants into the work force; employers may have refused to hire women who were guaranteed a higher wage. From this perspective, the great victory for women was not the fact that fifteen states adopted minimum wage laws for women workers but that the entire Progressive movement after 1914 stopped agitating for legislation that singled women out.

This alternative reading of these early programs also offers a different account of mothers' pensions. Like other legislation passed under the sign of separate spheres, these pensions were based on the idea that certain classes of women, unable to protect themselves, needed the protection of others. Some people, of course, do need the help of others. But the upper-class women who agitated for mother's pensions could not sustain the campaign in such a way that the pensions were adequately funded. Under-provisioned and moralistic, mothers' pensions became a foreshadowing not of the welfare state but of welfare: a demeaning system that singled people out for disgrace instead of bringing them up to the level of others. Such a system made a clear distinction between the deserving and the undeserving poor.[17] Skocpol tends to absolve women reformers of advocating such a distinction, but the ideology of separate spheres led naturally to the idea of welfare as charity rather than welfare as right.

If our goal is the creation of a universalistic, nonstigmatizing welfare state, in other words, then the materialistic welfare state lauded by Skocpol needed to be destroyed before a modern welfare state could come into existence. I do not mean to suggest that Skocpol ignores alternative interpretations, or even that she argues against them. She is often her own best critic. At many points in her narrative, she acknowledges the importance of arguments against her general conclusions; and it is her own enormous amount of information that enables the critic to challenge her interpretations.

But because Skocpol then offers her conclusions anyway, the reader comes away frustrated by arguments that appear to be on all sides of the issue. Does it make sense to say that Civil War pensions were "not really a 'welfare state' in any objective or subjective sense" (151) and that "through Civil War benefits, the federal government—long before the New Deal—became the source of generous and honorable social provision for a major part of the American citizenry"? (101). If Skocpol rightly accepts that "the original supporters of mothers' pensions accepted categorical and behavioral rules defining which husbandless mothers were 'worthy' of public aid," how can she also conclude that "a generous and caring American welfare state" was "inherent in the maternalist policy breakthroughs of the Progressive Era and the early 1920s" (524)?

There is nothing necessarily wrong in taking positions on both sides of an issue: historical realities are complicated, and often there are truths on both sides. The problem with Skocpol's contradictory analysis seems to reflect the conflicts between her social science findings and her critical concerns. History offers her the picture of active women reformers fighting for their goals, which she likes, but if also offers a picture of those women operating out of a political philosophy which was not universal and egalitarian, which she does not like. An account which was true to such a historical record ought to conclude that the lessons for the present from the story told by Skocpol are mixed: yes, there has been an underappreciated "gendered" dimension to the origins of the welfare state, but no, it has not been a "progressive" one which contains powerful lessons for present debates.

This is not, however, the account that Skocpol finally gives. Instead, she claims repeatedly that the women reformers she discusses can serve as role models for the building of a more generous welfare state today. That idea is more fully spelled out in a reply Skocpol wrote to one of her critics, Linda Gordon, in which she identified the Children's Defense Fund, led by Hillary Clinton and Marion Wright Edelman, as "the clearest contemporary voice for ideals similar (though of course not identical) to those espoused by female social policy advocates in earlier periods of U.S. history."[18] When she reinterprets the goals and motives of women reformers as if they foreshadowed the modern welfare state, Skocpol takes these women out of the context of their time; upper-class women reformers of the late nineteenth and early twentieth centuries, Linda Gordon wrote in her review of Skocpol's book,

> came from a charity and social-work tradition that combined genuine pity for the poor with social-control impulses, particularly for children and for mothers alone. . . . The "maternalist" aspect of their vision thus required supervision of the morals and mental "hygiene" of the poor, with rehabilitation where they deemed it necessary.[19]

Skocpol believes that history supports the case for a more active welfare state in the present, but her defense of the welfare state in the present also shapes her understanding of history. Skocpol the social critic speaks as often in *Protecting Soldiers and Mothers* as Skocpol the social scientist.

This conclusion is also reenforced by Skocpol's intervention into debates among feminists. Skocpol has very definite sympathies, not of all of which will be well received by other feminists.[20] Her commitments are of two kinds. She is, first of all, a believer in economic equality rather than what Helen Haste, whom I discussed in Chapter 5, called cultural feminism. From Skocpol's perspective, the world would be a better place if we thought less about glass ceilings in the executive suite and more about helping mothers who cannot afford to raise their children. One can easily imagine Skocpol cringing at a feminist movement that puts the celebration of lesbian lifestyles or ecofeminist consciousness ahead of bread-and-butter economic issues. Certainly her somewhat elliptical criticism of the women's movement for making abortion its major issue is courageous. The large majority of American women want to be able to contribute to the support of their families. Skocpol rightly thinks public policy should help them.

Far more controversial is the second aspect of Skocpol's feminism. Like the nineteenth- and early twentieth-century reformers she discusses, she is sympathetic to the notion of separate spheres for women and men. Although there is a good deal of emphasis these days on women's difference from men, very few feminist historians have tried as explicitly as Skocpol does to find value in nineteenth-century versions of women's difference. This is in many ways the most interesting aspect of her book. When the battle for separate spheres was lost, we lost a political discourse that emphasized care and responsibility for others. Indeed, the notion of separate spheres represented the last major challenge to the liberal ideology of atomistic individualism in America.

Precisely for this reason, however, a defense of nineteenth-century separate spheres requires an extended theoretical discussion of what paths the welfare state might have taken, had it not incorporated the universalistic, individualistic, legalist, and egalitarian assumptions of contemporary liberalism. Skocpol is not averse to such counterfactual speculation; her entire book is premised upon it. We can, of course, never know what might have happened, but one thing seems clear: had the twentieth-century welfare state been based on the notion of separate spheres, it could have evolved in a number of ways vaguely compatible with what today is called communitarianism, but the one thing it could never have become is a universalistic, nonmoralistic, and generous social democratic welfare state. There is simply too great a tension between the notion that women and men act best in different spheres of life and the notion that public policies can be designed in a universal and egalitarian fashion. If we want the latter, we must reject the former. Skocpol wants both. This is the most serious tension in her book.

Neither soldiers nor mothers are, in themselves, synonymous with citizens, in the liberal understanding of that term. Soldiers have far fewer rights than ordinary citizens, and they have far greater benefits. They live in an ideal socialist society, trained, fed, and clothed by government while on active duty, and given aid by government for the rest of their lives in the form of college tuition, mortgages, and burial space. In return, they give up many of their rights. They sacrifice the status of liberal citizen, and sometimes suffer a curtailment of their rights, because they have a special duty to the nation, and their service is considered so valuable that extra benefits are justified.

And mothers are, in interesting ways, similar to soldiers. They do not—or at least did not—fight in wars, but they, too, have a special duty to society, without which society cannot survive. Because they are the agents of its reproduction, society has an interest in mothers, one that, on occasion, may conflict with their own rights as citizens of a liberal order. Mothers, like soldiers, cannot do whatever they want with their bodies, at least not in the post-*Roe v. Wade* environment. Of course mothers do not receive the same benefits that soldiers do. But that is precisely the point: if the maternalist welfare state described by Skocpol had continued into this century, we could not have developed a modern welfare state. We would have developed something much more like a modern army. Mothers would be supported by government, as would their children. But in return they would not be treated as liberal citizens. It is not even clear that they would have the right to vote.

Women's suffrage destroyed the maternalist welfare state. If women are citizens entitled to the rights enjoyed by all citizens, then among those rights—at least at the time about which Skocpol is writing—is freedom of contract. In *Adkins v. Children's Hospital* (1923), Justice Sutherland wrote that the passage of the woman's suffrage amendment meant that it was no longer possible to grant "restrictions on their liberty of contract which could not lawfully be imposed on men" (cited in Skocpol, p. 423). In the peculiar language of the day, this meant that legislation restricting working hours for women was now as unconstitutional as it had been for men. The matter could not be clearer. Women can have protection or rights, but they cannot have both. Most women wanted the right to vote, but with it went the end of protective legislation.

If the ideology of separate spheres is incompatible with formal legal equality for women, it is also incompatible with the principle of universalism. For how can spheres be separate when policies are pursued without respect to difference? Never mind that policies designed for women could not apply to men. Consider whether such policies could apply even to all women. For one thing, not all women are mothers. One could easily imagine working women who do not have children objecting to policies that benefit those who do have children as nonuniversalistic.

Moreover, it is even harder to imagine such policies benefiting all mothers. The notion of separate spheres contained the implicit understanding that women were responsible for the family, which was composed of a wife, a husband, and children. Building a welfare state upon that model would make the provision of benefits to unwed mothers on the same basis as married mothers enormously difficult. To be sure, unwed mothers also raise children in which society has a stake; but nineteenth-century efforts to help mothers were based on an explicitly narrow vision of the nuclear family. That vision made possible federal programs to help mothers, but they came with judgments about the moral behavior of the mothers who were helped. Dependency, as opposed to a liberal conception of citizenship, can be like that.

Protecting Soldiers and Mothers is an important corrective to earlier accounts of the welfare state, which generally leave out the fact that there were historical precedents for the welfare state in soldier's pensions and support for mothers. But these were precedents in the loosest possible sense of the term. As an engaged scholar and political advocate, Theda Skocpol makes an important case for a universalistic welfare state. But she cannot find support for that case in the history of maternalist legislation. A greater recognition on her part of the ways in which her historical narrative and her political concerns are in tension would have produced a more satisfying, and less contradictory, book.

Social Theory and Social Criticism

There are theoretical issues raised by *Protecting Soldiers and Mothers* which are as important as the historical and political ones. How many rights ought people to sacrifice in return for how many benefits? Is it more important to have the right to vote or to have a pension? Does the liberal notion of rights, including the right to one's own body, foreclose a communitarian obligation to others? Can social rights be provided in the absence of political rights, or will the absence of political rights mean that any social rights provided will be contingent and subject to reversal? In dealing with such theoretical concerns, Skocpol's different commitments once again enter into unsatisfactorily resolved conflicts. Just as she was unable to balance her role as a social scientist with her position as a social critic, she is unable to keep in balance her historical knowledge with her previous theoretical commitments.

Every important treatment of the welfare state in recent years has been built around T. H. Marshall's seminal essay "Citizenship and Social Class."[21] Marshall distinguished between economic, political, and social rights, each conveniently associated with one century since the eighteenth. Rights in property were established before the right to vote; and the right to vote made possible the preservation of the right to a decent life. Skocpol never discusses Marshall's essay in her book. If she had, she would have been forced to reflect on the question of whether the social rights won by women in the nineteenth century, in the absence of the political right to vote, were really worth winning. I am not prejudging the answer. We all might want to believe that the right to vote is far more important, which makes the case for providing an alternative point of view even more essential. But Skocpol simply does not rise to this level. We are left with an account that, for all its length, is frustratingly incomplete.

Skocpol's treatment of the role played by independent women's organizations in the struggle for nineteenth-century social policies is no less interesting and no less problematic. Her focus on organizations such as the National Congress of Mothers, the Consumers League, and other groups that fought the fight for protective legislation and the Children's Bureau makes it clear how important political mobilization is to accomplishments in social policy. Just because women did not have the right to vote did not mean they were powerless and victimized. Their political capacities were, Skocpol rightly emphasizes, astonishing. Especially in contrast to the conservatism of the labor movement at this time, the story of the women's movement makes any believer in progress proud.

One can draw a number of conclusions from the story that Skocpol tells. Surely one of them would be that things do not happen in politics in predetermined ways. They occur, rather, when real people take matters into their own hands, sensing opportunities and using their political and coalitional skills to maximize them. A second lesson, moreover, is that pressures from groups independent of government force political leaders to respond. I read the story of how soldiers and mothers obtained benefits as an argument against structuralist and state-centered thinking in the social sciences. But alas, one of the leaders of structuralist and state-centered thinking has been Theda Skocpol. She made her reputation with two ideas: that revolutions happen independently of the wishes and talents of revolutionaries; and that states are actors in and of themselves, often leading social change from the top down rather than from the bottom up. *Protecting Soldiers and Mothers*, therefore, raises the question of how much of Skocpol's previous theoretical contribution to the social sciences will have to be jettisoned to incorporate the stories told in this book.

States and Social Revolutions, Skocpol's first book, which appeared in 1979, examined the French, Russian, and Chinese revolutions in order to understand when and why they took place. It concluded that the breakdown of the old order "was *not* because of deliberate activities to that end, either on the part of avowed revolutionaries or on the part of politically powerful groups within the Old Regimes."[22] Revolutions happened, rather, when the imperial states in these societies were unable to meet military and other challenges from outside, given their particular agrarian and precapitalist structure inside. Moreover the story of a revolution is, ironically, the story of the state, for what emerged in all three cases was a stronger governmental system than the one offered by the old regime. Revolutionaries may think of themselves as a vanguard, intensifying the class contradictions that bring revolutions about, but they are really pawns in a structuralist universe. If the structural conditions are not ripe, Skocpol implied, there would be no revolution.

Skocpol has applied the same perspective to the triumph of the welfare state, not only in America but also in Europe. It was not the working class and the political power of labor that created the system of public benefits; it was the actions of state officials. As she put it, together with Ann Shola Orloff, in 1984:

> Overall we maintain that the politics of social welfare provision are just as much grounded in the process of statebuilding and the organization and reorganization of political life as in those socioeconomic processes—industrialization, urbanization, demographic change, and the formation of classes—that have traditionally been seen as basic to the development of the modern welfare state.[23]

This takes the notion of the relative autonomy of the state to new heights. Now the state can be understood not only as powerful enough to adjudicate between classes but also as a force in its own right. "Bringing the state back in"—the title of a collection of essays edited by Skocpol and others—tried to shift the debate away from "society" and toward "the state."[24]

But the stories that Skocpol tells in *Protecting States and Mothers* stand in tension with her earlier work. On the one hand, she insists that nothing has changed. "Because states are authoritative and resourceful organizations—collectors of revenue, centers of cultural authority, and hoarders of means of coercion—they are sites of autonomous action" (42), she writes. This leads her to argue that, contrary to what many writers have claimed, there really was a state in late nineteenth-century America. On the other hand, *Protecting Soldiers and Mothers* is a criticism of early Skocpol. There is very little discussion of the structuralist assumptions of her earlier book, yet clearly Skocpol is arguing here that American women made a difference, a point of view that stands in sharp contrast to her argument that Russian, French, and Chinese revolutionaries did not. Moreover, even the arguments for state autonomy are now presented as part of a complex causal chain that includes social forces. "I am not trying to substitute 'political determinism' for 'social determinism,'" (47), she writes. She is clearly correct. For *Protecting Soldiers and Mothers* tries to find ways in which the activities of independent groups such as women's organizations "fit" the realities of governmental institutions and party systems. "We must make social policies the starting points as well as the end points of analysis. As politics creates policies, policies also remake politics" (58).

Skocpol clearly wants to admit revisions into her theories about the independent role played by the state, but she also does not want to acknowledge that critics of her earlier emphasis on the state may have been right. This ambivalence persists even after others have pointed out the tension in her work. In her response to Linda Gordon, for example, Skocpol argues that both Gordon and I "are both juxtaposing the present Skocpol book *not* to the arguments I made at earlier points, but to simplified stereotypes each of them had formed about my work" (168), yet Skocpol herself, in *Protecting Soldiers and Mothers*, refers to "the 'state-centered' theoretical frame of reference for which I had already become known" (viii).

It is that very frame of reference which can no longer stand if we are to believe the accounts told in *Protecting Soldiers and Mothers*. Skocpol will now be quoted against Skocpol for some time. I must confess to appreciating the new Skocpol. Painted in this book is a picture of reality far more nuanced than the one for which she has been known. In her new picture, real people move across the stage, people who know that their actions and their emotions matter. Still, this new Skocpol has not resolved the theoretical tensions that her shift in emphasis has produced. Theoretical commitments, like political ones, once developed, are difficult to abandon. Because she never addresses directly what is obviously a change in perspective over the course of her work, she achieves her new realism, and her new appreciation of contingency and chance, not by integrating the findings of her historical research with her previous theoretical claims but simply by putting one next to the other and blending them together.

Learning from Criticism

As important as the standards of social science are for the social critic, an appreciation of the rules of social criticism is essential for the social scientist. Most social critics know that, for all their advocacy, they have to try and meet the test of empirical verifiability. But not all social scientists appreciate the fact that, when they enter onto the terrain of social criticism, they have much to learn from previous works in that genre. For there are rules of social criticism just as there are rules of sociological method.

One such rule, I would argue, is to avoid a good-versus-bad view of history. The social critics of the golden age, inspired by leftist politics, constantly tried to discover one progressive historical agent after another. But whereas they generally looked toward the working class for their hopes, Skocpol offers women as exemplary historical actors. She describes her discovery of the role of gender as a "gestalt switch that enabled me to put together *Protecting Soldiers and Mothers*" (x). The discovery that women could play such a major role in social change "was like doing the last parts of a huge, complex, jigsaw puzzle: the pieces were finally fitting together, and the emerging picture was (to me, at least) lovely" (x).

But do pictures ever fit together? Historians in general caution against readings of the past which suggest that there is one clue which reveals a well-constructed story. The real question raised by these events, according to Linda Gordon, is: "Why did women design inferior programs for women?" To answer that question, we must avoid "a romantic view of women's generosity and an overly dichotomized view of gender which in turn assumes a kind of unity among women that was never present."[25] Although Gordon does not address this criticism to Skocpol, it does seem to apply. As Gordon concludes, appropriately citing T. H. Marshall, it was the social insurance advocates—primarily men—who moved closer to the idea of "social citizenship." This is not to make a judgment that men were better than women in this period—or vice versa. It is more a plea for the social scientist to recognize the realistic complexities of historical accounts.

A second rule of social criticism is this: avoid didacticism. History does not necessarily have lessons, but Skocpol is nonetheless determined to find them. Even as she was deeply into the research for her book, she writes, "there was still no hint that gender would play a central role in my understanding of U.S. political history" (viii). By transforming gender from a footnote to the center of her story, Skocpol is able to have "positive stories to tell" (x). Yet what a price she pays. While there is much to admire in the upper-class women who devoted so much of their energies to social improvement, it strains credibility to believe that they were completely altruistic. An earlier generation of social scientists—James Q. Wilson, Robert Merton, Richard Hofstadter—taught us to question the motives of Protestant reformers bent on straightening out the character of the many and the unfortunate.[26] Determined to rewrite the history of the welfare state in a way that preserves a role for reformers (and, to a lesser degree, for state officials), Skocpol ignores the skeptics and plunges ahead, oblivious of the fact that not all statist reformers were quite so honorable.

A third rule involves an appreciation of modesty, a rule that the social critics of the golden age generally flouted. Angry at the society, convinced of its hypocrisy and unfairness, the "heroic" social critics of the 1950s rarely stopped to consider that they might be wrong. Theda Skocpol views herself as more of a social scientist than a social critic, but she, too, is anything but modest in her claims. *"Protecting Soldiers and Mothers* tells some new stories about the history of social policy in the United States," and does so, moreover, in "fresh" and "innovative" ways,[27] Skocpol begins her response to Linda Gordon, addressing, oddly, one of the historians who told many of those stories before Skocpol. Excited about what she believes to be "the discovery of startling new facts and the reworking of preconceived notions to accommodate new possibilities" *(Protecting,* p. vii), Skocpol becomes as unwilling to respond to criticism of her social scientific ideas as the social critics of the 1950s were to their political and normative beliefs. Certain that she is right and her critics wrong, Skocpol debates in the no-holds-barred manner associated with polemic and ideological controversy—a way of engaging ideas that is as unsatisfactory for social science in the 1990s as it was for social criticism in the 1950s and 1960s.

Protecting Soldiers and Mothers is a landmark book that will continue to generate controversy and discussion. It is also a book that illuminates through subtext as well as through text. For all her enormous energy, fine sense of narrative, and wealth of historical data, Skocpol never reconciles her hopes as a social critic with her scholarship as a social scientist. No one can doubt Skocpol's commitment as a critic: even in the Republican-dominated 1990s, when the political air is filled with talk of cutbacks and retrenchment, Skocpol's desire to see a more universal and generous welfare state—especially one that achieves its objectives by extending benefits currently received by the elderly to families with children—is made explicit in nearly all of her writings on social policy. Yet it is simply not true that "the roots and consequences of the earliest phases of modern American social policies hold lessons applicable to the politics of social provision in the United States right down to the present day" (11). Earlier experiences with civil war and mothers' pensions are interesting in their own right. The social scientist has an obligation to understand them for what they were, not as overtures for what she would like them to be.

THE CERTAINTY OF SOCIAL CRITICISM

The Treachery of Knowledge

Social criticism is more effective the more it is grounded in knowledge; eloquence and rhetorical skills can take the critic just so far. Yet as essential as it may be for the social critic, knowledge about human behavior is rarely able to settle any moral and political controversy by itself. This is not just because the social sciences, when compared to the natural sciences, are limited in what they can discover; the natural sciences themselves convey an aura of uncertainty when applied to arenas of social contention. Scientists still do not know, to take just one example, whether homosexuality has a genetic basis,[1] and, even if they did, it would not be clear what such a fact would mean, for the degree to which homosexuality is socially or biologically determined is one of those issues on which left and right seem to switch positions depending on the uses to which such knowledge would be put.[2]

Because knowledge is both essential to social criticism yet unreliable for resolving disputes, social critics who are also social scientists have to be aggressive in accumulating data yet circumspect in interpreting them. The social critics of the golden age could rightly be faulted for failing to honor this injunction. A crucial ingredient of "heroic" social criticism was the notion that the forces of conformity and repression succeeded only by keeping ordinary people ignorant of their power, motives, and resources. The mere accumulation of knowledge about how the world worked, from such a perspective, served radical goals. Knowledge was inevitably on the side of the critic, who would make public the facts that the powerful wanted suppressed. Finding the right information might be difficult, but once found, knowledge itself was unproblematic.

The social scientists of the 1950s, by contrast, disdained social criticism. Their task, as they saw it, was to build the social sciences on models supplied by the natural sciences. Yet although they stood on the other side of the fact-value distinction from social critics, they shared with the latter a belief in the certainty of knowledge. It might take some time to accumulate reliable knowledge about society, and there would be many false steps along the way, but eventually social scientists would accumulate vast inventories of the knowable. When they did, social engineering would be more rational—based, as it would come to be, on indisputable facts about human behavior. As Talcott Parsons expressed it, in one of the most immodest statements ever made by a social scientist:

> Do we have or can we develop a knowledge of human social relations that can serve as the basis of rational "engineering" control? . . . The evidence we have reviewed indicates that the answer is unequivocally affirmative. Social science is a going concern; the problem is not one of creating it, but rather of using and developing it. Those who still argue whether the scientific study of social life is possible are far behind the times. It is here, and that fact ends the argument.[3]

In this chapter I review efforts by social scientists and social critics to obtain knowledge that might help settle disputes about the good life and how to lead it. I begin with a discussion of academic psychology in the 1940s and 1950s, a discipline convinced that it had already found the secrets of human behavior. The arrogance of that way of approaching knowledge is something we ought to avoid, yet not all contemporary social scientists do. I next discuss one of the leading American writers on contentious moral issues, James Q. Wilson, in order to point out the degree to which he relies on problematic scientific knowledge for some of his assertions. Finally I will contrast two books that deal with the question of how much we know about human behavior, in order to conclude that it is possible to know something, so long as we do not claim that we can know everything.

Psychological Hubris

Every modern political era has been shaped by a special social science. Classical liberalism and economics grew together. So did sociology and the welfare state. In the contemporary period, when identity politics is all the rage, psychology, at least of a particular kind, has become a growth industry.

Ellen Herman's *The Romance of American Psychology* tells the story of how this academic discipline became so entrenched in American culture.[4] Actually, the book tells two stories, for this is a discipline thoroughly divided between its experimental and clinical wings. Both the scientists and the therapists get their due in Herman's treatment, although this leaves her subject so vast that she is forced to become selective, and often cursory, in what she examines and what she ignores. But these are flaws of ambition; Herman's book deserves attention, for it reminds at least this nonpsychologist of the extraordinary gap between what psychologists of both persuasions knew about human behavior and what they were nonetheless prepared to say.

That gap made its most dramatic appearance during World War II. Called upon to offer insights under emergency conditions, most psychologists had no difficulty making sweeping generalizations with astonishing confidence. Here is Gardner Murphy endorsing the frustration/aggression hypothesis: "Fighting in all its forms, from the most simple to the most complex, appears to derive from the frustration of wants. . . . Satisfied people or satisfied nations are not likely to seek war. Dissatisfied ones constitute a perennial danger" (38). Murphy was not the only psychologist convinced that there was a direct link between individual and national behavior. "Societies move on the feelings of the individuals who compose them, and so do countries and nations," Alexander Leighton wrote in *The Governing of Men*. Leighton proposed that behavioral "weather stations" be established around the world, in Herman's words, "to constantly monitor levels of national and international aggression and hostility" (76). Whether psychologists were aware of how self-serving this linkage was is irrelevant; convinced that they could understand individual actions, they had no doubts whatsoever that they could also understand national ones.

Although Murphy and Leighton belonged to the more "tough-minded" scientific wing of psychology, their point of view was little different from that of the Freudians and anthropologists. "It is as if the German nation as a whole could be likened to a not uncommon type of adolescent who turns delinquent" (49), Erik Erikson wrote in 1940. Margaret Mead concluded that national morale could be enhanced by strengthening aspects of individual character—providentially those aspects which most overlapped with Mead's own liberal political views. Clinicians brought into military service had to make spot decisions, often on the basis of one or two questions, about the mental health of recruits. Although some, such as Harry Stack Sullivan, had qualms, most complied; 12 percent of all recruits (and 38 percent of all rejections) were turned away for psychological reasons. Unable to practice the psychotherapy for which they were trained—Freudian treatment often takes at least ten years, while the war only lasted five—therapists recommended the use of common sense in dealing with severe mental health problems of soldiers, but this, as Herman correctly points out, undermined the rationale for their own expertise.

Psychology was nonetheless one of the major winners of World War II. Every problem that faced the world in the aftermath of the war seemed to have a psychological dimension. David McClellan proposed that Third World countries would succeed economically to the degree that they possessed the right kind of achievement motivations; foreign aid, McClellan recommended, should be administered with respect to its "psychological multiplier effect" (141). Lucien Pye applied the same kinds of insights to political development. "Fears of failure in the adventure of nation building create deep anxieties, which tend to inhibit effective action" he wrote. "The dynamics of such psychological inhibitions . . . can permeate and restrain the entire process of nation building" (145). Psychology could also prevent revolution. Like Leighton's "weather stations," Project Camelot was designed to use behavioral science indicators in the development of models capable of predicting when revolutions and internal wars would break out.

Domestic life furnished even more compelling examples of the usefulness of psychology. Convinced by their experiences during war that racism and anti-Semitism were psychological in nature, the experts attacked segregation with vigor. It was a psychologist, Kenneth Clark, who furnished the dramatic evidence cited in *Brown v. Board of Education,* even though Clark had serious doubts about how generalizable his research with black and white dolls could be. Gunnar Myrdal's *An American Dilemma* was rooted in the latest psychological wisdom; three years later, the Truman administration's 1947 document *To Secure These Rights* endorsed the frustration/aggression hypothesis as an explanation for racism. Right-wing politics were found by Theodor Adorno to be a product of psychological deprivation, while Gabriel Almond treated the "neurotic" background that led people to become communists. No matter what the question—family dynamics, inequality, delinquency, race riots—psychology had an answer.

The same is true of clinical psychology. In 1940, only about 300 members of the American Psychological Association called themselves "clinical." By 1970 there were roughly 20,000 clinical psychologists in America. To a significant extent, this growth, like that of highways, was attributable to the federal government. Herman reminds us of the National Mental

Health Act of 1946, the rise and fall of community mental health, and the (new to me) fact that the 1958 National Defense Education Act established 60,000 jobs for school guidance counselors.

But something in the culture also worked to the advantage of clinical psychology, most likely the desperate search for what Erik Erikson—one of the first to do so—was to call "identity." Herman concludes her book with an examination of "the curious courtship" (276–303) between psychology and one of the identity movements: feminism. In its earlier phase, contemporary feminism was suspicious of psychology; its models, experimental or clinical, were held to be based on the experience of men, leading to the inevitable conclusion that something was psychologically amiss with women. Yet feminists quickly adopted consciousness-raising groups which were, despite occasional claims to the contrary, rooted in therapeutic ideas. If psychology became part of America's "public culture," its affinity with movements of liberation was surely part of the reason.

Still, only a minority of Americans identify with identity, which suggests that, for all their self-proclaimed insights into human behavior, psychologists, even when they remain convinced that they have found the secret of human behavior, are unable to convince everyone else that they have. One illustration of the declining legitimacy of psychology is the publication of *The Bell Curve*, one of whose authors, Richard Herrnstein, belongs in the classic tradition of psychometrics, a tradition ignored by Herman.[5] Herrnstein and Murray, like the psychologists of World War II, are convinced that science has given them answers to age-old problems of equality and inequality, but, unlike in that period, the culture now is far more skeptical of such claims. Psychology has been victimized by its own arrogance. Certain that it has put matters of public debate beyond debate, it only generates more debate—as, indeed, *The Bell Curve* has done. Whatever one concludes about the heritability of intelligence, one can surely conclude that *The Bell Curve* has not settled anything.

The same reaction against the certainty of knowledge has also affected clinical psychology. Psychotherapists were once so self-confident that they closed ranks against nonphysicians and never had to worry about filling their institutes. But drugs can accomplish in weeks what takes talk therapy, even at its best, years. Psychopharmacology plays as little a role in Herman's history as psychometrics, yet how can one understand psychology's relationship to American culture without discussing lithium— let alone Prozac? Although therapeutic methods are deeply embedded in American culture—and although they are believed by their advocates to hold the secrets to such dark matters as childhood sexual abuse—they have generated as furious a public debate as the findings of *The Bell*

Curve.[6] And the verdict appears to have come in; many of the individuals convinced of sexual abuse on the testimony of children who were "coached" by therapists have been released from jail; stories of Satanic sacrifice simply are not believable, even though juries and prosecutors recently believed them.

The rise and fall of psychology contains important lessons for the social critic. Psychology is a valuable discipline; it would be impossible to imagine modern life without the insights it provides into the self, its needs, and its relationship to other selves. As a behavioral science, moreover, psychology teaches a great deal about the ways in which human beings think, learn, remember, and act. The discipline of psychology has every right to claim that it ought to be the basic science of human behavior. But psychology does not have answers to the things we care about most. It cannot explain war and peace, let alone happiness and well-being. Its findings must always be tempered, contextualized, and treated with a certain skepticism. Then it will have an appropriate role to play in balancing the need to know with the need to find the right way to live.

Making Sense of Moral Sense

One area in which contemporary psychology has done extensive research and theorizing is the nature of moral behavior. Why, and under what conditions, psychologists ask, will people act altruistically, take responsibility for their society, and restrain their self-interest for the larger good?[7] James Q. Wilson, who appeared in these pages earlier, has long been concerned with these questions. In a book called *The Moral Sense*, he seeks to understand the sensibilities that enable individuals to live together. His wants to show that "we have a moral sense, most people instinctively rely on it even if intellectuals deny it, but it is not always and in every aspect of life strong enough to withstand a pervasive and sustained attack."[8] Wilson addresses timeless themes for timely reasons. He thinks that Americans no longer know how to talk about morality; to help them out, he offers them the benefit of wide reading in fields ranging from evolutionary biology to animal ethology and pharmacology.

If these seem odd subjects, this is because Wilson believes that science—not just social science—has much to teach us about humans, including their moral behavior. "However much the scientific method is thought to be the enemy of morality," he notes, "scientific findings provide substantial support for its existence and power" (xii). Through science we learn that one specific part of the brain—the cingulate gyrus of the limbic system—may be the locus of our sociability. Individual differences in aggressive behavior are probably linked to enzymes such as monoamine oxidase or to neurological transmitters such as serotonin. Darwinian theory suggests that "the moral sense must have an adaptive value; if it did not, natural selection would have worked against people who had such useless traits as sympathy, self-control, or a desire for fairness in favor of those with the opposite tendencies" (23).

Wilson is not only reporting on the findings of science, he is also one of America's leading conservative scholars and intellectuals. The same question can be asked of him that I asked of Theda Skocpol: how do we know, in reviewing his findings, whether it is science or politics that is speaking? This question applies even though Wilson backs up his claims, not with the "soft" fields of sociology and history, but with the "hard" findings of biology and neuroscience.

The trump card that for Wilson demonstrates the importance of biology for understanding human society is the bonding that takes place when a new infant is born. "The mechanism underlying human moral conduct is the desire for attachment or affiliation. That desire is evident in the instinctively prosocial behavior of the newborn infant and in the instinctively caring response that parents make to that behavior" (127). Just as Labradors are born to fetch, Wilson writes, we are born to bond. Infants naturally seek out human contact from a very early age. Parents bond to the cuteness of babies, as if Darwinian evolution produced just those physical features in infants that gladden our hearts and make us cry for joy. ("Scientists," Wilson comments, "have not, in my view, taken the concept of 'cute' sufficiently seriously" [127].) The origins of nothing less than all of human society seem to lie in the first six months of life.

Innate drives to bond create a universal moral imperative. "If culture were the all-powerful source of human character that some imagine it to be, then cultural differences would cause bonding differences to a greater extent than seems to be the case" (153). Everywhere people tend to their own first and strangers, when tended to at all, long after. Fortunately for those who live in the West, the family developed in such a way to transform the natural sociability of the infant into care for distant others. (This is not the only explanation of the Western advantage, according to Wilson; religion, the rise of commerce, and the ideology of individualism all played a role.) Wilson argues that we should not confuse moral rules, which vary between cultures, with moral dispositions, which, because natural, are constant. People are preprogrammed to be prosocial, but that does not mean that the machine is always turned on. Only when families carry out their moral training satisfactorily will the innate moral sense be activated.

In assigning such an important role to the family, Wilson engages directly the question of sex roles. (Oddly, he calls this chapter "gender," a term popularized by feminists to make the point that sex roles are defined by culture.) Starting from birth, the bonding process that makes human society possible is disproportionately the mother's business. Fathers, not naturally inclined to bond, have to be roped in. "Since human infants require a long period of care after birth, a central problem for women living anywhere but in the most nurturing environments is to find ways of inducing the male to supply the resources necessary to make this care possible" (167). Women are a sex while men are a gender; because they have nurturing instincts, women belong to nature, whereas men, because they have to be taught to be human, are a product of culture. To get men to play a role in nurturance for which nature has poorly equipped them, women use social conventions such as courtship to test out the commitments of their prospective males. A stable society is one that links the natural morality of women with the socialization of men's aggressive drives. Families do this best, but schools and other social institutions can help. Whatever institutions are called upon, "the habitual performance of duties" (249) rather than adherence to moral precepts is more likely to guarantee results.

In short, Wilson's argument is that bonding is a necessary but not sufficient condition for the preservation of moral order. On the one hand, everything flows from it:

> Our moral senses are forged in the crucible of this loving relationship and expanded by the enlarged relationships of families and peers. Out of the universal attachment between child and parent the former begins to develop a sense of empathy and fairness, to learn self-control, and to acquire a conscience that makes him behave more dutifully at least with respect to some matters. (226)

On the other hand, moral sentiments—duty, self-control, and fairness—have to be taught, and they are not always taught well.

These are strong claims; how do we know they are true? Wilson believes that science tells us so. "The single most important discovery has been the importance to the child of having a strong and affectionate bond to the parents, especially to the mother" (145), writes Wilson, citing the work of John Bowlby and Mary Ainsworth. "There is some controversy over how this measurement is done and what the measure implies," he adds, "but relatively little over the importance of what is being measured —the mother-child bond" (145).

Relatively little controversy indeed. In fact, research seeking to prove the importance of the mother-child bond has been subjected to as extensive a critique as any scientific finding has ever encountered. And the critique has been a persuasive one. For one thing, not all mothers bond with their children; in situations of extreme poverty, in fact, they do the exact reverse, understanding that too close an identification with a child that may not live would serve no one's interest.[9] For another, even when studies do show long-term positive effects from early infant bonding, they are often filled with methodological errors, unexamined assumptions, and shifting conceptualizations.

Diane Eyer's *Mother-Infant Bonding* tells the story of how it came to pass that psychiatrists, psychologists, pediatricians, nurses, and, finally, the general public accepted the idea that very early contact between mother and infant could prevent antisocial behavior sometime later on.[10] As Eyer relates it, John Bowlby had become interested in the question of maternal deprivation as early as 1927. Working as a child psychologist at the London Child Guidance Clinic, he argued that delinquent boys became that way because institutionalization deprived them of the mother love required for full human adjustment. Heavily influenced by psychoanalytic theory, Bowlby believed that only the mother could serve as a substitute ego and superego for an infant lacking in any self-conception.[11]

Mary Ainsworth was not persuaded by Bowlby's psychoanalytic explanation of attachment, but she added substantial empirical evidence for the proposition that small infants need their mothers. Her studies in Uganda, first carried out in 1955, demonstrated that infants became attached to their mothers by six months and showed fear of strangers at about nine months. Ainsworth also hypothesized that the more responsive the mother was to her infant, the more likely the infant was to attach itself to her.[12] This finding, replicated among Baltimore infants, came to be known as the "strange situation" test. Small infants could adopt more easily to such situations—for example, the mother leaving the room—when their attachments were secure. If their attachments were insecure or what Ainsworth called "avoidant," strange situations became more traumatic.[13]

The findings of both scholars have been seriously challenged. Psychoanalytic theory, upon which Bowlby based his argument, was anything but uncontested; most of the leading interpreters of its latest wrinkles, including Anna Freud, Melanie Klein, and D. W. Winnicott, dismissed

Bowlby's conjectures as simpleminded. Whether in response or not, Bowlby began to shift his theoretical ground. When Harry Harlow discovered that baby monkeys miss their mothers, Bowlby quickly adopted his finding. When Darwinian ideas once again became popular explanations of why some human practices survive and others disappear, Bowlby began to argue that attachment was a mechanism of evolutionary survival.[14] When Bowlby wrote that a working mother is the moral equivalent of "death of a parent, imprisonment of a parent, war, famine" (cited in Eyer, p. 50) and other forms of devastation, ideology more than science seemed to characterize his work.

In a similar manner, Ainsworth's work has also been subject to extensive scrutiny by developmental psychologists such as Michael Lamb (one of her students) and Jerome Kagan. Ainsworth's samples were extremely small—twenty-four dyads in Africa and twenty-six mother-infant pairs in Baltimore, for example—and, at least in Baltimore, socioeconomically and ethnically homogeneous. Lamb pointed out that human infants bonded to blankets, pictures of their mothers, and other inanimate objects.[15] Kagan challenged the strange situation test on many grounds. For one thing, as we shall see later in this chapter, Kagan believes that some behaviors of infants are born with them, which would undercut attachment to the mother as an explanation for what they do. Moreover, mothers attempt to control the anxiety of their children, and how effectively they do so will determine whether the children are classified as "avoidant" or "insecurely attached." Finally, West German children were far less "securely attached" than American, which must reflect cultural differences in the way infants are treated.[16] (Wilson acknowledges these controversies and agrees that there is "no consensus yet in sight [146].")

As a result of these disagreements, the idea of bonding underwent a significant transformation. Maybe it was not important that the mother provide the bonding, researchers began to argue; any kind of bonding will do. If this were true, then one-half of the biological basis for the theory—the half which says that the mother instinctively bonds as much as the child—might have to be significantly revised. Bonding, which began as a precise concept defined down to the smallest details of contact, changed its meaning every time it was challenged, until it wound up meaning the opposite of its original intent. As Eyer summarizes, "Today, the attachment concept has broadened almost enough to describe the successful development of babies being raised by multiple caretakers—a situation originally thought to cause maternal deprivation" (69).

Mother-infant bonding, then, is too flawed a concept upon which to build a theory of much of anything, let alone the origins of modern morality. But James Q. Wilson remains enthusiastic about it. In turning to science, Wilson presumably hopes to make a stronger case for the importance of the moral sense than can be made by simply stating that it is a good thing which we all ought to appreciate. But does it make sense to address moral dilemmas on the basis of scientific findings? Can we learn what to do about single-parent families, delinquency, gay rights, or even ecology by brushing up on biology? And even if we are skeptical of the ability of the natural sciences to help us resolve moral issues, can we rely on the conclusions of the social sciences, which seem even more uncertain?

It is, after all, deeply controversial issues about which Wilson is writing. *The Moral Sense* generally refrains from taking on the issues of the day, but Wilson is a social critic as well as a social scientist: he clearly believes that moral people will lead their lives in some ways and not in others. In a section of his book dealing with moral sentiments, Wilson argues for a society in which individuals are brought up to respect other people. They will keep their instincts under control. They will be concerned with issues of equity and fairness, which means rewarding people proportion to the efforts they expend. And they will have a sense of duty that will lead them "to honor obligations even without hope of reward or fear of punishment" (100).

Wilson wrote *The Moral Sense* to make the point that science undergirds his view of human beings and undercuts the view of those he opposes: value relativists, liberal social scientists, the media elite. But if mother-infant bonding is the foundation of his argument, as his language at points seems to claim, it is as shaky a foundation as one could find. Wilson himself undermines his grounding when he acknowledges, from time to time, that the mother may not be essential to the bonding process. Moreover, there is virtually no research on children that predicts later behavior; for example, IQ before five has little to do with IQ after the age of five. Even the most convinced attachment theorists would be very unlikely to accept what Wilson proposes in their name, for they are more concerned with establishing correlations than they are with generalizing the results to "large" questions of historical development and social policy. Wilson is widely read in the scientific literature and generally captures the spirit of scientific skepticism, but, in trying to reach morality through science, he simultaneously fails to grasp the larger sensibility of science. Nature has no politics.

Wilson's language indicates that he knows he is often on shaky ground when he bases his moral claims on scientific findings. Is human personality genetically based? Here is Wilson's response, with my emphases: "A *good deal* of evidence suggests that *certain* aspects of personality . . . are *to some degree* genetically determined" (135). Later in the same paragraph Wilson argues that the study of twins and adopted children demonstrates that "much but not all" of personality is inherited, that altruism "may" also be inherited, and that the notion that religiosity has a biological root is a "possibility" (135). This is the appropriate language to use in describing these findings, but is it not the language of certainty.

The same is even more true for social science. For example, some evidence exists that being raised in a one-parent family causes long-term academic or even emotional problems later on. Still, cause and effect are murky enough, and other evidence inconclusive enough, that one social scientist quite properly notes that "There will never be anything like conclusive proof for this proposition unless we randomly assign babies at birth to single- and two-parent families of various economic and ethnic circumstances and then watch them grow up."[17] The social scientist is Wilson himself, in a recent article on the family values debate. Nonetheless, Wilson then goes on to cite studies demonstrating the harmful effects of one-parent families, writing as if the truth of this proposition, while not provable in some ultimate sense, is becoming clearer every day.

All of this indicates that we ought to be cautious in making political and moral conclusions on the basis of presumably scientific—or social scientific—findings. One simply cannot begin with biology and end with a position on women in the work force, crime in the streets, condoms in the schools, or drunks in the driver's seat. This is not an argument for ignoring the findings of science. It is rather a reminder to social critics and social scientists to use the findings of science in the same way that scientists offer them: tentatively, inconclusively, and always with the acknowledgment of possible error.

How Little We Know

As the social sciences broke away from moral philosophy, they dropped one of the central preoccupations of eighteenth- and nineteenth-century thought: whether there was such a thing as human nature. The social sciences which flourished in the United States after World War II treated human nature as they did national character—a subject best left unaddressed, primarily for political reasons. Man was what we made of him. Culture replaced nature as he first cause of social life. Although the aims of social science were ambitious, the theorizing was modest. Rather than large truths about the human condition, investigators sought "middle range" theories that could be subject to empirical verification. In more recent years, the postmodern skepticism that distrusts the social science project has not questioned its lack of interest in the question of human nature. Indeed contemporary statements about the social construction of everything leave nothing outside artificially created realities.

Intellectual fashion being what it is, human nature is now making a comeback. Biological and genetic factors, once considered illegitimate, are increasingly used in explanations of crime, intelligence, and self-destructive activity. Every social science discipline has been influenced by rational-choice theory, which generally treats self-interest as if it were hardwired into the brain. Sociobiology—now called evolutionary psychology or Darwinian anthropology—has moved slightly closer to the academic mainstream. There will surely emerge a consensus to the effect that culture has been overemphasized; obviously, biology plays a role in how and why we act. But just as surely this consensus will leave wide open the important questions: are biological and genetic factors background influences or proximate causes? what policy implications follow from the emerging interest in these explanations? can biological factors really be treated as distinct from cultural or environmental ones?

Two recent books not only illustrate very different ways of approaching these questions, but the contrast between them also suggests what is and what is not knowable about human behavior. Jerome Kagan, a psychologist committed to observation and measurement, is cautious and balanced in his conclusions.[18] Robert Wright, a journalist, cheers evolutionary theory from the sidelines, as if one idea could explain everything in the world.[19]

Kagan believes that ancient speculation about temperament—Galen divided people into the phlegmatic, the melancholic, the sanguine, and the choleric—was close to a fundamental truth: human beings are born with a disposition to act in certain ways. Although parental choices will surely influence a child's development, some children are fundamentally shy and withdrawn while others are outgoing and unflappable. Kagan, who like most social scientists was skeptical of biological explanations of human behavior, is convinced by fifteen years of experimental work that physiology does play a role in determining which children will be inhibited and which will not.

For Kagan, psychology is a natural science. He distrusts parental reports about their children's behavior as imprecise and biased. Only direct observation will do, leading Kagan and his associates into careful study of the facial gestures and bodily reactions of ever-younger infants as they confront strange situations. Even at the age of four months, differences in temperamental style can be detected. Moreover, the level of fear present in four-month-olds predicts similar levels at nine, fourteen, and twenty-one months. Correlations with gender were established; girls were more fearful than boys. There were few direct links between temperamental style and physiological states, but there were some. Highly reactive infants in general possessed high heart-rates, even when in the womb in the last weeks of pregnancy. The evidence is, as evidence will be, mixed, but there clearly is a style in which some infants are less fearful, have low heart-rates, smile a good deal, and are less reactive, while others manifest all the opposite characteristics.

Do these findings establish a case for the biological origin of temperament? Kagan answers positively, but hardly exuberantly. Psychologists face an unresolvable dilemma in these matters, he notes. If we want certain insight into the neurology and physiology of our subjects, we have to study other animals. But what we learn about one species of rats may not only be irrelevant to humans, it can also have little to do with other species of rats. Kagan would rather retain human subjects, but, as a result, he also must retain what he calls"the ancient method of indirect truth" (204). Hence the less than startling conclusion: after years of work, countless experiments, and obsessive scrutiny, Kagan not only limits his focus to the smallest of problems—whether infants show fear—but also finally hedges his bets. After all, 40 percent of the fearful four-month-olds did not develop into inhibited infants, and only 10 percent possessed all the characteristics of an uninhibited style. There is, it turns out, no iron-clad proof of the biological origin of temperament, merely suggestive possibilities.

In a book that seeks to make the case for biology, Kagan concludes by emphasizing everything but. The biological origin of temperament should be viewed as a disposition, not a determination, Kagan argues: "There is no determinism in the early temperamental bias; no genetic conductor coordinating all the players into one unchanging melody" (271). Temperament cannot be reduced to physiology, even though physiology is important. The fact is that psychology, as a science, has no general principles comparable to those of physics or biology. Because it exists in a "pretheoretical era" (279), psychology must be modest. It must give up any pretense, at this time, of generalization. Facing the great questions of will and the human condition, it must insist on ambiguity. Kagan's book is hardly a manifesto for its subject or even its findings. Its subtext is understated but important: don't jump to conclusions until you know what you are talking about, and since you can't possibly at this time know what you are talking about, don't jump to conclusions at all.

If only Robert Wright had taken that advice. Wright believes that evolutionary fitness explains everything. There really is such a thing as human nature; we are born to maximize our genetic inheritance in our offspring. Of course culture plays a role. No doubt individual choices matter. Circumstances, in short, always vary, but operating all the time and with relentless (and unconscious) perspicacity, at all times and in all places, is one thing: genes acting selfishly, concerned only with reproducing themselves in the maximally effective way.

The premises of what used to be called sociobiology are not, for Wright, hypotheses that will or will not be verified by empirical investigation. They are rather comparable to revelation: blinding insights into our condition so dazzling that they must be accepted as truth, even—especially—when they appear not to apply. As Wright breezily acknowledges, his book is "a sales pitch for a new science" (11). What he sadly fails to realize is that real science doesn't need salesmen. Its evidence speaks for itself. Because he writes as an advocate and enthusiast, Wright actually demonstrates that evolutionary accounts of our actions are sheer speculation—and rather unconvincing ones at that.

Relations between the sexes are the most fertile ground on which to apply the insights of sociobiology, according to Wright. Human sexual life is dominated by the fact of unequal parental involvement with respect to offspring. The genes of men, wanting only to proliferate, force men toward greater promiscuity. But men are not simply Don Juans, for they also need to insure that their offspring will flourish. Men therefore strategize their sexual search. One way they do this is to divide women into two types, the Madonna and the Whore, a dichotomy that may be "built into the male brain" (122) and which serves, in modified form, as an "efficient adaptation." "It leads men to shower worshipful devotion on the sexually reserved women they want to invest in—exactly the sort of devotion these women will demand before allowing sex. And it lets men guiltlessly exploit the women they don't want to invest in, by consigning them to a category that merits contempt" (73).

Women pursue men quite differently than the ways men pursue women. Their main interest is not in having sex but in judging whether the men to whom they give themselves can be trusted to share in the raising of children. This leads them to spend inordinate amounts of time sending out signals and testing the water. Once hooked, women tend to stay hooked, but this does not mean that monogamy developed because it was in the interests of women. Actually women would be better off under polygamy, especially now when there are so many women without husbands. Monogamy is rather "a grand historical compromise" a cartel arrangement that "was cut between more fortunate and less fortunate men" (97). It is therefore absurd to discuss a moral ideal such as faithfulness divorced from the functions it serves (or does not serve) in reproduction. For what is morality other than the conventions humans adopt to adjust themselves to the presence of the selfish genes within them?

Wright goes on to apply similar ideas to the formation of families and social inequality, but it is worth pausing at this point to ask how much of his analysis is rooted in something that can be called science. The answer is: almost none. There is very little to be gained by generalizing about the behavior of men and women throughout all time and across all cultures; while one can indeed be struck by certain universals, it is also the case that sexual relations in the West have changed dramatically in just the past thirty years. And even if the descriptions of male and female behavior are true, there is a more parsimonious explanation for them. Pregnancy costs more for women than men. Therefore they will be more sexually conservative. Unless of course they have access to birth control (mentioned only in passing by Wright) or abortion (never mentioned by Wright).

Wright actually knows that he is on thin ground scientifically. The evidence for the Madonna-Whore dichotomy, he writes, "rests on strong, theoretical expectation, and considerable, though hardly exhaustive, anthropological and psychological evidence" (77). In short, it may not exist. The theory on which all this is based, we learn, "will likely be vindicated" but only "eventually." "The problem isn't a shortage of plausible theories; it's a shortage of studies to test the theories" (83). The contrast with Kagan's approach could not be greater. Wright not only jumps to conclusions, he even leaps over buildings in a single bound, so sure is he that the secret of human existence has been found.

When you do this sort of thing, you usually find yourself in the position of explaining completely contradictory facts by the same theory. If people compete, that is because of their genes. But if they cooperate, their genes have found a more rational way of being selfish. Telling the truth has evolutionary advantages; so does telling lies. Homosexuality, the naive observer may believe, should not exist under Darwinian logic, for if men are programmed to maximize their offspring, why would they engage in sex that did not produce offspring? Yet, Wright argues, "the fact that some people's sexual impulses get diverted from typical channels is just another tribute to the malleability of the human mind" (383). Oddly, Wright concludes that "for moral purposes" (384) the fact that homosexuality does not harm others ought to end the discussion—odd only because Wright has already written that "The question may be whether, after the new Darwinianism takes root, the word *moral* can be anything but a joke" (324).

None of this should be taken to mean that sociobiology is worthless or even unscientific. A great deal of the behavior of many species, though not ours, has been explained in interesting (if not conclusive) ways by sociobiologists. Moreover there may even be something of relevance to humans in this school of thought—so long as we remain at the level of vast statistical description and confine ourselves to periods in the distant past. Once we move closer to home, culture and mind replace biology as the main determinants of our evolution, as both Edward Wilson and Richard Dawkins acknowledge.[20] When we begin to realize the importance of the way human beings take cognizance of the world around them and make choices with the help of their (unique) minds and brains, little is gained by insisting on the relevance of a theory premised on multigenerational effects.

Finally, the one thing that sociobiology, and any of its offspring, cannot do—and which any serious scientist in this tradition would never try to do—is to explain the behavior of one specific person, a historically situated individual such as you or me, as if that person's actions were determined by his genes' insistence on perpetuating themselves.

Yet this is exactly what Wright chooses to do. The figure he selects makes terrific reading for literary and rhetorical purposes, even if, for scientific purposes, the notion is absurd. Let's see, Wright muses, what Darwinianism tells us about the life of . . . Darwin himself. It turns out that the oddities of Darwin's life—his rational search for a wife, his monogamy, his illness, his delay in publishing the theory for which he became famous—all can be explained by sociobiology. Darwin, for example, is often praised as saintly because of his willingness to give credit to Alfred Russel Wallace for jointly discovering the theory of natural selection. Such a view fails to appreciate "the adaptive beauty of Darwin's conscience (306)." What Darwin really did was to develop a brilliant strategy by which he would be remembered both for his scientific accomplishments and for his generosity. On the one hand his delay in publishing his theory made Wallace a real threat he could not ignore. On the other hand, he knew that when the history was written, Wallace would be forgotten and Darwin remembered. Of course Darwin was not "a perfectly adapted animal," but still "lots of odd and much-discussed things about Darwin's mind and character can make a basic kind of sense when viewed through the lens of evolutionary psychology" (308).

Wright has established a nonproblem for which he offers a nonsolution. There is no reason why social scientists should return to discarded nineteenth-century efforts to develop grand theories that explain everything. When Auguste Comte, one such thinker, approached the world, he first practiced "cerebral hygiene"—his notion was to purge himself of every idea ever offered by anyone else so that his theory would retain its purity. The world is better off because scholars now try, not only to learn from others, but also to accumulate knowledge modestly and with acute awareness that they might be wrong. In this sense, searching for a theory that explains everything is a meaningless task. How could it be otherwise that the solutions to the puzzle fail to convince when the puzzle makes no sense in the first place? "A new worldview is emerging," Wright exclaims (4). As if we need one.

If there is indeed a return to theorizing about human nature, it should keep in mind that these are humans whose nature we are interpreting. Kagan reminds of this truth and, in saying little, says a great deal. For the message of his book is that knowledge about humans never comes easy. Wright's book, designed to get us to think in a new way about human nature, actually denies that there is a nature specific to humans. Whatever nature we may have has nothing to do with our particularity as a species and everything to do with our similarities to other species.

There is little to be gained by trying to understand human nature as a biological constant. This is not because biology is unimportant but the reverse. One of the great insights of biology, and one of the reasons it can never be a science like physics, is that the dynamics of each and every species found in nature are different. Humans beings are one such species found in nature. Respect for this species demands respect for the culture it has built. Social scientists ought to think about humans as plastic in nature—capable of many different actions under many different circumstances—because only that view corresponds with the actual experiences we have. In their own way, both Kagan and Wright demonstrate the limits of biology as an explanation of human conduct, the one by honest admission, the other by exaggeration. Human nature really exists. What makes it human is that it can never be reduced to one thing.

Degrees of Confidence

For social critics interested in backing up their judgments about how society ought to function with knowledge about how it actually does, the question of whether or not we can ever have confidence in findings about human behavior is of central importance. Opinions on that question have swung full circle from the self-confident arrogance of the golden age. Now, under the influence of postmodernism, the possibility that we can ever know anything is widely discounted. But such lack of respect for knowledge can be asserted in ways fully as dogmatic as Talcott Parsons' belief in social science and social engineering; the move from complete certainty to complete uncertainty is not much of a move at all. Knowledge, one wants to respond to the postmodernists, may be treacherous, but it is not *that* treacherous.

Social scientists do know about some things, even if they do not know much about others; social criticism informed by what we know is preferable to social criticism that springs full-blown out of the theorist's head. The issue is not whether social facts are knowable in some absolute sense, but rather how knowable they are. Social knowledge can be organized by degrees of confidence: we can have great confidence in some findings and less in others.

Generally speaking, the less vital an issue is to the question of how we ought to live, the more confidence we can have in findings which support our position. Jerome Kagan has demonstrated fairly conclusively that infants have an inborn propensity to show or not show fear, but that has little or nothing to do with whether they will support more spending for prisons when they become adults. If one were to summarize the major findings of the literature on mother-infant bonding, it would be that infants need close attachment to someone or something, but not necessarily to their biological mother. That finding, alas, tells us very little about how we create a system of moral trust and mutual accountability among strangers. In both cases we know something, but in both cases the something we know takes us only so far.

It also follows that the more we care about an issue, the less we can rely on science to tell us what is right, a dictum well illustrated by James Q. Wilson's *The Moral Sense.* As a citizen with articulate and well thought-out views on some of the most controversial issues of the day, Wilson has many interesting things to say about moral matters. To give just one example, he writes movingly about why most people understand drug addiction or alcoholism as a moral failure; self-control is so important a moral sentiment that we inevitably attach a stigma to those who so evidently lack it. But this means, as Wilson recognizes, that for most people such addictions cannot be written off as having a biological or neurological cause; if they could, the importance of families and friends in reenforcing self-control would not matter.

Wilson speaks best on morality, in other words, when he writes as a moralist, not a scientist. If Wilson wants to argue that women, for the sake of their children and thereby the rest of society, should stay at home rather than work, he should say so rather than engaging in highly speculative notions about sexual selection. Indeed, the comments that both

Wilson and Robert Wright make about biological bases of sexual selection indicate that the gap between what biology teaches us about sexual difference and the political concerns raised by feminists is about as broad as the gap between individual behavior and the aggressiveness of nations which was announced by academic psychologists after their participation in World War II. Scientific evidence simply will not help us decide whether, in today's culture wars, the left or the right has the better position.

Social critics have little to fear from science; its findings are not going to make their judgments obsolete. But that does not mean that social critics should ignore science; they ought to welcome the knowledge that scientists accumulate, a welcome best achieved by recognizing that facts about human behavior are a part of what we need to know if we are going to hold our institutions and practices up to criticism, but never the whole of what we need to know.

THE MORALITY OF CRITICISM

Social Criticism and Political Liberalism

Even when the social critic does not write about morality directly, the act of criticism itself presupposes a certain moral posture toward the world. By their very nature, social critics promote disagreement, which means that consensus cannot be among their highest priorities. They subject the ideas of another person to attack, so empathy is not a quality they value highly. No matter what their politics, they cannot accept the argument that whatever exists must exist; critics, even when they are conservative, will always tend to be skeptical. Truth, for the critic, is valued more than solidarity, the individual conscience takes priority over the collective conscience, the ultimate standards for judging the truth of an idea or an institution are established by rational and cognitive faculties, and priority must be given to political and economic systems which place value on the free exchange of ideas. The morality of criticism is neither communitarian nor authoritarian, but liberal—understood in a broad philosophical sense that might include many who, on the issues of the day, would call themselves conservative.

Yet liberal morality is increasingly felt to be problematic for modern societies. With its emphasis on abstract conceptions of justice, legal formalism, neutrality toward the good life and individual rights, liberalism, its critics charge, cannot provide rich traditions of meaning and belonging for individuals already disposed, by the conditions of their lives, to anomic aloneness.[1] A wide-ranging debate between liberals and communitarians characterizes contemporary political theory, one that has important implications for the theory and practice of social criticism.[2] For if we feel that the collectivities to which we belong are threatened—requiring that our obligations to them take precedence over our individual desires and needs—then we would likely restrain our urge to criticize institutions and practices for the sake of the common good. If, on the other hand, we assign a higher priority to the individual voice than to group solidarity, we are likely to conclude that the suppression of criticism in the name of cohesion is too high a price to pay for community.

Although liberals and communitarians argue at the level of theory, their debates have important implications for the everyday lives of most people. Criticism is not something that just takes place in the pages of intellectual magazines. American society is felt by many to be excessively litigious. Its politics, increasingly partisan, seems to place too much emphasis on negative campaigning. Disrespect for authority, many conservatives believe, has gone too far, as criticism becomes more highly valued than obedience. This negative disposition toward criticism is reenforced by a generally positive image of conciliators. Especially at a time when Americans seem divided from each other—and when those divisions take the form, as increasingly they do, of murdering one's opponents— the moral superiority of cooperation seems self-evident. Critics of criticism believe they are doing everyone a favor. Their objective is to build consensus by helping disputing parties to see the common interest they have in solutions which avoid zero-sum situations.[3] In such ways can the anger and frustration which characterizes American politics be overcome.

Yet, as befits a society still committed to liberalism, every position just enumerated has been itself criticized: litigation is a way in which the aggrieved can have recourse; restrictions on negative campaigning violate free speech; self-interest offers a surer guide to long-term cooperation than guided consensus; and institutions that do not deserve respect ought not to have respect. Critics often believe themselves to be serving a higher cause than obedience or tradition; for the critic, exposure is the moral legacy of the Enlightenment. Not only is criticism good, many critics insist, cooperation, under some circumstances, can be bad. If consensus comes about before critics have had a chance to hold the adopted ideas up to scrutiny, a society could easily take steps down the wrong path, with potentially far worse results later on. No one has to like criticism—or, for that matter, critics. But they ought to view them as necessary evils; criticism is just another word for freedom.

Social critics, who by the nature of their work engage in an activity about which Americans have such ambivalent feelings, inevitably have to speculate about the morality of what they do. Is criticism always the appropriate attitude to take toward existing social practices and institutions? Can criticism cause harm to those being criticized? Under what conditions should solidarity matter more than criticism? In this chapter I will address questions involving the morality of criticism by examining the ideas of a social scientist whose views on these matters have reached more Americans than perhaps any other in America. Like Margaret Mead of the golden age of social criticism, Deborah Tannen, a sociolinguist, uses the insights of anthropology to address issues on the minds of most Americans. Unlike Mead, she does not write about exotic foreign cultures; her research involves primarily Americans. Although her ostensible subject is how we talk, her main concern involves issues of agreement and disagreement. There are times and places, she feels, when criticism is justified. But these are generally asides in her argument, the clear thrust of which is that criticism is nearly always wrong, destructive, and especially harmful to women.

Tannen claims that her arguments in favor of cooperation and against criticism are rooted in both good science and good therapy. We criticize others because we do not understand them, yet communication, as we learn from sociolinguistics, always involves some miscommunication. Once we realize that communication is anything but a straightforward proposition, we will be less predisposed to criticize others and will therefore accord them greater respect. A proper understanding of how language is shaped by cultural assumptions, Tannen concludes, can therefore strengthen the social bond, from husbands and wives all the way to the international community.

Tannen's use of language to discuss larger issues of cooperation and conflict is an ingenious idea. She writes about the single most common social activity in which people engage; everyone talks, although not everyone reads, reasons, or writes. She brings knowledge of an academic discipline, and a relatively obscure one at that, to the general public. Questions of political philosophy which might seem abstract are brought to life by illustrating them through the way we talk; Tannen's anecdotes are like parables, easily understandable and fascinating to discuss. Yet, as ought to be clear from my treatment of social scientists like Theda Skocpol or James Q. Wilson, the notion that we can draw moral lessons from social science findings ought to be treated with some skepticism; Tannen, I will argue, is unable to muster as much scientific support behind her analysis of language as she claims. And for that reason the advice she gives has no special standing. There may well be good reasons why cooperation ought to have the moral benefit of the doubt over criticism, but Tannen does not provide them. This is not to conclude that being critical is always the right thing to be, but it does suggest that there are moral virtues associated with criticism which ought not to be overlooked in our desire to understand and empathize with one another.

Deborah Tannen: Sociolinguist

"I got hooked on linguistics," Deborah Tannen wrote in her first best-seller, *That's Not What I Meant*, "the year my marriage broke up."[4] The breaking point came over a simple matter of visiting a relative. "Do you want to go to my sister's?" Tannen asked her then husband. "Okay," he responded. Not completely satisfied that this was a positive answer, Tannen chimed in: "Do you really want to go?" (6), at which point he exploded, driving her into desperate anger. Groping to make sense of what happened, she heard a lecture by a prominent linguist named Robin Lakoff and "a floodlight fell upon the stage of my marriage" (8). It seems that different people have different styles of talking. Her style was literal: "I took it for granted that I would come out and say what I wanted, and that I could ask my husband what he wanted, and that he would tell me." His style was indirect; "he assumed people hint at what they want and pick up hints" (8). The problem was not that they were dishonest with each other, for each was speaking truthfully. The problem was that they did not understand why they misunderstood. Talking through their problems only made matters worse because the problem was how they talked.

That's Not What I Meant constructed upon this example a catalogue of miscommunication, an inventory to all the ways that conversational style causes confusion. The world of talk is filled with devices and designs that send messages other than the ones we think we are sending. How loudly or softly we speak, when and how we pause, whether we use irony or humor, whether we make a request in the form of a question or a declaration, how we take turns, whether we interrupt, the forms of address we use, how we frame what we say—all are capable of being misunderstood. Linguistics, by teaching us to be more aware of these things, is a path to self-discovery. "I don't know if my marriage would have continued had I discovered linguistics before the breakup instead of right after. But I would have understood better what was going on" (14). The same is true for all of us. "This book is meant to assure you that when conversations seem to be causing more problems than they're solving, you aren't losing your mind. And you may not have to lose (if you don't want to) your friendship, your partner, or your money to the ever-gaping jaws of differences in conversational style" (14).

Tannen's book shot to the top of the best-seller list, to be followed by the equally popular *You Just Don't Understand* and her latest contribution, *Talking from 9 to 5*.[5] But in spite of her celebrity status, Tannen makes it clear that her academic side is important to her. Her best sellers always list the Ph.D after her name. Even in her most popular books, she introduces herself as an academic. *Gender and Discourse* assembles some her major scholarly papers.[6] No doubt Tannen's academic credentials are also important to her readers. This is not just your ordinary self-help maven telling you these things. The always reasonable tone of voice, the reliance on technical terms, even the odd markings used by linguists when they analyze a conversation—all convey the message that the author of these books is a someone whose advice is based on more than just her opinion; there is significant theory and research to back it up.

Tannen was trained at Berkeley, primarily by John Gumperz and Robin Lakoff. Gumperz argues that linguists get language wrong when they study speakers as individuals rather than as "members of specific groups."[7] Not only does group membership shape language, but language also shapes group membership; as Gumperz put it with Jenny Cook-Gumperz, "social identity and ethnicity are in large part established and maintained through language."[8] Lakoff added conversational style, the idea that people, especially men and women, speak in different ways.[9]

Both Gumperz and Lakoff were part of a reaction against the search for universal constants in human behavior. Their ideas seem close to the Sapir-Whorf hypothesis that language shapes thought, "an idea," Tannen notes, "that has been central to linguistics" (*TNWIM*, p. 187). It has also been thoroughly disproven; Steven Pinker, a linguist of quite a different persuasion than Tannen, makes mincemeat of the notion that the Eskimo have lots of words for snow or that the Hopi are oblivious to time.[10] Nonetheless, when properly toned down from the extreme cultural relativism of the early years of anthropology, there is considerable truth in the idea that what we say is in part determined by who we are.

This kind of linguistics lies closer to the "softer" social sciences than to the cognitive sciences or phonetics and morphology. Its aim is not parsimonious explanations of universal features of language but the description, as carefully done as possible, of local situations. Tannen herself wrote her doctoral dissertation on one dinner party: a two-and-a-half hour Thanksgiving feast shared by three New York Jews, two California Christians, and a Brit.[11] Her goal was not to generalize about all talking, let alone all Thanksgiving dinners. Her approach is ethnographic— critics (of which, on this point at least, I am not one) would say anecdotal. This kind of approach defends itself through the claim that human behavior is so complex that a universalizing science is inappropriate to understand it.

Local knowledge can yield general insights. But the qualifications and exceptions that make for local knowledge, already at odds with parsimonious explanation, are also at odds with popularization. Who wants to know about one dinner party? We want to know about ourselves, and since Deborah Tannen, who has not studied us, wants to tell us about ourselves, she can only do so by making vast generalizations from the cases she has studied. In her academic work, Tannen writes about specific people; in her popular work, she writes about generic people. There is little relationship between the two.

The generic individuals that populate Tannen's best-sellers are only identified by first name: Samantha, Maxwell, Minerva, Jay, Eric. One's first reaction on being introduced to them is to wonder how representative they are. The fact that Maria thinks Gordon can't take a joke might be of interest only to Maria and Gordon, depending upon how many wives think of their husbands as dunderheads. In shifting from specific cases to generic individuals, Tannen shifts the grounds of proof. The test of ethnography is insight, but the test of universality is generalization. How representative is Maria? Such questions can only be answered in the form of bell-shaped curves; ironically, it is the popular Tannen whose work requires the harder scientific technique. But no such answers are forthcoming; indeed no such questions are ever asked. The only question that matters is whether Maria reminds the reader of herself.

This shift from local description to universal generalization would be difficult for any social scientist, but for one who believes in the power of culture over communication it is peculiar to say the least. Linguistic strategies, Tannen writes, are influenced by ethnic and national background; Jews are "high involvement" speakers, while California Christians strive for "high considerateness" (*YJDU*, p. 196). But the generic individuals in her popular books generally lack marks of identification; readers are rarely provided the local detail that might make sense of what the speakers say. We have no idea whether these figures are real people, composite portraits, or pseudonymous stand-ins. And, in truth, it does not matter, for by invoking their existence, Tannen transforms herself from ethnographer to fabulist. These figures can be stripped of their identity because they have no identity. They are not interesting for who they are but for what they illustrate. In her academic work, Tannen begins with individuals and ends with generalizations. In her popular work, she begins with generalizations and realizes them through individuals.

There is one exception to what I have just said: we do know their gender. In giving us only this information, Tannen seems to be saying that gender is not only one form that culture takes, but it is, for all intents and purposes, the only form. This is actually strange, for Tannen is not a militant feminist. Feminism is not her ideology; nonjudgmentalism is. The discovery of linguistic style means that men should not be blamed for their aggressiveness nor women for their indirectness. Nonjudgmentalism is simultaneously academic (objectivity, scientific detachment) and popular (twelve-step recovery, self-help). Cool down, everyone, and let's listen to the reasonableness of everyone's position—this is her message, and it is not a message that has been well received by those feminists for whom men are the enemy.

Yet nonjudgmentalism is just another way of making judgments, and a poor one at that. Tannen's judgments are predictable: women's way of speaking is better. After all, if men and women talk differently, whose language should we use to reconcile their differences? Tannen believes that miscommunication is tragic and that we should make sincere efforts to understand each other. But she also claims that "the role of peacemaker reflects the general tendency among women to seek agreement" (*YJDU*, p. 167). For men and women to communicate they have to do so in a style that favors women.

Tannen the scholar and Tannen the popularizer differ somewhat in the emphasis they give to gender. Her academic writings note that the feminist claim that men dominate women in conversation is hard to reconcile with the feminist complaint that men never talk. Nor is it true that men interrupt women to dominate them; what appears to be interruption can simply be "overlap," two or more people talking at the same time, which is quite common in some cultures. One of the classic articles seeking to prove that men dominate women in talk is strongly, and effectively, criticized by Tannen, for it simply counts interruptions without recognizing ethnographic context;[12] in some cases, overlapping can be "cooperative," not a "fight for the floor" (*GAD*, pp. 60, 62).

Yet even in her scholarly writings, gender determinism creeps into the analysis. *Gender and Discourse*, her collected academic writings on this theme, contains an essay (originally coauthored with Robin Lakoff) that relies entirely on the screenplay of Ingmar Bergman's *Scenes from a Marriage*. Social scientists usually examine real-life events, not artistically created ones. But even granting that a genius like Bergman can tell us something about reality while writing fiction, he is, after all, a Swede.

One would think that a cross-cultural linguist would be the first to point out that the way Swedes talk may have little to do with the way Americans talk. To argue that Bergman has nonetheless created a marriage that tells us about all marriages is to conclude that, as cultural categories, men and women are more important than Swedes and Americans. Whether or not this is true is unimportant; what is important is that, if it is true, then the categories of men and women are no longer cultural but universal. All men will act in a certain way, regardless of culture, as will all women. Culture has to disappear if gender is to be treated as a culture; Tanner begins with Gumperz only to deny his major insight.

Gender determinism, hinted at in Tannen's academic writing, becomes the rule in her popular writing. Even here, Tannen insists, with benumbing regularity, that she never blames anyone, yet there is clearly more to the matter than these disclaimers. *You Just Don't Understand*, which concentrates entirely on gender, endorses "difference feminism" much more strongly than *Gender and Discourse*. Men and women speak different languages—genderlects, Tannen infelicitously calls them—because they think in different ways. Females think sideways; they try to make connections, be supportive, and focus on details, whereas men, thinking up and down, strive for logic, abstraction, and directness. Men engage in report-talk, women in rapport-talk, the one more public, the other more private. A man and a woman had an argument over an article in the newspaper which claimed that students were less idealistic than they were in the 1960s. The man accepted the claim, presumably because the story offered evidence to that effect. The woman was not so sure because her niece and her friends were quite idealistic. Since our society validates abstraction, we ought to value women's ways of speaking more highly. Because gender equality doesn't exist, only by giving special weight to female speech can we be fair. We have to judge in order to be nonjudgmental.

In an afterword to one of the scholarly papers collected in *Gender and Discourse*, Tannen writes that she added new examples to *You Just Don't Understand* "to avoid the false impression that my intention was to deny that interruption exists, that overlap can be intended to interrupt, or that men can use interruption to silence women" (*GAD*, pp. 74–75). There is a good deal of truth in this statement. Although only one of the ten chapters of *That's Not What I Meant* dealt formally with gender, the war between the sexes provided the bulk of the illustrations in every chapter. Tannen comes closest to her own sentiments when she writes that "we cannot take a step without taking stances that are prescribed by society and gender specific. We enact and create our gender, and our inequality, with every step we make" (*YJDU*, p. 283). Whatever the truth or falsity of such statements, they are neither neutral nor nonjudgmental.

Deborah Tannen: Conversational Therapist

For a host of reasons, there is little if any scientific basis to Tannen's claims about the way we talk. It is simply impossible to make a moral claim for consensus based on the fact that conflict, at least with respect to language, is built into cultural difference, especially if gender is viewed as a source of cultural difference. But this academic criticism may be unfair. Whatever the state of sociolinguistics as a science, Tannen is simply trying to help people. Shouldn't we judge her by the clinical standard of whether she does rather than by the scientific standard of whether she has reality right?

Tannen the clinician proceeds in two steps. First, she asserts the existence of a problem: people miscommunicate, causing conflict. Then she offers a solution: an understanding of miscommunication will facilitate cooperation and lessen conflict. There are major problems with both claims.

People do miscommunicate—sometimes. They also communicate perfectly well at other times. Moreover, miscommunication often leads, not to conflict, but to an ambiguous result that allows both sides to cooperate; this is called diplomacy. And even perfect communication can cause deep and resolvable conflicts to emerge. Recall Tannen's story about her first marriage. Her former husband became angry, and Tannen became depressed, because she asked him a second time whether he really wanted to go to her sister's. This was not miscommunication. The conflict was a product of their anger toward each other. The communication, which expressed perfectly their mutual distrust, simply brought it out into the open.

Tannen gets the idea that miscommunication is ubiquitous from an anthropologist, Gregory Bateson, whose first wife, Margaret Mead, perfected the anthropologist's technique of making the strange seem vaguely familiar, only to render it strange again. Tannen is an anthropologist in reverse. She makes the familiar seem strange, only to render it familiar again. To accomplish this task, she relies heavily on Bateson's ideas and terminology: metacommunication, framing, the double bind, and complementary schismogenesis.

Metacommunication refers to talk about talk. As a naturalist, Bateson noted not only that various animals communicate with each other but that they first communicate about the kind of communication they will have.[13] It is as if a monkey—Bateson formulated this insight after a 1952 visit to the Fleishhacker Zoo in San Francisco—would say something like the following: my next gesture is meant as play, so don't take it as hostility. Humans, obviously, do this too. We signal in many ways whether our words are meant to be ironic or to be taken as uttered, for instance. One way in which metacommunication takes place is by framing: a pause in what we are saying indicates a change of context. This can be direct: "Let's get serious," we might say. Or it can be indirect; we move to a darker part of the room in order to say our next thoughts, thereby suggesting greater confidentiality.

Tannen consistently misuses Bateson's terms in her best-sellers. When you give someone a gift, you are not only conveying the actual thing you bought but the "metamessage" that you care, Tannen writes (*TNWIM*, p. 58). Or, she points out, the failure of one person to match her friend's complaint with a similar complaint sent a "metamessage" lacking in solidarity (*TNWIM*, pp. 47–48). These are not, technically speaking (and Bateson's terminology is extremely technical) metamessages; she should say "subtext," as when we say one thing but mean another. Both metamessages and subtexts involve the relationship between the speakers, but Bateson's point about metacommunication, a highly abstract one, was an exercise in the theory of logical types, not an empirical observation.

Bateson, indeed, was anything but an empirical social scientist. In the 1936 epilogue to his anthropological study of an Iatmul congratulatory ceremony in New Guinea, he wrote that "my fieldwork was scrappy and disconnected—perhaps more so than that of most anthropologists."[14] Bateson, like many of the social critics of the golden age, took great pleasure in shocking convention, which is perhaps why he proposed that the only reason not to have an incestuous relationship with his (and Margaret Mead's) daughter was the possibly negative genetic consequence.[15] Such inclinations also help explain his disdain for his empirically oriented professional colleagues in anthropology who believed that their discipline was a science. Unlike them, Bateson was "sceptical of historical reconstruction." His theories, he wrote, "proved too vague to be of any use in the field." "I did not clearly see any reason why I should enquire into one matter rather than another," he commented, so "I either let my informants run on freely from subject to subject, or asked the first question which came into my head" (*Naven*, p. 257).

No wonder that Bateson scandalized the professional community of anthropologists. As his biographer David Lipset points out, Bateson's work was dismissed as unreliable because it was excessively auto-biographical.[16] Many of the heavy hitters in the field joined the attack. In his preface to Firth's *We, The Tikopia*, Bronislaw Malinowksi wrote that "we are suffering from a surfeit of new anthropological theories" in which "the reality of human life is being submitted to some queer and alarming manipulations"; among these was the work of "another writer" who analyzes "cultures in terms of Schismogenesis." Compared to such speculation, Firth's book was "an unaffected piece of genuine scholar-ship, based on real experience of a culture and not on a few hypostatized impressions."[17] As influential as Bateson's ideas may be, they are not based on any firm empirical reality.

With his disdain for description, Bateson is an odd choice for building a theory dealing with everyday life. But Tannen's reliance on him is even more puzzling because Bateson was explicitly uninterested in the ordi-nary; whatever else dolphins and schizophrenics—his two favorite subjects—have in common, they are not Maria and Gordon. There is little doubt that schizophrenics have communication problems; in a widely cited metaphor, Bateson illustrated "complementary schismo-genesis" by asking us to imagine a couple lying under an electric blanket with the controls reversed. Every time he tries to make himself warmer, he makes her warmer instead, so she responds by making him colder. An interesting idea—but is all marital communication like this? Bateson himself noted that the process can be reversed so that "a balance will be reached when the forces of mutual dependence are equal to the schis-mogenic tendency," with the result that "instead of leading to an increase in mutual hostility, the inverse process leads rather in the direction of mutual love."[18] These qualifications are not found in Tannen, for their implication is that women and men can communicate without her help. Moreover the destructive form of schismogenisis appears most often in cases of "psychodeviance," which, by definition, is not the typical pattern.

Why does Tannen rely on Bateson so much? My guess is that citing Bateson, even if incorrectly, gives her the advantage of claiming that ev-eryday life, far from being a simple affair in which things mean what they seem to mean, is treacherous, filled with traps, waiting to surprise (and harm) the innocent. If one believes, by contrast, that most of the time people actually mean what they say—that they know their own motives and have sufficient control over language to express them clearly—then Tannen's entire diagnosis of miscommunication, and the Batesonian structure upon which it improperly lies, collapses.

Whether conflict is caused by miscommunication or perfect communication, is it bad? Although Tannen offers the strong opinion that it is, the case is anything but clear-cut. Psychological health, self-respect, equality—all may require in certain situations that conflict be encouraged.

Tannen devotes a chapter of *That's Not What I Meant* to "the intimate critic"; our relationships, which we form for support and for solidarity against the outside world, turn critical within. Partners respond to each other with an arsenal of critical devices: sarcasm, repeating what others say, asking indirect questions, even praising in the wrong way. "The tragedy of all these forms of criticism is that they make one feel unheard or even unloved, and the sense of incompetence they engender can long outlive the arguments or discussions that spawned them" (*TNWIM*, p. 153). Fortunately, this tragedy can be avoided. Critics should recognize "that some forms of criticism are more destructive than others" (163). The criticized ought to remember "that criticism is a common by-product of closeness." In addition, "one should mount self-defense on the level of the pain—the effect of feeling criticized—rather than skirmishing about the validity of the criticism" (164).

Tannen's advice to avoid the substance of criticism in relationships is bad advice. It would turn all relationships into therapeutic encounters, not intellectual partnerships. And good relationships, irrespective of social class, *are* intellectual partnerships; marriage is as much about jointly solving the intellectual demands of life as it is about warmth and intimacy. This is especially the case when children are involved; being a parent demands hard thinking, at nearly every moment, about some of life's most intractable moral dilemmas. Since every parent is a moral philosopher, isn't it better for husbands and wives to argue about the substance of their disagreements, and to argue as heatedly as the situation demands?

A strong dose of criticism is also necessary for self-respect. Here is some more of the clinical Tannen. A man and a woman meet, like each other, and spend the night together. Since it was a weekday night, his suggestion that they dawdle a bit and have a leisurely breakfast together is taken by her as romantic and exciting. No sooner does she agree than he picks up the newspaper, into which his head is soon buried. "Had she known nothing of the gender differences I discuss," Tannen writes, "she would simply have felt hurt and dismissed this man as yet another clunker. She would have concluded that, having enjoyed the night with her, he was now availing himself of her further services as a short-order cook" (*YJDU*, p. 86). Luckily, however, this woman had heard Deborah Tannen lecture. Hence she realized that, "unlike her, he did not feel the need for talk to reenforce their intimacy. The companionabilty of her presence was all that he needed" (86).

To which I can only respond: on this point feminist critics of Tannen are right. This woman had every right to throw the creep out of her house. If she wanted a relationship with him, she should have torn the paper out of his hands and told him that his oafish ways had better change fast. Any other response not only undermines her self-esteem but also shows no respect for him. Surely Tannen is correct that criticism can be out of place. But so can a failure to criticize. Being in relationships is about learning when to criticize as much as it is about tinkering with the way criticism is given.

In his book *Pluralism*, the philosopher Nicholas Rescher says that consensus has no moral benefit of the doubt. The same is true of cooperation. "It makes good sense to revise beliefs to accommodate them to other *evidence*," Rescher continues, "but it makes no rational sense to revise them to accommodate other *people*."[19] Of course this is a man talking, one no doubt influenced by Kant, for whom moral judgments based on the idiosyncratic characteristics of "mere" individuals were inevitably wrong judgments. Yet one need not adopt Kant's high-minded standards to realize that the respect we have for other people is as much respect for what they say as how they say it.

Treating people's style as more important than the substance of what they say, for all its seeming reasonableness, fails to take people, and their ideas, seriously. This sounds like a heavy burden to lay on Tannen's shoulders. After all speaking is empowerment; when we give voice to an idea, we are also, to use Albert Hirschman's term, giving voice[20]—that is, we are expressing our opinion about the way our institutions are run rather than exiting from them in search of better opportunities elsewhere. One of Tannen's goal is to make speech more fair; if men speak one way and women speak another way, and if our society gives more respect to the former than to the latter, then fairness demands that we design our institutions so that women's voices can be heard.

This, at least, is the main argument of Tannen's latest book, *Talking from 9 to 5*. In it, she concentrates on the world of work, especially in large, and hierarchical, organizations. As her focus moves from bedrooms to boardrooms, the question of whether cooperation or conflict is preferable becomes crucial.

Talking From 9 to 5 argues that much of what we attribute to gender discrimination can also be viewed as asymmetries of communicative style. One reason why the glass ceiling exists is that promotion within firms is based on certain expectations of how people will talk—decisively, in a take-charge manner—which themselves are gender biased. Women are more interested in getting the job done than they are in boasting about their accomplishments. But the world of work establishes a premium on self-promotion. Women not only fail to brag, they also tend not to demean others; as Tannen says of herself, "I am always careful not to make anyone look bad" (*TFNTF,* p. 145). No wonder that women are stopped before they reach the top.

Some do reach the top, but this does not end the problems that flow from the incompatibility between women's way of talking and corporate culture. A boss exercises authority, "but the very notion of authority is associated with maleness" (167). Women respond to the authority they have by downplaying it. If, on the other hand, they relish their power, they are accused of being a Dragon Lady—of denying their femininity. The result is a classic Batesonian double bind.

Unlike private relationships, where people have more power to jointly determine the nature of their interaction, "someone who takes a job is entering a world that is already functioning, with its own characteristic style already in place" (23). That world is, from top to bottom, biased against female conversational styles. Women apologize more than men. They speak more indirectly. They tend not to dominate meetings. They are left out of the sports talk and the dirty jokes. Their concerns about sexual harassment make men wary of them. Great gains have been made by women in the world of work, but if these different evaluations of conversational style are allowed to persist, those gains will go for naught.

What to do? "I would not advise women to adopt men's styles to succeed—although, in some cases, in some ways, this might work" (125), Tannen writes. The fault lies not in men and women, nor even in sexism. The problem is that our culture values men's way of speaking more than women's; hence what we have to do is to revise our institutions to give more recognition to women's ways of talking. What we need is communicative affirmative action; procedures that will distribute equally the opportunity to speak.

Tannen believes that unstructured groups—meetings in which the rules for turn-taking in speech are unspecified—are unfair. "Running a meeting in an unstructured way seems to give equal opportunity to all. But in practice, conversational-style differences result in unequal opportunity" (293). Instead, time should be devoted at meetings to discussions of process; group leaders ought to encourage those who are silent to speak out. We also might "invite individuals to submit their opinions in writing either before or at the meeting, so they will not be unduly influenced by what others say before their turn comes next" (305). The point is to avoid giving disproportionate attention to those who argue most vociferously, even most persuasively, for their point of view. Even negotiation can be a trap; "it may be in the interests of companies to allow more decisions to be made independently by individuals whose judgment they trust, so that those judgments will not be subject to negotiations with others whose styles may give them an advantage, regardless of whose ideas are superior" (306).

Tannen's proposals for corporate governance build upon this distaste for consensus from below. Inclusion cannot be trusted to happen by it-self; for everyone to speak, facilitators are required, and they need the backing of regulatory rules. Ultimately, democracy itself may be trap un-less it is correctly structured; as Tannen writes, " 'democratic' principles, which seem to be self-evidently desirable, don't always end happily for everyone and—most important—may not always result in the best deci-sions being made" (292).

This skepticism toward democratic principles may be why Tannen in-cludes in her book some rather unfocused, but nonetheless revealing, re-marks on Japanese management style:

> Americans tend to assume that hierarchy precludes closeness, so employers and employees cannot "really" be friends, and if they do become friends, complications arise that must be worked out. I myself was inclined to assume that hierarchy is distancing, so that taking a one-up position is synonymous with pushing some-one away. But the Japanese perspective made me rethink that as-sumption. (214)

It turns out that Asians think differently about hierarchy than Americans. For the Japanese, dependency is not necessarily a bad thing, since "there are obligations as well as privileges that go along with both the superior and the subordinate roles" (215). If we Americans were open to the way other cultures think about these things, we would realize that hierarchy can be "close and mutually, not unilaterally, empowering" (216). We even have such relationships in our own culture: mother-child bonding and sibling relationships are hierarchical, but also loving.

We tried such things once: they were called paternalism. Not much is gained by calling them maternalism. What was abusive about them is precisely what Tannen likes: they did not allow for conflict and argument. When conflict came, it took the form of labor unions—organizations based on the premise that conflict is preferable to cooperation when it comes to issues of distributive justice. Conflict—deep-seated antago-nism toward the other, suspicion of his intentions and motives, a wari-ness even about talking to him—is the stuff of democracy. Cooperation—procedures that focus on style rather than substance, efforts to elicit participation from all, reasonableness in tone and mutual regard—is the stuff of elite control.

Tannen would like more meetings to adopt the Japanese practice of *nemawashi.* "The Japanese," she writes, "believe that people are much more likely to express their true feelings (*honnē*) in private, informal conversations than they are in a meeting, which is public, formal, and likely to elicit more "false fronts" (*tatemaē*), or socially acceptable feelings" (305). *Nemawashi* is a system in which "managers in neutral or intermediate positions go around, talk privately to each person who will be at the meeting, get everyone's opinions, and coordinate everyone's interest" (305). We tend not to do this, to our detriment. "The history of the Gulf War might have different if our leaders had practiced *nemawashi*" (306).

If *nemwashi* works, it does so by sacrificing accountability. Decisions made in public have to be exposed to the countering views of all sides. Such decisions, subject to the give-and-take or argument and disagreement, may not be perfect, but they are tested, moderated, broadened, and, when necessary, altered. They also come prejustified, for the very process of hammering them out is what guarantees that they will have public support. As the political philosopher Stephen Macedo has argued, "liberal virtues" are the virtues of debate and public justification. Ideas that go through the kind of screening to which liberal democracy subjects them have a kind of built-in resilience.[21] Public justification involves both speaking and listening—it is as important to hear what others say as it is to have one's own say.

In Tannen's world, by contrast, everyone can speak, but no one need listen. Since consensus-building takes place behind the scenes, there is no argument with the ideas of others because those ideas are never heard. It would no longer be necessary to persuade others, to make a compelling case for one's beliefs, or even to articulate one's thoughts with the help of others. *Nemawashi,* applied to America, would encourage gossip, false accusation, cowardice, rumor, disinformation, and elite manipulation. McCarthyism was a kind of *nemawashi.* Rely more on that way of making decisions in the corporate world, and greater equality between men and women might be the result—both would be treated in equally irresponsible ways.

The Politics of Tannenism

As Tannen quite rightly acknowledges, the corporate world that provides the setting for *Talking from 9 to 5* is not, and is not meant to be, democratic. She entered that world, she tells us, because she wanted to leave behind the world of private speech for what she calls "private speaking in a public context" (8). If this trend continues, her next book will be about public talk in public settings, bringing her to the question of politics and public debate. When she does, she will have to deal with the problem of democracy, for as inapplicable as it may be to large, hierarchical corporations, it remains the operative ideal for an open and public political system.

When Tannen turns more explicitly to politics, we already have an idea what she will say. Even in her first best-seller, Tannen understood that her work had political implications. For what is politics but talk, and what is political conflict but disagreement? The flaws in our politics, like the flaws in our marriages, can be fixed, if we understand that "the processes of conversational style that play themselves out in private conversations are also at the heart of public and international relations" (*TNWIM*, p. 191). Affirmative action, she suggested "has not worked as well as expected (191)" due to miscommunication. "Most Americans genuinely believe that everyone should be given equal opportunity. But they balk in confusion, disillusionment, and dismay, when culturally different people, having been optimistically admitted, do not behave in expected (and they think self-evidently appropriate) ways (192)." What's true for the country is true for the world. "International relations are largely a matter of individuals sitting down and talking to each other" (193). Linguistics can help prevent nuclear war.

Language, in short, has become the language of politics. We don't speak because we disagree; we disagree because we speak. Hobbes believed that people would inevitably be at war, requiring a sovereign to keep the peace. Tannen thinks that people would inevitably be at peace, except that communication keeps them in a state of war. We ought to turn our attention from substance to style. Get our national conversation on the right track, and political civility will follow. If marriages can be made to work, so can Congress.

The politics of Tannenism cannot be overlooked in any effort to account for her success. Truly American politics seem to have reached a new stage of partisan ugliness, as not only the parties, but every potential interest group, weighs in by exaggerating its own case while denigrating its opponents. There is considerable evidence from surveys that Americans are disgusted by the whole spectacle. Responses which emphasize that this kind of public bickering is as old as the Republic, and can actually have healthy consequences for the body politic, fall on deaf ears. Americans hate politics because they detest the conversational style in which it takes place.

Are Tannen's ideas about language therefore appropriate to American politics? Although a sociolinguist, Tannen, a professor at Georgetown University, is not averse to an occasional foray into the public limelight. She got her big break in 1992, when fifty power-wielders—including Senators Gore, Mikulski, Bradley, Robb, Pell, Lieberman, Fowler, Biden, Simpson, Kassebaum, and Spector as well as numerous wives and daughters—listened to her discussion of male/female miscommunication as penance for their roles in the Hill-Thomas hearings. Shortly thereafter, Bill Clinton was elected president, and Tannen the pundit for the powerful came into her own.

Speaking at the December 31, 1993, Renaissance Weekend in Hilton Head, S.C., Tannen told her guests that "a culture of critique" has overtaken America; like a bad marriage, we scream at each other instead of cooperating to find the truth.[22] Three months later, she was more specific in an essay in the *Los Angeles Times*. The Clintons are just trying to do their jobs, she wrote, especially the job of providing health care for everyone. But the media won't leave them alone, hounding them with Whitewater, a trivial event that "was dragged to light by reporters digging in Little Rock garbage, searching for something—anything—to provide the exposure of errors that our public discourse now requires." Her main message was that she was opposed to opposition. After the by-now familiar disclaimers that journalists should ask tough questions and that intellectuals should point out the weaknesses of each other's arguments, she said this:

> But when opposition becomes the overwhelming avenue of inquiry, when the lust for opposition exalts extreme views and obscures complexity, when our eagerness to find weaknesses blinds us to its strengths, when the atmosphere of animosity precludes respect and poisons our relations with one another, then the culture of critique is stifling us. If we could move beyond it, we would move closer to the truth.[23]

As these remarks indicate, there clearly are important political implications in Tannen's writings. The question she poses is whether cooperation and consensus, presumably virtuous in private relationships, ought to have moral priority in public ones as well. Through an analysis of language, Tannen ends up a strong communitarian—our respect for each other, she concludes, should outweigh our individual need to find fault.

Yet Deborah Tannen's efforts to wrestle with the moral value of agreement and disagreement illustrate why we ought not jump to the conclusion that empathy and understanding are always morally preferable to criticism. There certainly is cause to worry that disagreement may be getting out of hand in America; the rants of talk-radio hosts can be frightening in their violent simplicity. Political differences have already taken too many lives and destroyed the dignity of too many individuals. One of America's great accomplishments was its victory in our first significant culture war: the agreement by Protestants to accept the legitimacy of Catholics and Jews in America,[24] and it would be a shame beyond measure if similar agreement were not to be found among new ethnicities and religions in American life. Agreement ought to be the objective of any stable political system.

But everything depends on how the goal is reached. Too hasty a conclusion, and disagreement is prematurely foreclosed. The Supreme Court made a serious mistake when it tried to stop disagreement around abortion by declaring it a fundamental right in *Roe v. Wade*. Congress did its job, and did its job properly, when it subjected the Clinton health plan to critical scrutiny. We have not yet achieved anything close to consensus on welfare reform, and until we do, critics ought to take out their knives and dissect the ideas of their rivals. And, despite anything Tannen said in Los Angeles, an opposition party in a democracy has the duty to investigate seeming improprieties in the conduct of its opponents. On any of these issues, advocates of agreement have no special claim to virtue. If agreement is essential to a stable political system, disagreement is essential to a liberal democratic one.

Is Tannen right that sometimes criticism can get out of hand? Of course she is. But this in no way means that we need to search for a political philosophy that will make consensus, rather than conflict, its basic goal. Too great an emphasis on unity, as I argue in the following chapter with respect to the ideas of Norman O. Brown, runs the risk of trampling on liberty. Deborah Tannen is no Norman O. Brown, but her criticism of criticism does contain antidemocratic and antiliberal features. We are much more likely to preserve liberal democratic values by trying to reach consensus through conflict and criticism than by upholding consensual values and allowing criticism within them.

Fortunately for the social critic, there are two aspects of the liberal commitment to criticism which set limits on the dangers of conflict spinning out of control. First, there is nothing to prevent liberals from agreeing, through democratic procedures, to place criticism out of bounds on certain issues. As Stephen Holmes has argued, liberalism is compatible with "gag rules"—agreements made *not* to criticize some things in the interest of making discord over other things possible.[25] If we understand liberalism as a positive philosophy of community building, and not just an ethic of opposition, then liberalism implies not only rules that prevent a majority's desire for consensus to override a minority's right to criticize but also rules that determine the conditions under which criticism can take place. Liberalism is not an agreement that criticism will *always* trump consensus; the American Civil War settled that.

A second aspect of liberalism that works to keep criticism within bounds is its commitment to self-criticism. As the political theorist Mark Hulliung has emphasized, the Enlightenment's ability to turn its gaze on itself is one of its most valuable legacies.[26] Effective social criticism is rooted in the willingness to confront one's own political position with as much gusto as one gives to an attack on the positions of one's opponents. Self-criticism is a rare quality. Communitarians who elevate consensus over criticism do not have it; I found myself constantly wondering whether, if I followed Tannen's advice and held in check my criticism of others, I would still be able to examine critically my own motives and ideas. But liberals who attack communitarian ideas as always and inevitably dangerous do not have it either, for they never examine the first propositions of their attack.[27] If critics never turn their gaze on themselves—which ideologues and polemicists rarely do—they are not acting as critics.

There are no simple answers to any of the questions raised by Deborah Tannen's analysis of the way we speak with each other. No one can doubt, after reading her books, that Tannen is a well-meaning, empathic, and sincere person who is genuinely concerned with our ability to hurt one another. Her injunction that we try as hard as we can to avoid being cruel is itself one of the key principles of liberal morality.[28] But there are many ways of being cruel, and one of them is by refusing to take the ideas of another person seriously enough to subject them to criticism. Criticism may be unpleasant, and it can certainly be overdone, but without it there cannot be a society premised on the notion that everyone counts.

SOCIAL CRITICISM AND POLITICAL POWER

The Arrogance of Powerlessness

Social critics should be willing to apply the same scrutiny to their own ideas as they do to those of others. Alas, they generally do not. And one of the reasons they do not is an unfortunate legacy of social criticism's golden age: the conviction that while critics may not have power on their side, at least they have truth.

Inherent in the moral stance of the "heroic" social critic was a firm belief in Noam Chomsky's oft-cited dictum: "it is the responsibility of intellectuals to speak the truth and expose lies."[1] But, Chomsky continued, while this dictum "may seem enough of a truism to pass without comment," actually this was "not so" (325). The reason had everything to do with power—or, more precisely, with two kinds of power. Intellectuals were "a doubly privileged elite" (28); first, because America exercised power over the rest of the world and, second, because intellectuals in America had become powerful in their own right. Chomsky's conclusion was harsh:

> At least this much is plain: there are dangerous tendencies in the ideology of the welfare state intelligentsia who claim to possess the technique and understanding required to manage our "post-industrial society" and to organize an international society dominated by American superpower. (125)

Intellectuals had once been independent, free-floating, critical of existing regimes. Now there were little more than "scholar-experts" (348), their scholarship and expertise both compromised by their devotion to the state.

For social critics of the 1960s, the war in Vietnam constituted apt proof of Chomsky's perspective. Henry Kissinger was a particularly compelling example of an intellectual so committed to power that he lost his ability to do not only what was right but also what was smart. Because the powerful lied—so relentlessly and so consistently—the moral stance of the war's critics remained relatively untainted. The war in Vietnam was one case where the equation of power with mendacity made sense. To be sure, critics of the war might have scrutinized their own motives and tactics more than they did, but the compelling rightness of their cause gave them the moral high ground even to this day.

If power, in Chomsky's view, was bad, serving the cause of truth was good. At one level, this is obvious: intellectuals indeed have an obligation to prefer truth to lies. But there is a flip side to Chomsky's certainty, one that complicates the moral position of the social critic. Devoted to the truth as he sees it, why should the heroic critic ever examine his own ideas with the same passion that he expends in the exploration of the ideas of his opponents? The convinced critic, after all, only weakens his cause and gives comfort to his enemies by questioning his first premises. Heroic social criticism is rarely, if ever, introspective. The task of the critic is to expose "their" lies, not "ours." We don't lie; therefore we need never ask ourselves whether we are lying. The righteously indignant critic questions everyone's motives but his own. Classic social critics so often rejected liberalism because the liberal's commitment to autocritique seemed an unnecessary luxury that the war of ideas rendered unaffordable.

So long as good and bad are as clearly delineated as they were during Vietnam, the failure of critics to engage in self-criticism rarely becomes a problem. But what happens if the opposition between truth and power does not hold? There are, after all, reasons to question the assumption that truth is *always* on the side of the powerless and untruth on the side of power. For one thing, writing itself is a form of power; intellectuals, including even Chomsky, do not take up social criticism because they reject power but because they desire the power to change the world according to their liking. For another, exercising power can be a sobering lesson in understanding how the world works. Kissinger is not the only example of an intellectual in power; Vaclav Havel seems to have been able to serve truth and power without the one necessarily undermining the other.

If truth and power are not in conflict, the critic's refusal to scrutinize his own positions becomes a serious flaw. What was once a heroic virtue becomes a debilitating vice. Now the critic seems, not principled and morally pure, but rigid, hypocritical, sanctimonious, and, worst of all, illiberal. Social criticism unwilling to criticize itself is on the way toward intellectual oblivion. It not longer serves justice; it only serves itself. Unable to recognize the arrogance of its presumptions, it denies the very truthfulness around which its moral claims are built, for it lives the lie of incorruptibility, even while being corrupted by its hubris.

In reexamining the legacy of golden age social critics, it is important to ask whether their conviction that power and truth were in opposition led them astray; if truth and power do not always work at cross-purposes, then the critic's claim to be exempt from the necessity for self-scrutiny collapses. To shed light on this issue, I will compare the way two radically different writers approached the question of power and truth. One is Raymond Aron, whose commitment to *realpolitik* was as strong as Kissinger's, but who also was a significant sociological theorist. The other is Norman O. Brown, a social critic who was even more extreme in his rejection of power than C. Wright Mills or Herbert Marcuse.

Both writers, enormously popular in their time, went through an eclipse, only to be rediscovered in very recent years. Both were also flawed; certainly neither can be considered introspective, self-critical, or modest. But their contrasting approaches to the question of power produced surprising results: Aron, who tended to defend power, gave critics of the status quo a weapon to use against it, while Brown, who distrusted power, wound up defending an organic conception of authority which allowed little room for individual liberty, including the liberty to challenge power. Criticism came from Aron, the one generally believed complacent, while Brown's self-styled critical ideas led only to complacency. The contrast between their ideas undermines the case for an exemption from self-criticism. If we cannot equate powerlessness with virtue and power with corruption, then the critic is indeed obligated to consider his own position to be as open to criticism as those of his opponents.

Aron and The Irony of Realpolitik

Alone among the intellectuals of his generation, Raymond Aron found his milieu among power holders and policy elites. He was as sympathetic toward the United States (whose leaders, Mills claimed, were "crackpot realists")[2]—and as hostile toward the Soviet Union—as most intellectuals were the other way around. His books, including his most academic ones, were not so much the products of long hours in the library as they were personal essays dealing, even when the subjects seemed remote, with current affairs. The publication of his memoirs therefore raises the question of *realpolitik:* do intellectuals concerned with human affairs come to understand the world better if they put themselves in the position of those making political decisions or if they stand outside in judgment of them?[3]

Aron competed with such luminaries as Jean-Paul Sartre and Paul Nizan to be the most brilliant young Frenchman of his generation. But after military service from 1928 to 1930, he did not go to the French provinces. He went to Germany instead, working as a teaching assistant in French at the University of Cologne. This was the decision that changed his life; Germany, as Rolf Dahrendorf once said, was Aron's fate.[4] "Despite everything," he realized, "my reading of the great works on idealism and realism interested only my mind, not my heart" (39). What he found in Germany was politics; indeed for him the discovery of Germany and the discovery of politics were the same thing. Instead of the universalistic morality of Durkheim, it would be the *realpolitik* of Max Weber that would structure his thought. "Thanks to him," Aron writes of Weber, "my future course, glimpsed on the banks of the Rhine, took shape" (46).

Returning to France in 1933, Aron produced three important books in rapid succession: *German Sociology, The Critical Philosophy of History,* and *Introduction to the Philosophy of History.*[5] Through his confrontation with German thought, Aron was able to introduce a far more tragic view of historical fate than those to which French thinkers were accustomed. "History," Aron wrote, "consumes individuals at a frightful rate, a consumption we see no way of avoiding so long as violence is necessary for social changes."[6] But if history is tragic, it does not follow that its course is always predetermined. One of the major purposes of Aron's *Introduction to the Philosophy of History* was to argue that things—especially "big" events like the Battle of Marathon—may have been otherwise. It is as if we can choose between our tragedies; the best is never possible, but we can, under the right conditions, avoid the worst.

Aron found attractive in Weber's thought a way of understanding the conditions that make possible one fate rather than another—Weber's emphasis on action. Individuals are not cogs in a structure, as they are in Marx (and even more in Durkheim); from Weber's perspective, choices are available, but not to everyone. By trying, in Aron's words, "to present the world as it was" (40), the sociologist comes to appreciate the narrow, but nonetheless real, degrees of freedom available to elites at any historical moment. Weber's greatness, Aron wrote, lay in his being "a politician and a thinker at the same time."[7] It did not take much foresight to realize that Aron was establishing for himself the same objective, although he, like Weber, would never directly serve a prince.

Aron's entire career was dedicated to the proposition that to understand the social world, the social theorist must place upon himself the limits that those who would influence history place upon themselves. "I considered myself responsible at almost every moment, and I was always inclined to ask what I could do in the place of those in power" (30), Aron reflected. It was not long before the first test of his perspective would present itself. He left France for England in June 1940, becoming involved in *La France libre*, a resistance paper initiated by Charles de Gaulle. Each month, in the "Chronique de France," Aron the political analyst appeared. (He was called René Avord.) His articles were consistently characterized by razor-sharp reasoning, cold calculation of alternatives, and a strict avoidance of sentimentalism. At a time when the distinction between reporting and propaganda had disappeared, Aron's columns came to be widely appreciated for their balance and rootedness in the real world.

At the same time, the negative side to *realpolitik* began to make its first appearance in his thought. "We were not subject to censorship," he wrote, "although we practiced a kind of self-censorship." (122). Unfortunately what *La France Libre* left out was that World War II was not just another war. Caught up in the dilemmas of Vichy, Aron barely took cognizance of the anti-Semitism of the regime and paid little attention to the fate of the European Jews. Aron absolves himself of blame: "I cannot criticize myself for not having foreseen the execution of a plan of genocide, and for having written nothing about it in *La France Libre*" (123). Such self-justification is remarkably lame: the whole point of realism is to foresee what others cannot, a strategy that often works, but fails to do so when political leaders are themselves not guided by realism but by a fanatical effort to exterminate their enemies—even at the cost of destroying themselves. *Realpolitik*, in other words, must itself be guided by *realpolitik;* the theorist has to make a realistic decision when its principles apply. Indiscriminate *realpolitik* turns into its opposite.

Yet if Aron's perspective failed the test of fascism, it would pass, at least in the period from 1946 to around 1960, the test of communism. For one extended moment, *realpolitik* and reality would coincide in a way they did not during World War II (and would not again in the 1970s and 1980s). There were real issues at stake in the postwar division of Europe; as the collapse of communism demonstrates to all but the most cynical, freedom matters. It is impossible to imagine what the cold war was about without the shape given to it by thinkers of Aron's stature.

Happy in England, where he came into contact with the economists Lionel Robbins and Friedrich Hayek, Aron never considered remaining there after World War II. "The decisive reason for my choice almost went without saying: I would never change my country. I would be French or I would have no country" (133). Returning home, he rejected not only England but a traditional academic career as well. "Infected by the virus of politics" (139), he had discovered that it was reality, not approaches to reality, which stirred his soul. After a stint with Camus' *Combat,* he joined, in 1947, the staff of *Le Figaro,* surprising to those who would have assumed that a man of his background would have joined the more left-leaning *Le Monde.*

What, then, were Aron's politics? It is a sign of the complexity of his thought that the question is still difficult to answer. He was, in a sense, born on the left: "A Jewish intellectual of good will who chooses the career of letters, estranged from his fellows who remain in textiles or banking, can hardly do anything but will himself, feel himself, to be on the left" (34). Yet for Aron's generation, the issue that defined one's politics was one's attitude toward communism. From the start to the finish of his career as journalist and scholar, Aron never wavered from strongly anticommunist views. Numerous French intellectuals after World War II either apologized for Stalinism (as Merleau-Ponty did in *Humanism and Terror*) or—in the case of those associated with the *Rassemblement Democratique et Revolutionnaire*—opted for a "third camp" position between capitalism and socialism.[8] In this atmosphere, Aron's consistent anticommunism stood out as an act of courage, although then, as later, there would be more than a few Russian and Eastern European intellectuals living in Paris and warning of the possible fate of their countries. It is therefore easy to read into the polemics between Aron and Sartre as the East-West conflict writ large. In actual fact Aron's anticommunism raised two other issues that would, in the long run, prove more decisive. Anticommunism on the scale he envisioned meant a strong Germany and close Franco-American relations. Both positions were as uncomfortable for French intellectuals as a critical attitude toward Moscow.

Aron recognized quite early that a strong Germany was the key to European stability. In *The Century of Total War* he wrote: "Western Europe knows from of old, or should know, that it is disastrous to have as enemies both Germany *and* Russia." With the latter already defined as an enemy of the West, relentless logic demanded that the former be made a friend. The partition of Germany, Aron argued, was already a victory for the Russians: "The elimination of Germany immediately opens the West to the Russian menace." The French, in short, would simply have to swallow their distaste for their neighbors to the East and work to strengthen them:

> A reconstituted Germany would tend, in accordance with old traditions, to oscillate between East and West, and to extract as

much as possible from one side or the other in return for always uncertain co-operation. A precarious situation, it may be said. True, but how much better than that of today! The prospects of peace will be improved with the increase in the number of centers of force.[9]

Anticommunism and *realpolitik*, which need not work together, in this case did, but most French thinkers could not then and—now that a unified Germany has become a reality—do not accept today what Aron saw so clearly, that national pride has little to do with how balances of power work.

Even more difficult for French opinion to swallow was the need for Franco-American cooperation. Although the Vietnam years would seem to indicate otherwise, it is not the French left that is anti-American and the French right that looks toward Washington. The French left, especially in its contemporary postmodernist phase, is fascinated to the point of obsession with the United States. But the French right has never accepted Tocqueville's efforts to convince his fellow nobles that they had better make an accommodation with the new Atlantic power. Aron's insistence on reminding his countrymen of who won the war did not go down easily, for the more French ruling circles came to be indebted to American military intervention, the more they resented their increasing dependence. It was, in many ways, far more difficult to be pro-American in Paris than to be anti-Soviet; even Aron, in making the case that America had every right to be the dominant power in the West, felt the need to apologize for some of the peculiarities of American politics, such as the tendency of its political leaders to moralize when they ought to analyze.

Aron's *realpolitik* was as uncomfortable to French sensibility as Henry Kissinger's would later be to the American. But whereas Americans react negatively to *realpolitik* in favor of a Wilsonian idealism, the French reject cold calculation of interest when it seems to interfere with *la gloire*. *La Tragédie algérienne*, which came out in 1957, shocked polite French opinion.[10] People assumed that Aron, in criticizing French Algeria, was changing sides. As he rightly points out, they misunderstood his views. Sentiment played no role in his analysis. Geography and demography destined Algeria to be Algerian, and Aron could not help but direct contemptuous phrases at those whose passion for the idea of a greater France led them to think otherwise.

By the end of the 1950s, Raymond Aron had become a one-man truth squad in bringing European, and especially French, thought in line with the realities of world politics. There may have been no better journalist writing anywhere in the world at the time, certainly none with the

breadth of Aron's interests and the clarity of his purpose. Already a prolific author and increasingly influential figure, he had only one question
facing him as he contemplated a job so far well done: what would he do
next? Two things happened to Raymond Aron in the second half of the
1950s that would change, and ultimately weaken, his life's work. One was
that he returned to the university. The other was that America discovered
him.

Aron decided in 1955 to compete for an academic position at the Sorbonne. Not having served his time in the provinces, he stirred enough resentment to transform his appointment into a public controversy.
Georges Balandier was not the strongest competitor, however, and Aron
was able to win the job, entering the academic world in plenty of time to
witness the revolutionary changes that culminated in the events of 1968.
Although he continued his journalism, Aron obviously wanted more than
immediate influence. His appointments, first at the Sorbonne and later at
the Collège de France, gave him the opportunity to become a thinker of
world-class stature.

There is fascinating academic gossip in Aron's memoirs for those who
love that kind of thing: indeed the career of Pierre Bourdieu, who would
elevate academic gossip into a career, can be traced throughout Aron's
recollections. Pierre Hassner, who today occupies the role that Aron held
for so long, is described as the most brilliant mind Aron ever encountered. A too self-serving, but wonderfully entertaining, portrait of Talcott
Parsons giving a lecture in incomprehensible German is painted in acid.
Jon Elster, a Norwegian social scientist of enormous current influence, is
also an important character in Aron's milieu. If along the way we are told
too many times how wonderful such American sociologists as Robert
Merton and Edward Shils found Aron's ideas, it is a small price to pay for
the close-up look at inscrutable French academic institutions presented
in this book.

Yet as an academic Aron never achieved the stature he wanted. To be
sure, he wrote some very important books and is associated with some
very important ideas. His two-volume *Main Currents in Sociological
Thought* presented as clear an introduction to the ideas of Montesquieu,
Comte, Tocqueville, and Pareto as one could hope to find.[11] The publication of his academic lectures, furthermore, introduced into public discussion the notion that it was not the difference between capitalism and
socialism that shaped the world but the rise of industrial society in any
form.[12] Aron contributed as well to the discussions over totalitarianism
and democracy that shaped the postwar years. Finally, his massive *Peace
and War* and his reflections on Clausewitz would bring to sociology a concern with international relations and war-making that had been missing

in a discipline given to idealistic longings for harmony and cooperation.[13]

This was an impressive enough academic legacy by almost anyone's
standards, but Aron's standards were not those of anyone. Looking back,
as Aron's memoirs force us to do, one sees books written too fast, with too
little reflection, and with little or no original research. A tendency toward
pontification and elaboration of the obvious in numbing detail had already existed in Aron's work even before he turned to the academic world;
The Opium of the Intellectuals, for example, simply does not have the literary power of a book like Milosz's *The Captive Mind.*[14] Aron was caught
between two audiences, unable to satisfy either. As a popularizer, he
was no James Burnham. But as a systematizer, neither was he a Rolf
Dahrendorf. Recognizing his problem, Aron would sometimes attempt
to be more "philosophical" (that is, jargon-ridden and incomprehensible)
than Sartre, as he was in *History and the Dialectic of Violence.*[15] At other
times, he would introduce his books by saying, with unflattering frequency, that he was only bringing his thoughts to the public because of
the insistence of this or that publisher or friend. Of Aron it could be said
that few people have written more books whose main theme is impossible to summarize. He could, at his worst, rank with Toynbee or Spengler.

It was, furthermore, during this period that Aron's influence spread to
the United States. He became Washington's favorite European, irrespective of whether Democrats or Republicans were in power. Appearing at
Cambridge in 1960, he became an active member of the Harvard-MIT
seminar out of which Kennedy's foreign policy was created. Kissinger,
who would review Aron's *Peace and War* in the *New York Times,* became a
close friend, writing, as it turned out, the preface to Aron's memoirs.
Robert McNamara invited him to the Pentagon, carefully placing on his
own desk a copy of Aron's *The Great Debate.* Washington needed Aron to
add a dollop of *savoir faire* to its seemingly sophisticated, but in fact naive, approach to world affairs. Aron needed Washington because rootless
Jewish intellectuals—he describes himself as "de-Judaized, an unbe-
liever, nonpracticing, of French culture, with no Jewish culture" (336)—
are likely to be taken with more respect there than in Paris. Aron and
America were a marriage made in heaven.

Aron's flirtation with this country, however, did not have happy consequences for the quality of his thought. *Realpolitik* requires the theorist to
put himself in the position of abstract, not specific, policy-makers. The
point of realism is to look at the world clearly with a view toward adopting policies untainted by sentiment, emotion, and personal loyalty. Yet as
a theorist develops contacts, influential friendships, and intimate connections, he will inevitably be tempted to identify so closely with people

he knows that the advantages of clarity and honesty will be lost. "Was I more indulgent toward American diplomacy in 1969–75 because of my personal relations with one of its creators?" (388), he wonders of his close friendship with Henry Kissinger. Of course he was or he would not have asked. If intellectual quality is the measure, it should be Kissinger bragging that he knew Aron and not the other way around. Yet it is Aron who seems anxious for readers to know how close he was to the American secretary of state.

Aron's susceptibility to flattery led him to fail the test of Vietnam. While the American role in Vietnam could not be compared exactly to the French role in Algeria, in both cases the proper *realpolitik* strategy was one of cutting losses. Willing to confront the prejudices of his own country, Aron was unable to confront those of his new audience in Washington. Could Aron really care so little that the Kennedy people *always* put on their desks the books of the people to whom they were talking? (Norman Mailer was once bowled over when a primed John F. Kennedy, having learned from Pierre Salinger which of Mailer's books the author himself preferred, remarked that he liked *The Deer Park* best of all.) Aron had remarkably little to say about Vietnam and seemed, for so loquacious a writer, to want to leave the subject for other things. The Raymond Aron that Americans came to know in the 1960s and 1970s was but a shadow of the Parisian Aron of the 1940s and 1950s.

One can never know whether it was flattery or simply intellectual exhaustion that caused Aron's more ambitious writings of the 1970s to suffer as well as his commentary. *In Defense of Decadent Europe* is little more than a string of clichés, most of them ideologically rigid and correspondingly embarrassing to read. At a time when the Western European Communist parties were descending into decrepitude, Aron described them as part of a doctrinally rigid international movement prepared to take state power. "In the Soviet Union today," Aron wrote, "more coal and all other forms of energy resources are being produced than in the United States," as if Soviet communism was still on its way to burying American capitalism. Toward the end of the book, aware that perhaps his cold war ideology had become too rigid, Aron asks "Does it follow that the 'hour of liberalization' has struck in the Soviet Union?" and then answers with a most unambiguous no.[16] Granted almost no one could have foreseen the revolutions of 1989, but Aron in his last books saw them even less than most. His *realpolitik*, through which he had once defined freedom, had become a prison of his own making, no longer appropriate to a world in rapid change.

If Aron's thought was in the process of sliding into pathos, he rescued himself with one grand final effort: his memoirs. Though often pompous and self-justificatory, Aron's recollections take the reader through fascinating worlds in a fascinating way. For better or worse, they don't make intellectuals like this any more. Neither in France, nor, for that matter, in the United States, are we likely ever again to see such a cohort of brilliant minds, all of whom live in one city, have known each other since childhood, are in the process of creating, rather than reiterating, ideological positions, and are so equally at home in both academic and journalistic endeavors. By bringing that world to life, Aron more than vindicated himself. He left a document which reminds us that the life of the mind and the life of power need not be alienated from each other.

Raymond Aron was the author of some thirty-five volumes covering both journalistic and academic topics. The themes elaborated in nearly all those books would seem to be confirmed by world events. France lost Algeria. Germany will become the dominant power in Europe. Weber proved to be more prophetic in his analysis of industrial society than Marx. The West won, but it exhausted itself in the process. About the only one of Aron's themes that has not been proven by recent events is the biggest one of all: communism proved not to be a totalitarian menace to world peace after all. Yet it is not by a scorecard of correct predictions that we judge the importance of social theorists. It is by the standard of whether the words they wrote helped define the meaning of the world around us. Aron's—not all the time, but enough for any single person—did. The same cannot be said for most of the others of his country and generation.

Norman O. Brown: Authoritarian Anarchist

Norman O. Brown's writings could not be more different than Raymond Aron's. For the 1960s radical in incipient rebellion against all established power, Brown, along with Herbert Marcuse, offered an irresistible combination of familiar and exotic. Marcuse and Brown seemed to operate by a division of intellectual labor which corresponded to the split in the New Left generation to whom they spoke. Just as antiwar demonstrations had their political activists intent on organizing a mass movement against capitalism *and* drug-taking hippies interested more in Nirvana, so Marcuse was understood to be talking the language of politics and Brown the language of myth. Marcuse, after all, was a product of the legendary Frankfurt school, worked in the Office of Strategic Services during the war, taught the future communist organizer Angela Davis, and self-consciously identified with some of the political "heavies" among the younger generation. Brown, by contrast, was the poet and the mystic. "For the reality of politics, we must turn to the poets, not to the politicians," he wrote in *Love's Body*.[17] Brown was more likely to write about Blake and Yeats than Hegel and Marx. His favorite philosopher was the mysterious Spinoza. Islam and Buddhism occupied as much space in his books as Protestantism and Judaism. Reading Brown was like taking drugs, only more likely to lead to tenure.

The republication of *Love's Body*, plus the appearance of a collection of previously unpublished essays and current speculations,[18] makes possible a reevaluation of his influence on a generation's consciousness. Now that the dust of the 1960s has settled, it is Brown who has left a stronger impression than Marcuse. Yet if Brown has outlasted Marcuse, it is *not* because he was more mystical and less political. Indeed, any notions of a division of intellectual labor between these men is incorrect, for Brown is as "political" thinker as Marcuse. Moreover, Brown's politics, understood *as* politics and not as poetry, raise disturbing questions about how much liberty would have to be sacrificed in order to bring some spiritual or organic wholeness to the human race. Brown anticipated many of the themes that would dominate the French intellectual scene after Aron: the hermeneutics of suspicion associated with Derrida and Foucault. Because he did, it is fair to say that rarely has a thinker been so right in foreseeing trends that are so wrong.

Brown himself was clear about the political origins of his theoretical speculations. "My first historical identity, my Marxist ideology, was wrecked in the frozen landscape of the Cold War, the defeat of the simplistic hopes for a better world that inspired the Henry Wallace campaign for the Presidency in 1948," he told a California conference on the humanities in 1989 (*Apocalypse and/or Metamorphosis*, p. 158). But unlike many of his generation who turned from Marxism to liberalism, Brown turned to psychoanalysis. His concern would be the body, not the body politic. But bodies are what bodies politic rule. Brown, knowing this, invariably shifts his attention from one to the other. His goal is "the resurrection of the body; but not the separate body of the individual, but the body of mankind as one body" (*Love's Body*, p. 83). Psychoanalysis, in his hands, is a cure not for lost souls but for misdirected societies. "I wagered my intellectual life on the idea of finding in Freud what was missing in Marx," Brown wrote in 1990 (*Apocalypse and/or Metamorphosis*, p. 179). But this is not correct. It was what was *un*found in Freud that inspired him. Freud, for most of his life, was a doctor concerned with individual patients. Brown's concern is with *die Massen,* the collective person that absorbs, and renders irrelevant, individual persons and their dreams, desires, and fantasies.

Reflecting his primacy as a political theorist, Brown begins *Love's Body* with a discussion of Locke. (The book's first chapter is called "Liberty.") For Brown, as for Locke, the signifying fact of modern political life is the overthrow of feudalism with its rigid system of orders and obligations. But whereas Locke and other liberal thinkers such as Jefferson and Madison find in different estates and factions a protection against arbitrary authority, Brown believes that the struggle against authority is illusory. Just as the infant seeks to crawl back into the mother's womb and the young man engages in a futile rebellion against the father, modern people delude themselves if they believe they can lead disembodied lives.

Leaving the state of nature, Brown is saying, was our primal mistake. Liberal political theorists were not unaware of the terrors involved in so radical an act, for, with the exception of Hobbes, they tended to portray the state of nature as a rather pleasant place. And the resulting artificiality of society was not always an improvement, as Rousseau would consistently maintain. Nonetheless artifice is creative—it shares much linguistically with art—and what it creates is culture. Liberalism is, in that sense, a theory of the necessity of artificial culture, a way of understanding that if we are to live with the terrors of separation, we need to find a way to make modern life bearable.

Liberal social theorists, strongly influenced by the rise of sociology, found two answers to the riddle of modern alienation, both of which are rejected by Brown. The first was the group. If we understand individuals as bound to families, communities, ethnic enclaves, and associations, we can accept separation unblinkingly, recognizing that however much we have in common as humans, we also differ in the particularities that define group identity. (The term generally given by liberals to this strategy is pluralism.) Such a task leads inevitably into discussions of boundaries, classifications, and exclusions. (No one can be a member of a particular group unless others cannot be.) Indeed any theory of group membership is a theory of exclusion. Its concern with community, ethnicity, particularity, norms, and customs is all a way of talking about the necessity to put boundaries in place to keep some in and others out.

For Brown, however, boundaries are the very essence of what is wrong with modernity. This begins with the boundary between the self and the external world, a distinction made only "in the lunatic state called normalcy or common sense" (*Love's Body,* p. 142). That boundary, like all boundaries, is "an artificial construction . . . not natural, but conventional . . . based on love and hate" (42). Reality is not a spatial concept, to be found in places. It is rather energy or instinct. To separate, therefore, is to destroy. "A social order based on the reality principle, a social order which draws a distinction between the wish and the deed, between the criminal and the righteous, is still a kingdom of darkness" (152). Psychoanalysis as social therapy can help modern liberals overcome the boundaries that separate them. "The conclusion of the whole matter is, break down the boundaries, the walls. Down with defense mechanisms, character-armor, disarmament" (149).

The second sociological discovery that offered a solution to the loneliness of liberal society was an emphasis on the common representations and customs that override boundaries. Durkheim in particular stressed the importance of collective representations in solidifying the moral solidarity of a society, although—a sure sign of sociology's ambivalence—he was also a pluralist fascinated with classification. Collective representations can take many forms, but from the time of Durkheim and the discovery of anthropology, the most important of these representations has been understood to be culture.

What makes Norman O. Brown different is not his distaste for boundaries; division is usually dismissed by those who prefer union. It is that he couples his organicism with an attack on the one form that organic unity generally takes in modern society: the cultural. The importance of culture was of course stressed by Freud, and even more by contemporary writers, such as Lionel Trilling and Philip Rieff, influenced by Freud. Culture—"our ingeniously developed limitations," as Rieff defines it— makes order possible by preventing us from satisfying our drives and by providing substitute gratification. In Rieff's words, "Every culture is so constituted that there are actions one cannot perform; more precisely, would dread to perform . . . . sociology has not paid enough attention to what is not done, to the closed possibilities, to the negatives, the suppressed."[19]

Norman O. Brown knows and respects Rieff. (He met him at Herbert Marcuse's marriage to Inge Heumann.) But Brown understands that, although boundaries divide and culture unites, both repress, and he will have none of repression. Culture, in Brown's view, can never provide the unity that was lost with the transition from feudalism to modern liberal democracy. In *Life Against Death*, first published in 1959, Brown wrote that "there is an essential connection between being sick and being civilized,"[20] a theme he would never abandon. "The entirety of culture is projection" (170), he argued in that book. "Man in culture, *Homo sublimans*, is man dreaming while awake" (168). Culture is the tactic by which an ever more serious Oedipal complex is projected into the external world, "one vast arena in which the logic of the transference works itself out" (155). Culture is thus an illusion created by people to avoid the terror (and joy) of contemplating death. When man left nature for culture he sacrificed organic unity for the illusion of mastery.

Those who reach for the gun upon hearing the world culture generally insist on the rights of the person against the collectivity. The hostility that Brown (and Marcuse) show toward culture leads Nancy Chodorow to find an element of radical individualism in the thought of both men.[21] But Brown is as hostile to individualism, the key tenet of liberal political theory, as he is to culture. "There is no integration of the separate individual," he wrote in *Love's Body* (86). Since individuals understood as abstract rights bearers can live only in culture, and since culture is artificial, then persons are artificial as well:

> a person is always a feigned or artificial person, *persona ficta*. A person is never himself but always a mask; a person never owns his own person, but always represents another, by whom he is possessed. And that other that one is, is always ancestors; one's soul is never one's own but daddy's. This is the meaning of the Oedipus Complex. (98)

Every aspect of liberal theory that follows from the notion of individualism—rights, constitutions, privacy, property—is suspect. "The Western legal fiction, with its fetishism (personification) of the property, its reification of persons, eliminates the facts more completely, by eliminating the moment of truth, the interregnum, the search for the new incarnations" (102).

Nonetheless, Chodorow is right to emphasize Brown's individualism, so long as we understand that it is not real, flesh-and-blood people whose rights he is defending but the individual as larger-than-life hero. Brown's attack on culture is a by-product of the Eisenhower years, a time when it was *de* rigueur to believe that mass society, if not fascism, had arrived in the form of suburban tract-housing. (Betty Friedan's *The Feminine Mystique* contained a chapter on the home called "Progressive Dehumanization: The Comfortable Concentration Camp").[22] The radicalism born in the 1950s thought of itself as leftist, but its cultural criticism owed much to Gustav LeBon, Ortega y Gasset, Wilhelm Reich, and other antidemocratic theorists. Those who nodded knowingly at Malvina Reynolds's astonishingly arrogant dismissal of "little houses . . . made of ticky-tacky" were individualists who detested the lives of real individuals. Like existentialism, another all-but-forgotten philosophy of the beatnik era, the Brown and Marcuse treatment of culture enabled the social critic to reject liberal individualism and group obligations simultaneously, when most political theories argued the necessity for one at the expense of the other. Just as Marxism avoided the nitty-gritty details of how real societies worked in favor of a utopian vision of society without the division of labor, so Brown could ignore how real individuals thought and behaved in favor of a utopian individualism that only Nietzschean supermen could achieve.

One sees the same contempt for real people that characterizes Brown's cultural radicalism in his discussion of economics. All economic theory, Brown argues, even that of Marx's *Capital,* is premised on an elevation of the reality principle over the pleasure principle. "The prudential calculating character"—this is from *Life Against Death*—"(the ideal type of *Homo economicus*) is an anal character" (225). Like Georges Bataille, Brown understands economics through excrement. "What the elegant laws and supply and demand really describe is the antics of an animal which has confused excrement with aliment and does not know it, and which, like infantile sexuality, pursues no 'real aim'" (*Life Against Death,* p. 258). Capitalism "has made us so stupid and one-sided that objects exist for us only if we can possess them or if they have utility" (238). Individuals living under such conditions are thus unable "to distinguish real human needs from (neurotic) consumer demands" (253). (Again, Brown's thoughts range from the sacred realm to the profane considerations of 1950s social critics like Vance Packard.) Economics cannot be a real science, and market economics cannot be made whole, until those who study the former and those who live in the latter get in touch with death.

Since the classic work that links individualism, liberalism, and capitalism is Max Weber's *The Protestant Ethic and the Spirit of Capitalism,* much of Brown's work can be read as a commentary on Weber's hypotheses. The Protestant ethic, according to Brown, began on a toilet—Luther's, to be precise. There is "some mysterious intrinsic connection between the Protestant illumination and the privy" (*Life Against Death,* p. 206). For Brown, the link between them is the devil. Both Protestantism and capitalism are engaged in an anal effort to deny the diabolic. The concept of *beruf,* the inner-worldly asceticism which according to Weber makes it possible for the Puritan to be driven to accumulate, is best understood, Brown argues, as a coming to terms with the trickster Satan. "The inner voice, the personal salvation, the private experience are all based on an illusory distinction," he wrote in *Love's Body.* (p. 87). Such Weberian terms as "personality" and "character" are irrelevant to an understanding of the dynamics of liberal capitalism. Neither are innate. "A man's character is his *demon*, his tutelar spirit; received as a dream" (92). Personality is likewise "acquired. Like a mask, it is a thing, a fetish, a fetishistic object or commodity" (92).

For Brown, liberalism and literalism are the same, and Protestantism gave rise to both. *Love's Body*, like current literary theory, believes that "the letter killeth, but the spirit giveth life" (191). Brown engages on an extended critique of intentionalism, the belief that the meaning of a text lies in what the text's author intended. Textual criticism, "part of the search for the one true and literal meaning," is, according to Brown, an effort "to establish the text, *die feste Schrift*, a mighty fortress; the authoritative text" (193). Liberal societies govern themselves by authoritative texts; of all political arrangements ever invented, only liberalism is a product of the book. But Brown distrusts both authors and authority. He envisions a politics governed not by words on a page but by spirits in the air. Once we learn to think in symbols as opposed to words, that "would be the end of the Protestant era, the end of Protestant liberalism" (191).

"Jeremiads are useless unless we can point to a better way," Brown concluded at the end of *Life Against Death* (p. 307). And the better way, lest there be any doubt, is political perfection, not individual salvation. "The resurrection of the body is a social project facing mankind as a whole, and it will become a practical political problem when the statesmen of the world are called upon to deliver happiness instead of power, when political economy becomes a science of use-values instead of exchange values—a science of enjoyment instead of a science of accumulation" (317–18). What would it mean for politicians, those schooled in the realities of power, to deliver happiness rather than power? In the real world around us, it would most likely mean the death of individual liberty. Weber warned that the ethic of ultimate ends in religion should never be mixed with the ethic of responsibility in politics, an injunction that Raymond Aron made the credo of his entire life. Brown's writings demonstrate what would happen if that credo were violated.

This can be seen when Brown treats the ideas of the great philosopher Spinoza. Here is the advice Brown discovers in his ideas: "It is the task of the intellect to remove the doubt, to straighten out the confusion, to remove the ambivalence, to make a more perfect union, to make it all cohere" (*Apocalypse and/or Metamorphosis*, pp. 132–33). If one takes this message as a metaphor, it expresses little but the intellectual's desire for some consistency in the world. But when the subject is politics, and when politics is governed by the intellect, such advice can be dangerous indeed. In fact, Spinoza has been a most unreliable political guide in the twentieth century. One of Brown's essays on Spinoza begins with the story of how this philosopher became a sudden celebrity among Louis Althusser and his followers, such as Etienne Balibar, who once found the unified body in Mao. Moreover the "quantitative leap" (*Apocalypse and/or Metamorphosis*, p. 117) in the rediscovery of this Spinoza came about when Antonio Negri, a philosopher sitting in prison because Italian authorities believed him responsible for the violence of the Red Brigades, published a book on the subject. Spinoza's longing for an otherworldly unity, when translated into a this-worldly solution for the thinness of modern liberalism, comes out sounding suspiciously totalitarian.

There is an uncomfortable question lurking behind Brown's thought: is there, after all, no alternative to liberalism? Liberalism, for all its political success in the world, has had few friends among intellectuals. And, truth be told, it has not tried all that hard to make them. Jeremy Bentham and John Stuart Mill all too often went out of their way to make their thought unattractive to all but the logical; from Dickens' Mr. Gradgrind to present-day communitarians, the heartlessness of liberalism has been too easy a target to ignore. Rereading Norman O. Brown, however, is enough to turn any communitarian into a liberal. For in Brown's work the emphasis on unity becomes so all-absorbing that all human institutions and practices disappear. Brown's community is neither the *fraternité* of revolutionary France, nor indeed the close-knit ethnic enclaves admired by Christopher Lasch (who wrote the preface to *Life Against Death*). Both examples are, to borrow another phrase from the era that gave us Norman O. Brown, part of the problem, not the solution. Division, for Brown, began when man was divided from his collective unconscious. Intentional communities—those efforts by individuals to define for themselves the identities that will move them—only take us away from "that immortal sea which brought us hither" (*Love's Body*, p. 88). The best for which we can hope are "imitations" of real organic unity, which "are given in moments of 'oceanic feeling'; one sea of energy or instinct; embracing all mankind, without distinction of race, language, or culture; and embracing all the generations of Adam, past, present, and future, in one phylogenetic heritage, in one mystical or symbolical body" (89).

Brown insists that all this talk of unity should not be understood purely metaphorically. Psychoanalysis, he writes, is "visionary sans-cullotism," a political strategy, a way to "put down the mighty from their seats, and exalt them of low degree" (*Love's Body*, p. 236). The political agenda with which *Love's Body* begins is there at that end: "Every throne a toilet seat, and every toilet seat a throne" (236). Brown will not leave the profane world alone. Indeed the profane world, down to and including the bathroom, is where he prefers to focus his glance. Unlike sociologists like Erving Goffman, who draw sharp boundaries between the "backstage" areas where people can be themselves and front stages on which they perform for others, Brown's vision would give people no retreat from the demand for unity; one of the advantages of holism, from Brown's point of view, is that it abolishes the distinction between private and public which has been so central to liberal political theory. "Psychoanalysis is that revolving state which completes this revolution, disclosing the bedroom and the bathroom behind the bourgeois facade, disclosing the obscenity of the on-stage scene, abolishing the reality-principle and its unreal distinction between public and private, between head and genital" (236). Therapy for individuals may or may not help them; opinion is still divided. Therapy as a form of politics, because antithetical to boundaries, is unquestionably unhealthy. Even Marcuse, who rarely met a Dionysian he didn't like, warned of the danger of unity worship. Marcuse's first-ever publication in *Commentary* was a review of Norman O. Brown's *Love's Body*, in which Marcuse correctly pointed out that for Brown "the great leap into the realm of freedom and light is thus arrested and becomes a leap backward, into darkness."[23]

It thus should not come as a surprise that Brown, like so many contemporary deconstructionists, should have a problem with authoritarianism. Brown never wrote anti-Semitic articles for fascist newspapers, but he does admit that the Dionysian brew he finds so intoxicating can be discerned not only in the romanticism of Blake but also "in the upheavals of modern history—in the sexology of de Sade and the politics of Hitler" (*Life against Death*, p. 176). The worship of irrationality that led Georges Sorel, Georges Bataille, and Wilhelm Reich into the far corners of right-wing politics is no reason, from Brown's perspective, to abandon the worship. Whereas modernist literary critics loved Ezra Pound's poetry in spite of his fascist politics, Brown pays serious attention to Pound's periodical *The Exile*, published in 1927–28. Brown recognizes the "elitist pretension, the fascist potential" in Pound's attack on mass culture, yet he writes, "Pound's impudent candor makes me think twice before dismissing the thought because it is fascist" (*Apocalypse and/or Metamorphosis*, p. 160). When brought down from its mystical heights to the real world of twentieth-century politics, love's body looks suspiciously like an authoritarian state.

"Freedom is violence," Brown writes, again anticipating Derrida (*Love's Body*, p. 244).[24] It is not. It is rather the condition of character that enables economically and morally secure individuals to avoid violence, both the violence of others in the market and the violence that, as Weber knew, was always embodied in the state. We left the state of nature to be free, and the best proof that we succeeded is the effort by so many writers, typified by Norman O. Brown, who would have us go back. For if we are to return to nature, it will be because we choose to do so, an act in which only free men and women can engage.

Self-Criticism and Responsibility

In his radical anarchism, mysticism, and psychoanalytic inclinations, Norman O. Brown was the very model of a 1950s social critic. Playful, speculative, utopian—Brown's outpouring is a vast thought experiment, an effort to imagine a world without repression. *Love's Body* ends with the words, "Everything is only a metaphor. There is only poetry" (266). If true, no one can fault Brown for his romantic anarchism. But Brown knows that poetry and power are linked. "In 1968," he writes, "a world turned upside down, it seemed that the poetic imagination might come to power" (*Apocalypse and/or Metamorphosis*, p. 159). The metaphors of the poet can become the fighting words of the politician. And what would a politician make of Brown's metaphorical assertion that "The self does not belong to its possessor" (*Love's Body* p. 91)? Those are the kinds of words that anyone interesting in exercising power over real-life selves would want to hear.

Norman O. Brown speaks the language of the prophet, assuming, perhaps, that so long as there is oppression and inequality, the prophetic voice is always the appropriate one. Sometimes, indeed, it is, especially when the powerful, by dint of their own arrogant imperviousness to criticism, give to their critics the advantage of moral purity, if nothing else. But power is as necessary to serve the cause of eliminating injustice as it is to perpetuating injustice. If sometimes power is evil, most of the time it is both good and bad simultaneously. The social critic has to know something not about power in general but about the specific power of the society being criticized. Prophetic stances do not tell the critic the most important thing he needs to know: whether the evils he denounces are so rotten that rejection is the only course or whether there are levers of power, even within a hierarchical and unjust society, that can be exploited to abolish them. If the latter exist, the choice of prophetic criticism can be worse than irrelevant; it can also, as Brown's flirtation with authoritarianism reveals, be dangerous.

Raymond Aron, on the other hand, is a writer for whom the term "social critic" barely applies; at his worst, his books lack any critical edge, so intent is the author to convey to the holders of power how much he understands their situation. But whatever failures Aron had as a critic of power, and they were many, came not from his commitment to realpolitik but from his failure to honor its code. During Vietnam, Raymond Aron found himself unwilling to use the moral capital he had acquired to help bring an end to the disaster. The increasing ideological rigidity of his later years led him to misunderstand a world in which communism was on its way to collapse. These were times when Aron applied the principles of realpolitik to everything but his own presuppositions. The realist cannot speak truth to power without speaking truth to himself. Self-criticism makes realpolitik possible; without it, realpolitik becomes ideology.

One finds in the thought of neither Raymond Aron nor Norman O. Brown the kind of introspective self-criticism that defines a liberal social critic. But a comparison of their ideas ought to give pause to those who believe that advocates for the powerless have such virtue on their own side that they are under no special obligation to examine their own presuppositions. Dissidents, if less persuaded of the absolute rightness of their cause, might learn that they are as capable of deceiving themselves as any government official. Power-holders, once they start congratulating themselves on their perspicacity, become little different from the ideologues that challenge their rule. Self-criticism may not be necessary in a world which radically separates truth and power from each other, but because that is not the world in which (most of the time) we live, a little self-criticism can go a long way toward making more responsible the criticism one levels at others.

THE FUTURE OF SOCIAL CRITICISM

The Three Cultures

So long as there will be society, there will be social criticism. The golden age of social criticism may be over, romantic urges may have triumphed over realistic inclinations, the torch of social criticism may have passed from left to right, but some will always object to the direction their society is taking and will want to use the tools of social science to describe what is wrong and advocate what could be better. Social criticism never goes away; it merely changes its form.

What form, then, is social criticism likely to take in the near future? No precise answer is possible, but one can talk about the background conditions likely to affect its next versions. The critics of the golden age, I argued at the start of this book, found themselves torn between three competing urges: they wanted to be social scientists comfortable in the academy and familiar with methodological technique; they wanted to be public intellectuals, capable of reaching, if not a mass audience, then at least a nonacademic one; and they wanted to be politically relevant. Social criticism, in other words, is a product of three cultures: the political, the academic, and the popular. Each is undergoing important changes. A sense of the directions social criticism will take can be gleaned from understanding what some of those changes are.

Social Criticism and Politics

The political atmosphere of the United States is undergoing dramatic changes at the end of the twentieth century. The Republican Party, once a minority with little interest in reversing its fate, has begun to dominate Congress and may soon take over the presidency. The U.S. Supreme Court is reexamining principles of constitutional interpretation which have been settled for half a century: federalism, the separation of church and state, and oversight of congressional legislation. Ideas such as term limits and the balanced budget amendment raise fundamental questions of democratic theory and practice. Committed to the language of radicalism—even, in more effusive moments, revolution—the Republican Party is reexamining every aspect of how the public business has been conducted since the New Deal.

All this is healthy for a democracy. Parties that remain in power too long are not nearly as indispensable as they come to think they are. Moreover, many of the criticisms launched by Republicans against liberal policies and programs have found vulnerable targets. But despite the influence of neoconservative intellectuals, the Republican resurgence—a populist revolt from the heartland—is reactive more than reflective. Its manifesto is a Contract with America drawn after market-testing demonstrated the language and the themes that would have the greatest appeal.[1] Its leaders write books, but they are not sustained tracts containing arguments and evidence.[2] As a radical movement, it seems oddly out of touch with previous conservatisms in American history: Hamiltonianism, Calhoun's concurrent majorities, Henry Adams, agrarianism. It has no foreign policy. Louis Hartz once argued that conservatism could never really exist in this country, so automatic has been its commitment to liberalism.[3] Nothing proves the adage as much as the emergence of this new Republican majority, for whatever it is, it is not a movement guided by any coherent conservative understanding of how the world works.

On the left a new form of politics has also been emerging, one that is equally as radical in its rethinking of classic tenets. The left, since at least the eighteenth century, has stood for universal ideals, but now it defends the particulars of identity politics. Its major themes, once emphasizing economics, now focus on culture. Equality has been transformed from a vague, if nonetheless inspiring, ideal to a condition of legislative and judicial rule-making. No longer appealing to constituents whose main desire is to become bourgeois, the left articulates the ideals of the overclass to the oppressed of the underclass. Where the left once stood for the public good, now it stands for the right to be left alone. Most important of all, the left has become as conservative as the Republicans have become radical, protecting existing jobs, fearing innovation, preferring the imperfect status quo to a world in which an emphasis on greater responsibility would be accompanied by greater risk.

Right and left are further apart now than at any point since the New

Deal; for conservatives (especially religious conservatives) defenders of abortion and gay rights are the anti-Christ, while for radicals the Republican Party is understood to be flirting with fascism. Because these visions are so far apart, a considerable amount of future political debate will involve contrasting one with the other, as each side in the culture war quotes from the other in order to raise money and energize its troops. Yet more important for the future of social criticism may not be the differences between right and left but what they have in common, for they share assumptions about the nature of politics which would render criticism superfluous. Neither places a high priority on persuasion, communication, and the ability to change one's mind—all of which are essential for social criticism to flourish.

Right and left, to start with the obvious example, are both skeptical of assigning a high priority to free speech. The right has never been strongly committed to the First Amendment; loyalty to country, respect for authority, the need for discipline—these took priority over the right to make utterances deemed offensive to the majority. Nothing in the recent history of the right suggests a reexamination of this position; the Republican Contract with America contains sections on controlling crime and rolling back regulation, but nothing on creating conditions that would allow for widespread discussion and criticism of alternative policies. Newt Gingrich, the Republican Speaker of the House of Representatives, envisions the Internet as a model of political communication; electronic postings, like talk radio, the other favorite conservative means of communication, are indeed an expression of how Republicans view expression—angry gestures that never engage in an attempt to persuade others or to be influenced by the ideas of others in turn.

What is more surprising is the degree to which the left has come around to the right's position on free speech. The alliance between the Christian right and feminists against pornography is more than a marriage of convenience. Central to identity politics is the notion that marginalized groups do not need free speech because, lacking voice, their first requirement is to obtain power. Hence Charles Lawrence writes that "most Blacks—unlike many white civil libertarians—do not have faith in free speech as the most important vehicle for liberation."[4] Free speech, by equating the utterances of racists and victims of racism, is, according to this view, premised upon a false equality. The only reason to welcome free speech is tactical; oppressed groups may need it to get their points across, but groups which oppress them can properly have their utterances regulated in the interests not of the First Amendment but of the Fourteenth. Like conservatives, advocates of identity politics view speech as a form of declaration, not a means of persuasion.

Free speech is tangential to the goals of conservatives and enthusiasts for identity politics because both share an understanding of power in which communication across group lines becomes unnecessary. Political criticism and debate is based on the idea that, although we all have private or group interests, we also have interests in common which can be discovered through argument. Yet a key plank of the Republicans' new understanding of the world is that no such thing as a common interest exists. Republicans defend their position on the grounds that government, the vehicle for articulating what we have in common, tramples upon individual freedom. But as the political theorist Stephen Holmes has written, "The great threat to freedom . . . is the concentration of power. This is true whether power is concentrated in the public or in the private realm."[5] The Republican attack on the state is anything but an attack on power. Republicans know full well that weakening public authority strengthens private authority. The world they envision is not one which dispenses with the need for large-scale economic coordination or the division of labor, but one that seeks more efficiency through the elimination of cumbersome public input. The utopia of the right is a world without Ralph Naders. Its aim is a public sphere so weakened by private power that any public discussion about the direction of society, even if it took place, would have no impact on those whose decisions determine that direction. This is a vision more feudal than capitalist. Power will be increased by decentralizing it so that it cannot draw attacks on itself.

The left shares with the right a feudal vision of the state, one which defines and protects the interests of particular corporate groups, only this time the groups are defined by their place in the production of identity rather than by their place in the means of production. Michael Piore, an economist sympathetic to identity claims, writes that blacks "are the first of the new noneconomic corporate groups in American society,"[6] but others, such as gays, have joined them. All such groups "have the potential for violating the liberal conception of society" (21). One of those liberal conceptions involves the need for open communication to persuade others of the rightness of our ideas. Such an objective is unnecessary in a world of corporate identity groups. The political theorist Iris Marion Young argues that oppressed groups, although not those who oppress them, should be given a veto power over policies they deem counter to their interests.[7] One can well imagine the effect of such a proposal on political debate and argument. No unfairly treated group need ever collect data documenting its condition, nor issue eloquent pleas for liberation, nor expose the hypocrisies of the society to which it objects; all it has to do is to say no. Not only would social criticism disappear under such conditions, so would self-criticism; marginalized groups, so often criticized by others, will only be further marginalized if they admit their flaws. So long as power determines the world, criticism is redundant.

Social criticism flourishes under a system of representative government. Liberals have always known that populistic democracy, which seems to give people the power to influence the world around them directly, rarely works because the forms of communication it generates are unfocused and incapable of guiding policy toward its desired objectives. Direct democracy encourages frustration and resentment rather than criticism. It breeds politicians whose style relies on demagogic assertion, not argument and persuasion. Representative government, by contrast, limits the number of people with effective power but increases the requirement that they justify their actions and decisions to those who elect them. The more organized the political system into disciplined parties with responsible legislators, the more likely that political discussion and criticism will be effective.

This may be why neither the right nor the left, in their current manifestations, are strong supporters of representative government. Republicans, believing that people can never trust themselves, place the power of restraint not in argumentation but in rules: knowing that we may be tempted to vote for an long-term incumbent, we will prevent ourselves from so doing by invoking term limits; fully aware that we cannot restrain our demands for more spending by government, we will protect ourselves with a balanced budget amendment to the Constitution. This amounts to a full-scale critique of the idea that anyone can represent us adequately. Radicals usually view legislators as delegates carrying out the mandate of the people, not as independent thinkers with minds of their own. Supporters of term limits and the balanced budget amendment share this radical skepticism toward representation, but from a doubly radical assumption: even when our representatives slavishly carry out our will, we cannot trust them. It is a short step from term limits to no representative government at all. Why have anyone represent us if we are unwilling even to allow them to be our slaves? The Republican vision of government solves the problem of how we communicate with those who have power by abolishing power. It does not take much of a skeptic to realize that if power nonetheless remains, only our ability to communicate with it will wind up having disappeared.

This view is remarkably similar to the one shared by advocates of identity politics. Also suspicious of talk, leftists want to place authority in the hands of rules which do away with the need to communicate. Affirmative action assumes that white males will rarely do the right thing, making it essential that we prevent them from acting on the basis of instinct or sympathy. Multicultural agendas at universities are supported, often in secrecy, by administrators not responsible to any group. Hate-speech advocates share with neoclassical economic theory the notion that human nature cannot be trusted. Lani Guinier's convoluted tampering with voting rules was designed to guarantee the proportional representation of ideologies, rather than to have results emerge spontaneously from the give-and-take of political interests.[8] If the perfect symbol of the right's understanding of communication is the Internet, the perfect symbol of what the American left has become are congressional districts organized by race. The violation of liberal principles they entail is not so much their resemblance to apartheid as their epistemological assumption: blacks will not have to take whites into account to be elected and whites will not have to take into account blacks. If what we want is defined by who we are, there is no need for communication at all.

Social criticism is connected to a broad understanding of liberalism, for liberalism works best when we put ourselves in the vulnerable but also power-enhancing position of listening to arguments that might change our mind. How we get to the destination matters as much as whether we get there; the means—a constitution, political parties, interest groups, free speech, the possibility of representative government itself—are as important as the ends. Convinced that they know the best ends, both the new Republican right and advocates of identity politics downplay the significance of procedures to insure we reach these ends. Yet this focus on the ends of politics does not turn such advocates into consequentialists—those who would judge a policy by what happens because of it. For the ends sought both by the new Republican majority and identity politics often turn out to be more symbolic than real. Conservatives want three-strikes-and-you're-out without regard to its actual effects on crime and prisons. Leftists want to see more minority faces in Congress, even if the direct result is a more conservative Congress less hospitable to the concerns of minorities. A world of vibrant social criticism is marginal to both because, when all is said and done, they care neither about ends nor means. Their aim is to make a point, moreover a point determined by who we are or what we do; when the point has been made, the need for discussion stops.

If American politics continues to be divided between conservatives who want to dismantle public power and theorists of identity politics who want to reenforce the boundaries between groups, social criticism will undergo important changes. A polarized politics encourages solidarity in the ranks rather then internal dissent. Its model of criticism leans toward the polemical and the positional. Posturing substitutes for persuasion. Under such circumstances, social criticism is unlikely to be either inventive or interesting.

Yet such a politics also leads to dissatisfaction. When the ideologies that dominate political discourse close off debate, it usually breaks out somewhere else. Certainly one possible future for social criticism under the circumstances I am describing here will be a blending of the political, the social, and the cultural. Critics will spend less time talking about the details of policy and more time trying to identify the forces that have produced a political culture hostile to criticism. The position of the critic who cares about argumentation will only be enhanced to the degree that established ideologies assert rather than argue. Social criticism, in that sense, may continue to flourish; it just will be more likely to take place outside the framework of politics.

Social Criticism and the Academy

There are two different theories about the relationship between social criticism and academic life. One holds that the contemporary university, especially under the influence of leftist professors, has become a hotbed of criticism—an enclave of negativity in the otherwise positive culture of America.[9] The other argues that academic conditions are bad for social criticism. The best social critics have always been independent intellectuals living on the margins, this point of view maintains. When critics turn into academic careerists, more concerned with method than mendacity, social criticism has to suffer.[10]

Those who believe that academic culture is hostile to social criticism often point to two features of academic life which, they claim, encourage obscurantism and professionalization. One is academic specialization. The other is tenure. It is true that each has had an influence on social criticism. But it is also true those influences have been positive as well as negative. An additional point is even more important: however one judges the impact of specialization and tenure on social criticism, both are undergoing significant changes that point to quite a different academic future.

The highly specialized knowledge sought by academics in their neverending quest for professional respectability, critics of the university write, discourages the broad kind of speculative work which is usually associated with social criticism. So long as academic success is defined by publication in peer-reviewed journals dominated by disciplinary considerations, younger scholars lack the incentive and the time to write books that will influence ideas beyond the academy. This is a point made by writers from all sides of the political spectrum; as I argued in Chapter 2, in the 1960s it constituted the core of the left's critique of the academy, whereas in the 1990s, when the radicals are the specialists, it is typically asserted by the right.

Neither version of the critique tells the full story. For all the narrowness of academic specialization, it has produced a better body of work that the often eloquent, but also often empty, social science and social criticism of the 1950s. No one in the 1990s should be able to get away with the kind of unsupported statements about national character produced by the psychologists of the 1940s and 1950s, for example. Nor ought we to tolerate critics who believe that because their politics are right, their facts need not be. The American academy may produce fewer Richard Hofstadters and Lionel Trillings, but it also encourages more rigorous argumentation, more thorough empirical verification, and higher standards of publication than it did during the rapid expansion of the 1960s. Those who sit in judgment of candidates for tenure now are often less good at the business of scholarship than those they judge.

This general point is true of my own field; sociology is fragmented, politicized, and unable to define what it is, to the point where the entire field, according to Irving Louis Horowitz, has disintegrated.[11] I disagree, at least with half the indictment. Yes, the field is in awful shape organizationally, but it has also produced work that would meet any standard established during its "golden age" in the 1950s and 1960s.[12] To be considered serious social science, both quantitative and qualitative work has had to rise to a higher standard. A field that has seen the publication of serious works on a topic as contentious as race by William Julius Wilson, Christopher Jencks, Orlando Paterson, Douglas Massey and Nancy Denton, and Elijah Anderson cannot be all bad. Because the standard for sociology has risen, so has the standard for social criticism.

Whatever the relationship between social criticism and academic specialization, it is about to change. There are few constituencies with more power to shape the direction of higher education than consumers. For some time those who pay for education have not given all that much attention to the product they were buying. Now they do. Wherever tuition revenue drives the university, there pressures against specialization are building. Core curricula, for one thing, are making a comeback. Administrators everywhere, recognizing the need to keep tuition revenues high, have begun to sponsor centers for teaching excellence. Prestigious "multiversities," such as the State University of New York at Stony Brook, take out advertisements in the *New York Times* proclaiming their willingness to focus more on teaching. In those areas where presidents have some leeway—for example in filling endowed chairs standing outside departments—they search for generalists, not specialists, academics whose name-recognition (among the general public) will draw students.

As universities pay more attention to teaching, and as teaching itself returns to a focus on core curricula, the environment for social criticism may well improve; after all, such well-known critics of the golden age as Lionel Trilling and C. Wright Mills taught general education at Columbia. I certainly hope this is the outcome, for both sides in the current war over the university would find themselves somewhat put off by this development. The right, which attacks specialization for uncovering trivia and failing undergraduates, will hardly be happy with a general education that emphasizes the cultivation of a broad and critical sensibility. The left, which for two decades has based its academic legitimacy on its claims to theory, will not only have to reread classic texts in order to survive in the new environment but will even have to learn to think and write clearly. Yet the environment for social criticism will not improve if universities throw out the baby of knowledge and respect for evidence with the bathwater of specialization. If the university begins to place more emphasis on teaching and on general education, the result will be good for social criticism only if social critics remember that moral indignation is not enough.

Tenure is also held to be responsible for an academic environment in which critical tones become muted. This is not generally how conservatives see the matter; in their view, tenure protects radicals and allows them to be as critical as they want without taking responsibility for their ideas. Yet most academics who have been through the process of obtaining tenure know otherwise. Decades ago tenure may have protected radicals in the university from dismissal, but now a six-to-ten-year apprenticeship produces such caution that the candidate, once successful, is scarred for life. Tenure protects, not academic freedom, but academic complacency. So long as universities operate under a system which requires so insecure a probationary period, risk-taking books written with passion and devoted to sweeping themes are unlikely ever to see the light of day.

I am more persuaded by this point of view that I am with respect to critics of specialization. Tenure has always struck me as a mixed blessing at best: to be sure, some dissenting voices are protected by it (although these days they can come from the right as well as the left), but it also freezes the university into an institutional conservatism that simply cannot be good for the emergence of innovative ideas. Yet whatever the final balance-sheet on tenure, its future is as uncertain as the future of academic specialization. The American Association for Higher Education is studying the ways in which tenured academics might explore alternative career options. It has also entered the thicket of "post-tenure review": the issue likely to dominate administrative considerations over the next decade. Some institutions have abolished tenure. Some state legislators are calling for its abolition. It is no secret that tenure benefits elderly white males at the expense of minorities. There are even faculty members, many with tenure, who believe that the whole system has become little more than an excuse for irresponsibly self-interested behavior. So long as faculty are free to move from one university to another, tenure is unlikely to be abolished—at least for those who already have it. But one way or another, the system which exists now is unlikely to survive as legislators in the public realm and consumers in the private realm pay more attention to the priorities of concern to them.

What effect will the reform—some would say the restriction—of tenure have on social criticism? Without tenure, academics will find it harder to specialize, a development that could promote a genre of work less grounded in respect for reality. On the other hand, academics without tenure will find themselves with more incentives to write for the general public, a prospect that might produce works in social science more relevant to the issues about which Americans care deeply. There is little reason to believe that the abolition of tenure would produce an atmosphere of conformity so thick that social criticism would disappear. It is also possible that an academy without tenure will provide more free air for social critics to breathe.

Those who question the priorities of tenure and specialization belong to a tradition of social criticism of the university itself, one that has changed remarkably little from the days of Jacques Barzun to those of Page Smith and David Damrosch.[13] Such critics believe that the university, organized by departments and equipped with blinders, will never produce serious work devoted to large-scale themes. Yet, in writing their criticisms, each disproves the point. Social criticism has not done badly in the specialized university; it has a chance of doing ever better in the more general academic culture which is emerging, but only if it retains, rather than rejects, documentation and the testing of evidence, the tools of the kind of university with which it is presumably at odds.

Social Criticism and the Public Intellectual

Closely connected to concerns about the effects of academic specialization and tenure has been a worry about the future of the public intellectual. Russell Jacoby's argument is the most well-known; academics, spread throughout the United States and more likely to support themselves through teaching than by editing and writing, are a far cry from the intense, politically charged, and, above all else, critical world once symbolized by the New York intellectuals.[14] The question of whether we have reached the end of the era of the intellectual is much on the mind of intellectuals. There is the possibility that the intelligentsia may continue to be important, Steven Brint writes, "yet a good deal mitigates against it." Hence, "it is far easier to imagine a future in which the audience for broad social, cultural and moral argumentation will in effect gradually disappear."[15] If so, the future is not going to one especially receptive to a tradition of social criticism.

Yet if there has been a decline of the public intellectual, I have not noticed it. To be sure those independent quarterlies which have survived tend to be affiliated with universities. And New York is no longer a place in which one can live cheaply yet still be at the center of the intellectual action. But those who lament the passing of the public intellectual are generally lamenting the passing of a specific kind of intellectual, especially the intellectual of heroic dissent. The intellectuals of the golden age are, inevitably, a dying species, but they are being replaced. Some have pointed out that black intellectuals are not dissimilar from an earlier generation of Jewish intellectuals in their concern for large themes and their commitment to criticism.[16] Conservative intellectuals, an oxymoron during the 1950s, have become a vibrant reality in the 1990s, a phenomenon which can only help bring leftist intellectuals out of their academic torpor.

It is also important to emphasize that change does not mean decline. The conditions under which public intellectuals produce their social criticism has clearly changed since the golden age; David Riesman had his picture on the cover of *Time*, an honor which has escaped my generation of social critics. The fact that works of social science were published in the 1950s in understandable English (and sometimes flirted with the best-seller lists) reflects the "sociology of intellectual knowledge" at that time. It would be wrong to expect that different conditions at another time would produce the same kind of product.

Yet, perhaps surprisingly, intellectual and academic social criticism is not all that different these days from its "golden age" flourishing. To shed a little more light on this matter, I examined *Book Review Digest* in an effort to see the degree to which important works of social science then and now were reviewed, within two years of publication, by scholarly and popular journals (see table 1). Even with the limited value of these findings—some books were not reviewed until two years after publica-

Table 1 **Frequency of Reviews** Selected Works of Social Criticism

YEAR	TITLE	AUTHOR	POPULAR REVIEWS	ACADEMIC REVIEWS
1939	*Knowledge for What?*	Lynd	14	6
1950	*The Lonely Crowd*	Riesman	15	4
1951	*White Collar*	Mills	11	1
1955	*The Social System*	Parsons	1	4
1955	*Communism, Conformity . . .*	Stouffer	13	2
1956	*The Power Elite*	Mills	21	6
1958	*Philadelphia Gentlemen*	Baltzell	2	3
1959	*The Sociological Imagination*	Mills	12	2
1959	*The Presentation of Self . . .*	Goffman	0	0
1960	*Political Man*	Lipset	14	4
1960	*The End of Ideology*	Bell	6	3
1961	*Asylums*	Goffman	0	0
1962	*The Urban Villagers*	Gans	1	1
1963	*Outsiders*	Becker	2	1
1963	*Beyond the Melting Pot*	Glazer/ Moynahan	14	3
1963	*Invitation to Sociology*	Berger	0	0
1966	*Social Construction of Reality*	Berger	1	3
1967	*The Levittowners*	Gans	11	2
1967	*Interaction Ritual*	Goffman	0	0
1968	*The Academic Revolution*	Jencks/Ries	14	0
1970	*Coming Crisis . . .*	Gouldner	5	6
1971	*Relations in Public*	Goffman	5	1
1972	*Inequality*	Jencks	20	4
1973	*Coming of Post-Industrial . . .*	Bell	18	6
1976	*Everything in Its Path*	Erikson	8	0
1978	*Reproduction of Mothering*	Chodorow	2	1
1979	*States and Social Rev . . .*	Skocpol	3	2
1980	*Declining Significance of Race*	Wilson	0	0
1984	*Abortion and the Politics . . .*	Luker	8	3
1985	*Habits of the Heart*	Bellah	13	1
1985	*Canarsie*	Rieder	8	0
1987	*Public and Private High Schools*	Coleman	7	2
1987	*The Truly Disadvantaged*	Wilson	11	3
1991	*Acts of Compassion*	Wuthnow	4	3
1991	*Immigrant America*	Portes	2	3

tion, especially in scholarly journals, and *Book Review Digest* is not exhaustive—they indicate some decline in ability to reach general readers, but not all that much.

It is clear from even these cursory figures that *Habits of the Heart* or *The Truly Disadvantaged* are very much within the tradition of social criticism begun in the 1950s. (Nor has enough time passed at this writing to judge the impact on the culture of such new additions to the literature as Christopher Jencks's book on the homeless, Sara McLanahan's and Gary Sandefur's study of the economic effects of being raised by a single parent, or Herbert Gans's study of language and rhetoric directed against the poor).[17] Moreover, now, as then, sociologists are active in setting the public agenda: Paul Starr is an editor of *The American Prospect* and is widely regarded as one of America's leading experts on health care reform. Amitai Etzioni started nothing less than a political movement (communitarianism) that was taken seriously, not only in the United States, but in Great Britain and Germany as well. Starr and Theda Skocpol attended (along with myself) a meeting at Camp David to advise President Clinton on his 1995 State of the Union address. Contemporary feminism would be unrecognizable without the work of Nancy Chodorow and Arlie Hochschild. Not only are some of the critics of the golden age, such as Daniel Bell and Nathan Glazer, still writing and involving themselves in public affairs, but they have passed on their passion to my generation: Jencks worked with Riesman, Starr was a student of Bell's, Peter Skerry has learned from Nathan Glazer and James Q. Wilson, devotees of Alvin Gouldner make themselves heard through *Theory and Society*, and every feminist political theorist in the country seems to be coming to terms with the ideas of Hannah Arendt. In short, while we have no right to expect that this age should produce public intellectuals like the last one did, it actually has.

Finally, whatever the state of book publishing and reviewing, the culture of the intellectual magazine, certainly the weekly news-oriented magazine, is more alive today than it was in the golden age. In the 1950s, both *The Nation* and *The New Republic* focused almost exclusively on politics. Now both have significant "back of the book" sections dealing with intellectual and cultural themes. (Many of the chapters in this book originally appeared as essays in *The New Republic*.) *The New York Review of Books* was not in existence during the "golden age." Americans did not read, nor did they receive immediately on publication, *The Times Literary Supplement* then. At a time when innovation is supposed to be difficult, new magazines have been launched: *The American Prospect, Tikkun, Society, The Public Interest*. Even as I write, a new weekly magazine, *The*

Standard, has started publication, edited by William Kristol—doctorate in political theory from Harvard and son of two famous New York intellectuals, as is his collaborator, John Podhoretz. Surely this makes up for the loss of *The Reporter* or the decline of a handful of quarterlies, many of which, by the way, did not measure up to the standards of today's *Salmagundi.*

If it is an exaggeration to claim that the public intellectual has declined, it also misses the mark, as I suggested in the previous section of this chapter, to argue that academic work is so narrow, professionalized, and obsessed with ideology that it cannot possibly contribute to informed public debate. Critics such as Jacoby are prone to argue that just as intellectual work is good—as in broad and humanistic—academic specialization is bad—as in narrow and provincial. To be sure, academic writing is often convoluted and cautious, but intellectual writing can be bombastic and ignorant. There are few cultural artifacts more painful to contemplate than bad books by bad intellectuals—those which offer sweeping pronouncements about the end of this-or-that or the radical transformations taking place just as the author is writing about them. The last thing social criticism needs is more public intellectuals, if they are intellectuals unconstrained by an urge to check facts or to ground their ideas in readily available knowledge.

For decades, academics debated the relative weight that should be given to teaching versus research before it became obvious to almost everyone that the two are not in conflict; those who fail to renew themselves through some kind of research cannot possibly be good teachers. A similarly false debate is taking place between those who say that the university has no place for general intellectuals and those who attack academic publication as trivial and overly specialized. Although intellectuals are generalists, they can also be professional in their attitude, their discipline, and the use of the scholarship that forms their opinions. Although scholars view themselves as professionals, the best of them have something to say for a larger audience and a few are capable of saying it quite well.

Social criticism flourishes when both intellectual and academic work is done well. Critics of the university are right to suggest that there is something wrong with graduate education which teaches only how to write articles, so that candidates come up for tenure having published extensively yet knowing close to nothing. But there are also cases of the untenured assistant professor who chooses to write a popular book and receives widespread attention, only to be turned down later for tenure, yet whose work can be shoddy in its use of evidence, thin in documentation, and determined to make some larger point at the expense of a far more complicated reality. Being a public intellectual is not by itself a virtue.

If the quality of intellectual work is threatened, it is not because intellectuals are withering away, but because of the impact of their ideas on op-ed pages, television talk shows, weekly magazines, law reviews, and even on the university. Public intellectuals have been incorporated into American culture. Their terms—power elite, end of ideology, mass society, conspicuous consumption, authoritarian personality, counterculture—have entered the vernacular.[18] Their ideas have become the stuff of presidential speeches. One of them is a United States senator. The dangers which follow from this popularity are obvious; intellectuals generally make bad celebrities, and good celebrities are usually bad intellectuals. Yet it may be turn out to be the case that public intellectuals—even good ones—will survive even in spite of the demand for their ideas.

Every time a once independent publisher is bought out by a conglomerate, or a local bookstore closes after a superstore opens in its neighborhood, one hears laments about the decline of the generally educated reader—the obvious audience for the public intellectual. Yet for every indication of decline, there is also an indication of health: people still buy books, university presses rush in to fill the niches left by the withdrawal of commercial publishers, and neither the Internet nor the CD-Rom has replaced the age-old phenomenon of pages printed between covers. When Newt Gingrich really wanted to make his impact on American culture, he did it by publishing a book. In doing so, he joined a host of journalistic and popular writers—William Grieder, Jonathan Schell, Thomas and Mary Edsall, E. J. Dione, Alan Ehrenhalt, Roger Kimball, Susan Faludi, Hugh Pearson, James Traub, Jim Sleeper, Naomi Wolf, Michael Lind—who write about serious topics in a serious way for the generally educated reader. The economics of book publishing has changed since the 1950s, as has the technology, but there is evidently ample room left for commentary and critique.

Any society, even American society, has a need to understand itself. That need will surely be filled in different ways at different times. But these ought to be understood more as cycles than as declines and falls. It may very well be true that debate in America has become more facile, reduced to bumper-sticker slogans, shaped to fit the needs of television, personalized so that the MTV generation will pay at least some attention. But that only provides more grist for the critic's mill. Given the scenarios of doom that have written about public intellectuals, it is amazing that we still talk about them. Perhaps this should tell us that they are likely to be with us for some time.

The Next Critics

As public intellectuals go, so will social critics. What strikes me most about the sociology of social criticism is not that critics have disappeared but that they have become so ubiquitous. No longer tied to a few neighborhoods in Manhattan, social critics can be found in every corner of America. No longer automatically affiliated with the left, they can present themselves in any political form. No longer confined to the written word, they have television and radio at their disposal. No longer predominantly Jewish (or white, or male) they have larger potential audiences to address (which makes it that much more of a shame if they restrict their audiences by race or gender). No longer preoccupied by the themes of the 1950s—the problem of communism, the evils of racial segregation, the distortions of suburbia, the appeals of personal liberation—they face a more complicated, but also more challenging, set of issues.

None of this guarantees that the next generation of critics will be trenchant in their analyses, eloquent in their prose, and responsible in their recommendations. They surely face complications all around them (as, of course, did previous generations of critics). Still, I envy the next generation of social critics. They will have more than enough political issues on their plate to provide full meals for some time. They will, if they are academics, work in universities that will give them a chance to be both scholars and intellectuals simultaneously. Their main worry will not be marginality but popularity. The "golden age" of social criticism is over, which surely means that social criticism is due to thrive again.

Chapter One

1. Robert and Helen Lynd, *Middletown: A Study in American Culture* (New York: Harcourt Brace, 1929), and *Middletown in Transition: A Study in Cultural Conflicts* (New York: Harcourt Brace, 1937).

2. Robert Lynd, *Knowledge for What? The Place of Social Science in American Culture* (Princeton: Princeton University Press, 1939).

3. Arthur Vidich and Joseph Bensman, *Small Town in Mass Society: Class, Power, and Religion in a Rural Community* (Garden City: Doubleday, 1959); W. Lloyd Warner, *Democracy in Jonesville: A Study of Quality and Inequality* (New York: Harper, 1949).

4. Margaret Mead, *Coming of Age in Samoa* (New York: Morrow, 1928); Ruth Benedict, *Patterns of Culture* (Boston: Houghton Mifflin, 1934).

5. The most typical efforts along these lines were made by Erich Fromm, as in, for example, *The Sane Society* (New York: Rinehart, 1955).

6. See especially C. Wright Mills, *The Marxists* (New York: Dell, 1962).

7. David Riesman, in collaboration with Rueul Denney and Nathan Glazer, *The Lonely Crowd: A Study of the Changing American Character* (New Haven: Yale University Press, 1950); David Riesman, in collaboration with Nathan Glazer, *Faces in the Crowd: Individual Studies in Character and Politics* (New Haven: Yale University Press, 1952).

8. C. Wright Mills, *The Sociological Imagination* (New York: Oxford University Press, 1959), 195–226.

9. Noam Chomsky, *American Power and the New Mandarins* (New York: Pantheon, 1969).

10. Russell Jacoby, *The Last Intellectuals: American Culture in the Age of Academe* (New York: Basic Books, 1987).

11. Irving Howe, "This Age of Conformity," in *Selected Writings, 1950–1990* (San Diego: Harcourt, Brace, Jovanovich, 1990), 26–49.

12. Andrew Jamison and Ron Eyerman, *Seeds of the Sixties* (Berkeley and Los Angeles: University of California Press, 1994), 1.

13. Jacoby, *The Last Intellectuals*, p. 118.

14. Christopher Lasch, *The Revolt of the Elites and the Betrayal of Democracy* (New York: Norton, 1995), 193.

15. Derek Freeman, *Margaret Mead and Samoa: The Making and Unmaking of an Anthropological Myth* (Cambridge: Harvard University Press, 1983).

16. Michael Wreszin, *A Rebel in Defense of Tradition: The Life and Politics of Dwight Macdonald* (New York: Basic Books, 1994).

17. For example, see Edward Said's *Representations of the Intellect* (New York: Pantheon, 1994).

18. Michael Walzer, *The Company of Critics: Social Criticism and Political Commitment in the Twentieth Century* (New York: Basic Books, 1988).

19. The phrase belongs to Joan Scott, as cited in Russell Jacoby, *Dogmatic Wisdom: How the Culture Wars Divert Education and Distract America* (New York: Doubleday, 1994), 165. Paul Lauter calls such critics "marginal at best to the academy." Paul Lauter, "'Political Correctness' and the Attack on American Colleges," in Michael Bérubé and Cary Nelson, eds., *Higher Education Under Fire: Politics, Economics and the Crisis of the Humanities* (New York: Routledge, 1885), 82.

20. Lionel Trilling, "Preface," *Beyond Culture* (New York: Harcourt Brace, 1979), i-ix.

21. Kurt H. Wolff and Barrington Moore, eds., *The Critical Spirit: Essays in Honor of Herbert Marcuse* (Boston: Beacon Press, 1967).

22. Not one more insightfully than Philip Rieff, *The Triumph of the Therapeutic: Uses of Faith After Freud* (New York: Harper and Row, 1966). For just one more recent example, see Wendy Kaminer, *It's All the Rage: Crime and Culture* (Reading: Addison Wesley, 1995).

23. See Chapter 10 below, in which I deal with the ideas of Deborah Tannen.

24. Andrew Mecca, Neil J. Smelser, and John Vasconcellos, eds., *The Social Importance of Self-Esteem* (Berkeley and Los Angeles: University of California Press, 1989).

25. Alfie Kohn, *No Contest: The Case Against Competition* (Boston: Houghton Mifflin, 1986), and *Punished by Rewards: The Trouble with Gold Stars, Incentive Plans, A's, Praise, and Other Bribes* (Boston: Houghton Mifflin, 1993).

26. Frederick Crews, *The Memory Wars: Freud's Legacy in Dispute* (New York: New York Review of Books, 1995).

27. This is happening. For some excellent examples, see Daniel Horowitz, *Vance Packard and American Social Criticism* (Chapel Hill: University of North Carolina Press, 1994); Casey Blake, *Beloved Community: The Cultural Criticism of Randolph Bourne, Van Wyck Brooks, Waldo Frank, and Lewis Mumford* (Chapel Hill: University of North Carolina Press, 1990); and Wilfred M. McClay, *The Mas-*

terless: Self and Society in Modern America (Chapel Hill: University of North Carolina Press, 1994).

28. Ian Shapiro, *Political Criticism* (Berkeley and Los Angeles: University of California Press, 1990), 266. Too close an identification between democracy and opposition, however, can lead to the insupportable argument that democracy ought to be equated with left-wing political positions, since the left is usually in opposition.

29. Said's most accomplished reflections on his work, in my opinion, are contained in *The World, The Text, the Critic* (Cambridge: Harvard University Press, 1983).

30. Aijaz Ahmad *In Theory* (London: Verso, 1992), 159.

31. Christina Hoff Sommers, *Who Stole Feminism? How Women Have Betrayed Women* (New York: Simon and Schuster, 1994).

32. Morris Dickstein, *Double Agent: The Critic and Society* (New York: Oxford University Press, 1992), 155.

33. Michael Walzer, *Interpretation and Social Criticism* (Cambridge: Harvard University Press, 1987), 36.

34. Walzer, *The Company of Critics*, p. 226.

Chapter Two

1. This symposium actually was spread out over three issues. For the first one, see *Partisan Review* (July/August 1952).

2. George Nash, *The Conservative Intellectual Movement in America* (New York: Basic Books, 1976).

3. David Lance Goines, *The Free Speech Movement: Coming of Age in the 1960s* (Berkeley: Ten Speed Press, 1993), 526–62.

4. Charles Sykes, *Profscam: Professors and the Demise of Higher Education* (Washington, D.C.: Regnery Gateway, 1988), 12.

5. Martin Anderson, *Impostors in the Temple: American Intellectuals Are Destroying Our Universities and Cheating Our Students of Their Future* (New York: Simon and Schuster, 1992), 137–93.

6. Roger Kimball, *Tenured Radicals: How Politics Has Corrupted Our Higher Education* (New York: Harper and Row, 1990), 32.

7. Newt Gingrich, *To Renew America* (New York: Harper Collins, 1995), 219.

8. Michael Bérubé and Cary Nelson. "Introduction: A Report from the Front," in Michael Bérubé and Cary Nelson, eds., *Higher Education Under Fire: Politics, Economics and the Crisis of the Humanities* (New York: Routledge, 1995), 9, 10, 15, 19.

9. Ernst Benjamin, "A Faculty Response to the Fiscal Crisis: From Defense to Offense," in ibid., p. 65.

10. Linda Ray Pratt, "Going Public: Political Discourse and the Faculty Voice," in ibid., p. 38.

11. Gerald Graff, *Professing Literature: An Institutional History* (Chicago: University of Chicago Press, 1987).

12. Stanley Fish, "Being Interdisciplinary Is So Very Hard to Do," *Profession 89* (New York: Modern Language Association, 1989), 15–22, cited in Bruce Robbins, *Secular Vocations: Intellectuals, Professionals, Culture* (London: Verso, 1993), 238.

13. Stephen Park Turner and Jonathan H. Turner, *The Impossible Science: An Institutional Analysis of American Sociology* (Newbury Park: Sage Publications, 1990), 127.

14. Andrew Jamison and Ron Eyerman, *Seeds of the Sixties* (Berkeley and Los Angeles: University of California Press, 1994).

15. Of the entire group, only Mills and Marcuse could be said to have followed traditional academic careers. The other critics they examined include C. Wright Mills, Hannah Arendt, Fairfield Osborn, Leo Szilard, Herbert Marcuse, Margaret Mead, Allen Ginsberg, James Baldwin, Mary McCarthy, Saul Alinsky, Dorothy Day, and Martin Luther King, Jr.

16. See especially the essays collected in Stanley Fish, *Doing What Comes Naturally: Change, Rhetoric, and the Practice of Theory in Literary and Legal Studies* (Durham: Duke University Press, 1989).

17. These themes are explored in ways similar to those developed here in David Bromwich, *Politics by Other Means: Higher Education and Group Thinking* (New Haven: Yale University Press, 1992).

18. George Levine, Peter Brooks, Jonathan Culler, Marjorie Garber, E. Ann Kaplan, and Catharine R. Stimpson, *Speaking for the Humanities* (New York: American Council of Learned Societies Occasional Paper No. 7, 1989), 6, 8, 14.

19. Anderson, *Impostors in the Temple*, pp. 9–27.

20. John Gross, *The Rise and Fall of the Man of Letters: Aspects of English Literary Life Since 1800* (Chicago: Ivan Dee, 1992).

21. Andrew Ross, *No Respect: Intellectuals and Popular Culture* (New York: Routledge, 1989), 52.

22. Michael Bérubé, *Public Access: Literary Theory and American Cultural Politics* (London: Verso, 1994), 146.

23. Stanley Aronowitz, *Roll Over Beethoven: The Return of Cultural Strife* (Hanover: University Press of New England, 1993).

24. Meaghan Morris, "Things to Do With Shopping Centers," in Simon During, ed., *The Cultural Studies Reader* (London and New York: Routledge, 1994), 298.

25. William Warner, "Spectacular Action: Rambo and the Popular Pleasures of Pain," in Lawrence Grossberg, Cary Nelson, and Paula Teichler, eds., *Cultural Studies* (New York: Routledge, 1992), 672–88; Douglas Kellner, quoted in Bérubé, *Public Access*, p. 145.

26. For just one example, see Helen Haste, *The Sexual Metaphor* (Cambridge: Harvard University Press, 1994), 172–76.

27. Shannon Bell, *Reading, Writing, and Rewriting the Prostitute Body* (Bloomington: Indiana University Press, 1994).

28. bell hooks, *Outlaw Culture* (New York: Routledge, 1994), 118, 123.

29. Personal communication to the author.

30. Cited in Bérubé, *Public Access*, p. 148.

31. Richard Hofstadter, *Anti-Intellectualism in American Life* (New York: Vintage Books, 1963).

32. Paul Lauter, "'Political Correctness' and the Attack on American Colleges," in Bérubé and Nelson, *Higher Education Under Fire*, pp. 82, 84.

Chapter Three

1. For a statement of this position, see Dorothy E. Smith, *The Everyday World as Problematic: A Feminist Sociology* (Boston: Northeastern University Press, 1987).

2. Herbert Gans, *The War Against the Poor: The Underclass and Anti-Poverty Policy* (New York: Basic Books, 1995).

3. Jerry Z. Muller, *The Other God That Failed: Hans Freyer and the Deradicalization of German Conservatism* (Princeton: Princeton University Press, 1987); Arnold Gelhen, *Man in the Age of Technology,* Patricia Lipscomb, trans. (New York: Columbia University Press, 1980); Martin Heidegger, "The Question Concerning Technology," in *Basic Writings,* David Farrell Krell, ed. (New York: Harper and Row, 1977), 287–317.

4. Louis Wirth, "Urbanism as a Way of Life," in Albert J. Reiss, Jr., ed., *Louis Wirth on Cities and Social Life* (Chicago: University of Chicago Press, 1964), 60–83.

5. For an example, see Robert Nisbet, *History of the Idea of Progress* (New York: Basic Books, 1980).

6. Robert Bellah et al., *Habits of the Heart: Individualism and Commitment in American Life* (Berkeley: University of California Press, 1985).

7. Nels Anderson, *The Hobo: The Sociology of the Homeless Man* (Chicago: University of Chicago Press, 1923); Harvey W. Zorbaugh, *The Gold Coast and the Slum* (Chicago: University of Chicago Press, 1929).

8. The classic statement of this perspective is Herbert Blumer, *Symbolic Interactionism: Perspective and Method* (Berkeley: University of California Press, 1969). An exemplary treatment of the "exotic" is Erving Goffman, "Where the Action Is," in his *Interaction Ritual* (New York: Pantheon, 1967), 149–270. See also Jack Katz, *Seductions of Crime: Moral and Sensual Attractions of Doing Evil* (New York: Basic Books, 1988).

9. Howard Becker, *Outsiders: Studies in the Sociology of Deviance* (Glencoe: The Free Press, 1963).

10. Elliott Liebow, *Talley's Corner: A Study of Negro Streetcorner Men* (Boston: Little, Brown, 1967).

11. This is especially the case with Goffman's essay, "The Moral Career of the Mental Patient," in his *Asylums: Essays on the Social Situation of Mental Patients and Other Inmates* (Garden City: Anchor Books, 1961), 127–69.

12. Richard Shweder, "Anthropology's Romantic Rebellion Against the Enlightenment," in Richard Shweder and R. LeVine, eds, *Culture Theory: Essays on Mind, Self, and Emotion* (New York: Cambridge University Press, 1984); see also George W. Stocking, Jr., ed., *Romantic Motives: Essays on Anthropological Sensibility* (Madison: University of Wisconsin Press, 1989).

13. Frederick Thrasher, *The Gang: A Study of 1313 Gangs in Chicago* (Chicago: University of Chicago Press, 1928).

14. Martín Sánchez Jankowski, *Islands in the Street: Gangs and American Urban Society* (Berkeley and Los Angeles: University of California Press, 1991), 22.

15. Lilian R. Furst, *The Contours of European Romanticism* (Lincoln: University of Nebraska Press, 1979), 44.

16. Irving Babbitt, *Rousseau and Romanticism* (Boston: Houghton Mifflin, 1919), 139.

17. César Graña, *Bohemian Versus Bourgeois: French Society and the French Man of Letters in the Nineteenth Century* (New York: Basic Books, 1964), 99.

18. William F. Whyte, *Street Corner Society: The Social Structure of an Italian Slum* (Chicago: University of Chicago Press, 1955); Liebow, *Talley's Corner*.

19. Eric J. Hobsbawm, *Primitive Rebels* (New York: Norton, 1959).

20. Robert and Helen Lynd, *Middletown: A Study in American Culture* (New York: Harcourt Brace, 1929); Herbert Gans, *The Levittowners: Ways of Life and Politics in a New Suburban Community* (New York: Pantheon, 1967); Jonathan Rieder, *Canarsie: The Jews and Italians of Brooklyn Against Liberalism* (Cambridge: Harvard University Press, 1985).

21. George J. Becker, *Realism in Modern Literature* (New York: Frederick Ungar, 1980), 49.

22. Martin Bulmer, Kevin Bales, and Kathryn Kish Sklar, eds., *The Social Survey in Historical Perspective* (New York: Cambridge University Press, 1981); Jean M. Converse, *Survey Research in the United States: Roots and Emergence, 1890–1960.* (Berkeley and Los Angeles: University of California Press, 1987)

23. This urge culminated in Herbert Gans, *Middle American Individualism: The Future of Liberal Democracy* (New York: The Free Press, 1988).

24. James McKee, *Sociology and the Race Problem* (Urbana: University of Illinois Press, 1993).

25. Elijah Anderson, *Streetwise: Race, Class, and Change in an Urban Commu-*

nity (Chicago: University of Chicago Press, 1990); William Julius Wilson, *The Truly Disadvantaged: The Inner City, the Underclass, and Public Policy* (Chicago: University of Chicago Press, 1987).

26. See, for example, Adolph Reed, "The Underclass Myth," *The Progressive* 55 (August 1991), 18–20.

27. Andrew Hacker, *Two Nations: Black and White, Separate, Hostile, Unequal* (New York: Scribner's, 1992).

28. Douglas Massey and Nancy Denton, *American Apartheid: Segregation and the Making of the Underclass* (Cambridge: Harvard University Press, 1993).

Chapter Four

1. Mitchell Duneier, *Slim's Table: Race, Respectability, and Masculinity* (Chicago: University of Chicago Press, 1992). See also Alex Kotlowitz, *There Are No Children Here: The Story of Two Boys Growing Up in the Other America* (New York: Doubleday, 1991).

2. Andrew Hacker, *Two Nations: Black and White, Separate, Hostile, Unequal* (New York: Ballantine Books, 1992).

3. Glenn C. Loury, *One by One From the Inside Out: Essays on Race and Responsibility in America* (New York:The Free Press, 1995), 225–35.

4. Shelby Steele, *The Content of Our Character: A New Vision of Race in America* (New York: St. Martin's, 1991).

5. Reynolds Farley, *Blacks and Whites: Narrowing the Gap?* (Cambridge: Harvard University Press, 1984), 200.

6. Ibid, p. 202.

7. Roderick J. Harrison and Claudette E. Bennett, "Racial and Ethnic Diversity," in Reynolds Farley, *State of the Union*, volume 2: *Social Trends* (New York: Russell Sage Foundation, 1995), 141–210.

8. Frank Levy, "Incomes and Income Inequality," in Reynolds Farley, *State of the Nation*, volume 1: *Economic Trends* (New York: Russell Sage Foundation, 1995), 43. See also Gerald Davis Jaynes and Robin M. Williams, *A Common Destiny: Blacks and American Society* (Washington, D .C.: National Academy Press, 1989), 275.

9. Jaynes and Williams, *A Common Destiny*, p. 275

10. Harrison and Bennett, "Racial and Ethnic Diversity," pp. 174–75.

11. Paul Peterson and Christopher Jencks, *The Urban Underclass* (Washington, D.C.: The Brookings Institution, 1991).

12. Bart Landry, *The New Black Middle Class* (Berkeley and Los Angeles: University of California Press, 1987).

13. Cited in Gertrude Himmelfarb, *Poverty and Compassion* (New York: Knopf, 1991), 21.

14. David T. Ellwood and Mary Jo Bane, *Welfare Realities: From Rhetoric to Reform* (Cambridge: Harvard University Press, 1994), 111.

15. Christopher Jencks, *Rethinking Social Policy: Race, Poverty, and the Underclass* (Cambridge: Harvard University Press, 1992).

16. Elijah Anderson, *Streetwise: Race, Class, and Change in an Urban Community* (Chicago: University of Chicago Press, 1990).

17. United States Kerner Commission. *Report of the National Advisory Commission on Civil Disorders* (Washington, D.C.: Government Printing Office, 1968).

18. As one might expect, the story of race relations in New York is complicated. For some light, see Jim Sleeper, *The Closest of Strangers: Liberalism and the Politics of Race in New York* (New York: Norton, 1990), and Jonathan Rieder, *Canarsie: The Jews and Italians of Brooklyn Against Liberalism* (Cambridge: Harvard University Press, 1985).

19. Studs Terkel, *Race: How Blacks and Whites Think and Feel about the American Obsession* (New York: The New Press, 1992).

20. Thomas Byrne Edsall and Mary D. Edsall, *Chain Reaction: The Impact of Race, Rights, and Taxes on American Politics* (New York: Norton, 1991), 222–23.

21. Stephen L. Carter, *Reflections of an Affirmative Action Baby* (New York: Basic Books, 1991).

22. Hugh Davis Graham, *The Civil Rights Era: Origins and Development of National Policy, 1960–1972* (New York: Oxford University Press, 1990), 103–20.

23. William Julius Wilson, *The Truly Disadvantaged: The Inner City, the Underclass, and Public Policy* (Chicago: University of Chicago Press, 1987), and *The Declining Significance of Race: Blacks and Changing American Institutions* (Chicago: University of Chicago Press, 1990).

24. Lawrence Mead, *The New Politics of Poverty* (New York: The Free Press, 1992), 16.

25. Himmelfarb, *Poverty and Compassion*, p. 149.

26. James Q. Wilson, *On Character* (Washington, D.C.: American Enterprise Institute, 1991), 3.

27. Herbert Gans, *The War Against the Poor: The Underclass and Anti-Poverty Policy* (New York: Basic Books, 1995), 72.

28. Michael B. Katz, *In the Shadow of the Poorhouse: A Social History of Welfare in America* (New York: Basic Books, 1986), 291.

29. Ibid, p. 57.

30. Michael Katz, "The Urban 'Underclass' as a Metaphor of Social Transformation," in Michael Katz, ed., *The "Underclass" Debate: Views from History* (Princeton: Princeton University Press, 1993), 22.

31. Andrew T. Miller, "Social Science, Social Policy, and the Heritage of African-American Families," in Katz, *The "Underclass" Debate*, p. 288. Gans, *The War Against the Poor* (p. 58), believes that passing judgments on others is permissible, so long as it is not done in code words.

32. It is possible, however, to write in justification of the moral world of the 1950s, so long as one is honest in defending the hierarchical and authoritarian aspects of that world as much as the communitarian. See Alan Ehrenhalt, *The Lost City: Discovering the Forgotten Virtues of Community in the Chicago of the 1950s* (New York: Basic Books, 1995).

33. Douglas Massey and Nancy Denton, *American Apartheid: Segregation and the Making of the Underclass* (Cambridge: Harvard University Press, 1993).

34. Martin Carnoy, *Faded Dreams: The Politics and Economics of Race in America* (New York: Cambridge University Press, 1994).

35. Ellis Cose, *The Rage of a Privileged Class* (New York: Harper Collins, 1993); Patricia Williams, *The Alchemy of Race and Rights: Diary of a Law Professor* (Cambridge: Harvard University Press, 1991).

36. Howard Schuman, Charlotte Steech, and Lawrence Bobo, *Racial Attitudes in America: Trends and Interpretations* (Cambridge: Harvard University Press, 1985).

37. Andrew Kull, *The Color-Blind Constitution* (Cambridge: Harvard University Press, 1992).

38. Paul M. Sniderman and Thomas Piazza, *The Scar of Race* (Cambridge: Harvard University Press, 1993).

39. Richard N. Herrnstein and Charles Murray, *The Bell Curve: Intelligence and Class Structure in American Life* (New York: The Free Press, 1994). For my own critique, see Alan Wolfe, "Has There Been a Cognitive Revolution in America?: The Flawed Sociology of *The Bell Curve*," in Steven Fraser, ed., *The Bell Curve Wars* (New York: Basic Books, 1995), 109–23.

Chapter Five

1. Bryan D. Palmer, *Descent into Discourse: The Reification of Language and the Writing of Social History* (Philadelphia: Temple University Press, 1990).

2. For one example, see Michael Omi and Howard Winant, *Racial Formation in the United States: From the 1960s to the 1980s* (New York: Routledge and Kegan Paul, 1986).

3. Betty Friedan, *The Feminine Mystique* (New York: Norton, 1963).

4. Judith Stacey, *Brave New Families: Stories of Domestic Upheaval in Late Twentieth Century America* (New York: Basic Books, 1990); Kathleen Gerson, *No Man's Land: Men's Changing Commitments to Family and Work* (New York: Basic Books, 1993).

5. See, for example, Elaine Sorensen, *Comparable Worth: Is It a Worthy Policy?* (Princeton: Princeton University Press, 1994), and Barbara Reskin and Patricia A. Roos, *Job Queues, Gender Queues: Explaining Women's Inroads into Male Occupations* (Philadelphia: Temple University Press, 1990).

6. Any list is bound to be subjective. Mine would include, among very recent works, Linda Gordon, *Pitied But Not Entitled: Single Mothers and the History of Welfare, 1890–1935* (New York: The Free Press, 1994), and Kathryn Kish Sklar, *Florence Kelley and the Nation's Work: The Rise of Women's Political Culture, 1830– 1900* (New Haven: Yale University Press, 1995).

7. Sandra Lipsitz Bem, "The Measurement of Psychological Androgyny," *Journal of Clinical and Consulting Psychology* 42 (1974), 155–62.

8. Sandra Lipsitz Bem, *The Lenses of Gender: Transforming the Debate on Sexual Inequality* (New Haven: Yale University Press, 1993), 121.

9. Helen Haste-Weinreich and Don Locke, eds., *Morality in the Making: Thought, Action, and the Social Context* (New York: Wiley, 1983).

10. Helen Haste, *The Sexual Metaphor* (Cambridge: Harvard University Press, 1994).

11. Judith Lorber, *Paradoxes of Gender* (New Haven: Yale University Press, 1994).

12. Nel Noddings, *Caring: A Feminine Approach to Ethics and Moral Education* (Berkeley and Los Angeles: University of California Press, 1984); Mary Field Belensky, et al., *Women's Ways of Knowing: The Development of Self, Voice, and Mind* (New York: Basic Books, 1986); Wellesley College Center for Research on Women, *How Schools Shortchange Girls: The AAUW Report: A Study of Major Findings on Girls in Education* (Washington, D.C.: Association of American University Women, 1992).

13. Cited in Bem, *The Lenses of Gender,* p. 122.

14. Sandra Lipsitz Bem, "Gender Schema Theory: A Cognitive Account of Sex Typing," *Psychological Review,* 88 (1981), 354–64.

15. Judith Butler, *Gender Trouble: Feminism and the Subversion of Identity* (New York: Routledge, 1990).

16. See Gilbert Herdt, ed., *Third Sex, Third Gender: Beyond Sexual Dimorphism in Culture and History* (New York: Zone Books, 1994), and Anne Fausto-Sterling, "How Many Sexes Are There?," *New York Times,* March 12, 1993, p. A29.

17. Susan Faludi, *Backlash: The Undeclared War Against American Women* (New York: Crown, 1991).

18. Betty Friedan, *The Second Stage* (New York: Summit Books, 1986); Naomi Wolf, *Fire With Fire: The New Female Power and How It Will Change the 21st Century* (New York: Random House, 1993).

19. René Denfeld, *The New Victorians: A Young Woman's Challenge to the Old Feminist Order* (New York: Warner Books, 1995); Katie Roiphe, *The Morning After: Sex, Fear, and Feminism* (Boston: Little, Brown, 1993).

20. Daphne Patai and Noretta Koertge, *Professing Feminism: Cautionary Tales from the Strange World of Women's Studies* (New York: Basic Books, 1994), and Christina Hoff Sommers, *Who Stole Feminism? How Women Have Betrayed Women* (New York: Simon and Schuster, 1994). For a contrary view from an insider, see

Jean Fox O'Barr, *Feminism in Action: Building Institutions and Community Through Women's Studies* (Chapel Hill: University of North Carolina Press, 1994).

Chapter Six

1. Mari J. Matsuda, Charles R. Lawrence III, Richard Delgado, and Kimberlè Williams Crenshaw, *Words that Wound: Critical Race Theory, Assaultive Speech, and the First Amendment* (Boulder: Westview Press, 1993).

2. Andrea Dworkin, *Pornography: Men Possessing Women* (New York: Dutton, 1989), xxxvi.

3. Peter Brimelow, *Alien Nation: Common Sense About America's Immigration Disaster* (New York: Random House, 1995).

4. Richard Randall, *Freedom and Taboo: Pornography and the Politics of a Self Divided* (Berkeley and Los Angeles: University of California Press, 1989).

5. Linda Williams, *Hard Core: Power, Pleasure, and the "Frenzy of the Visible"* (Berkeley and Los Angeles: University of California Press, 1989).

6. Donald Downs, *The New Politics of Pornography* (Chicago: University of Chicago Press, 1989), 54.

7. Ibid, p. 99.

8. Attorney General's Commission on Pornography, *Final Report* (Washington, D.C.: U. S. Department of Justice, July 1986).

9. Robin Morgan, "Theory and Practice: Pornography and Rape," in Laura Lederer, ed., *Take Back the Night: Women and Pornography* (New York: Morrow, 1980), 139.

10. I am relying on the account of Downs, *The New Politics of Pornography*, pp. 34–94.

11. For arguments along these lines, see Ann Snitow, Christine Stansell, and Sharon Thompson, *Powers of Desire: The Politics of Sexuality* (New York: Monthly Review Press, 1983).

12. Sallie Tisdale, *Talk Dirty to Me: An Intimate Philosophy of Sex* (New York: Doubleday, 1994); Nadine Strossen, *Defending Pornography: Free Speech, Sex, and the Fight for Women's Rights* (New York: Scribner's, 1995).

13. Catharine A. MacKinnon, *Only Words* (Cambridge: Harvard University Press, 1993), 29,

14. Brimelow, *Alien Nation*, pp. 133–220.

15. Alejandro Portes and Reuben Rumbaut, *Immigrant America: A Portrait* (Berkeley and Los Angeles: University of California Press, 1990), 246.

16. Richard Alba, *Ethnic Identity: The Transformation of White America* (New Haven: Yale University Press, 1990); Mary C. Waters, *Ethnic Options: Choosing Identities in America* (Berkeley and Los Angeles: University of California Press,

17. Herbert Gans, "Symbolic Ethnicity: The Future of Ethnic Groups and Cultures in America," *Ethnic and Racial Studies* 12 (January 1979), 1–20.

18. Rosalie Pedalino Porter, *Forked Tongue: The Politics of Bilingual Education* (New York: Basic Books, 1990).

19. Peter Skerry emphasizes the political differences between the leaders of immigrant organizations and the immigrants themselves in his *Mexican-Americans: The Ambivalent Minority* (New York:The Free Press, 1993).

20. Robert N. Bellah, Richard Madsen, William M. Sullivan, Ann Swidler, and Steven M. Tipton, *Habits of the Heart* (Berkeley and Los Angeles: University of California Press, 1985), has been accused by many of its critics as sermonizing. I do not find this charge true, but it do think it applies to the follow-up volume, *The Good Society* (New York: Knopf, 1991).

21. Downs, *New Politics of Pornography*, pp. 56–73.

22. Dworkin, *Pornography*, p. 52.

23. Robert K. Merton, *Social Theory and Social Structure*, 1968 enlarged edition (New York: The Free Press, 1968).

24. C. Wright Mills, *The Sociological Imagination* (New York: Oxford University Press, 1959), 25–49.

25. Merton, *Social Theory and Social Structure*, pp. 92–96.

Chapter Seven

1. Representative of the genre are Jessica Mitford, *The American Way of Death* (New York: Simon and Schuster, 1963); Mary Adelaide Mendelson, *Tender Loving Greed: How the Incredibly Lucrative Nursing Home Industry is Exploiting America's Old People and Defrauding Us All* (New York: Knopf, 1974); and Robert N. Butler, *Why Survive? Being Old in America* (New York: Harper and Row, 1975).

2. As, for example, in Daniel Callahan, *Setting Limits: Medical Goals in an Aging Society* (New York: Simon and Schuster, 1987), and Phillip Longman, *Born to Pay: The New Politics of Aging in America* (Boston: Houghton Mifflin, 1987).

3. Thomas R. Cole, *The Journey of Life: A Cultural History of Aging in America* (New York: Cambridge University Press, 1992).

4. Betty Friedan, *The Fountain of Age* (New York: Simon and Schuster, 1993).

5. Cole, *The Journey of Life*, p. 228.

6. Gail Sheehy, *New Passages: Mapping Your Life Across Time* (New York: Random House, 1995).

7. Richard A. Posner, *Sex and Reason* (Cambridge: Harvard University Press, 1992).

8. Sherwin Nuland, *How We Die: Reflections on Life's Final Chapter* (New York: Knopf, 1994).

9. Richard A. Posner, *Aging and Old Age* (Chicago: University of Chicago Press, 1995), 1.

10. Tomas Philipson and Richard A. Posner, *Private Choices and Public Health: The AIDS Epidemic in Economic Perspective* (Cambridge: Harvard University Press, 1993).

11. As brought to our attention by Clifford Geertz in "Deep Play: Notes on the Balinese Cockfight," in *The Interpretation of Cultures: Selected Essays* (New York: Basic Books, 1973), 432.

12. Cole, *The Journey of Life*, p. 170.

13. Ian Hacking, *Rewriting the Soul: Multiple Personality and the Sciences of Memory* (Princeton: Princeton University Press, 1995).

14. My criticisms of Posner overlap with those articulated in Donald P. Green and Ian Shapiro, *Pathologies of Rational Choice Theory* (New Haven: Yale University Press, 1994).

15. Jack D. Douglas, *The Social Meanings of Suicide* (Princeton: Princeton University Press, 1967).

16. Jean Améry, *On Aging: Revolt and Resignation*, John D. Barlow, trans. (Bloomington: Indiana University Press, 1994), 67.

17. Jean Améry, *At the Mind's Limits: Contemplations by an Survivor on Auschwitz and Its Realities*, Stella Rosenfeld, trans. (New York: Schocken Books, 1986), 20.

18. Jean Améry, *Hand an sich Legen: Diskurs über den Freitod* (Stuttgart: Klett-Cotta, 1976).

19. This issue is explored in Martha Minow, *Making all the Difference: Inclusion, Exclusion, and American Law* (Ithaca: Cornell University Press, 1990).

Chapter Eight

1. C. Wright Mills, *The Sociological Imagination* (New York: Oxford University Press, 1959), 35–36. See also Hans Gerth and C. Wright Mills, *Character and Social Structure: The Psychology of Social Institutions* (New York: Harcourt Brace, 1953).

2. C. Wright Mills, *The New Men of Power: America's Labor Leaders* (New York: Harcourt Brace, 1948).

3. C. Wright Mills, *Sociology and Pragmatism: The Higher Learning in America* (New York: Paine-Whitman, 1964).

4. Alan Ryan, *John Dewey and the High Tide of American Liberalism* (New York: Norton, 1995), 271. See also John Patrick Diggins, *The Promise of Pragmatism: Modernism and the Crisis of Knowledge and Authority* (Chicago: University of Chicago Press, 1994), 280–321.

5. Paul Goodman, *Growing Up Absurd: Problems of Youth in the Organized System* (New York: Random House, 1960).

6. Edgar Z. Friedenberg, *Coming of Age in America: Growth and Acquiescence* (New York: Random House, 1986); Edgar Z. Friedenberg, *The Vanishing Adolescent* (Boston: Beacon Press, 1969); John Holt, *How Children Learn* (New York: Pitman, 1967).

7. Jules Henry, *Culture Against Man* (New York: Vintage Books, 1965), 183. Emphasis in the original.

8. See Thomas Sowell, *Inside American Education: The Decline, The Deception, the Dogmas* (New York:The Free Press, 1993), and William Kilpatrick, *Why Johnny Can't Tell Right from Wrong: Moral Illiteracy and the Case for Character Education* (New York: Simon and Schuster, 1992), both of which will be treated at greater length below.

9. Jonathan Kozol, *Savage Inequalities: Children in America's Schools* (New York: Crown, 1991).

10. Myra and David Sadker, *Failing at Fairness: How America's Schools Cheat Girls* (New York: Scribner's, 1994) and Peggy Orenstein, *Schoolgirls: Young Women, Self-Esteem, and the Confidence Gap* (New York: Doubleday, 1994).

11. Joseph A. Fernandez with John Underwood, *Tales Out of School: Joseph Fernandez' Crusade to Rescue American Education* (Boston: Little, Brown, 1993).

12. All quotations in this paragraph are from Steven Lee Myers, "Queens School Board Suspended in Fight on Gay-Life Curriculum," *New York Times*, December 2, 1992, p. B4.

13. Jane Roland Martin, *The School Home: Rethinking Schools for Changing Families* (Cambridge: Harvard University Press, 1992), 8.

14. Joan DelFattore, *What Johnny Shouldn't Read: Textbook Censorship in America* (New Haven: Yale University Press, 1992), 84.

15. Edward de Bono, *Teach Your Child How to Think* (New York: Viking, 1993), 16.

16. Lewis Perelman, *School's Out: The New Technology and the End of Education* (New York: William Morrow, 1992), 38.

17. Howard Gardner, *Multiple Intelligences: The Theory in Practice* (New York: Basic Books, 1993), 10.

18. Lewis V. Gerstner, Roger D. Semerad, Dennis Philip Doyle, and William B. Johnston, *Reinventing Education: Entrepreneurship in America's Public Schools* (New York: Dutton, 1994).

19. George H. Wood, *Schools That Work: America's Most Innovative Public Education Programs* (New York: Dutton, 1992).

20. Larry Martz, *Making Schools Better: How Parents and Teachers Across the Country Are Taking Action—and How You Can Too* (New York: Times Books, 1992).

21. Howard Gardner, *The Unschooled Mind: How Children Think and How Schools Should Teach* (New York: Basic Books, 1991), 202.

22. Ivan Illich, *DeSchooling Society* (New York: Harper, 1971).

23. John E. Chubb and Terry Moe, *Politics, Markets, and American Schools* (Washington, D.C.: The Brookings Institution, 1990), 32.

24. Seymour Flieger, with James MacGuire, *Miracle in East Harlem: The Fight for Choice in Public Education* (New York: Times Books, 1993).

25. James S. Coleman, *Equality of Educational Opportunity* (Washington, D.C.: Department of Health, Education, and Welfare, 1966).

26. David Guterson, *Family Matters: Why Homeschooling Makes Sense* (New York: Harcourt, Brace, Jovanovich, 1992).

27. Stephen Bates, *Battleground: One Mother's Crusade, the Religious Right, and the Struggle for Control of Our Classrooms* (New York: Poseidon Press, 1993).

28. Ibid., p. 311.

29. Diane Ravitch, *The Great School Wars: A History of the New York City Public Schools* (New York: Basic Books, 1974).

Chapter Nine

1. Richard Kluger, *Simple Justice: The History of Brown v. Board of Education and Black America's Struggle for Equality* (New York: Alfred A. Knopf, 1976), 557.

2. James S. Coleman, "Columbia in the 1950s," in Bennett Berger, ed., *Authors of Their Own Lives: Intellectual Autobiographies of Twenty American Sociologists* (Berkeley and Los Angeles: University of California Press, 1990), 75–103.

3. Richard A. Cloward and Lloyd E. Ohlin, *Delinquency and Opportunity: A Theory of Delinquent Groups* (Glencoe: The Free Press, 1960). The story is well told by Nicholas Lemann, who describes their concept as "the marriage of two great traditions in American sociology." *The Promised Land: The Great Black Migration and How It Changed America* (New York: Knopf, 1991), 120. Lemann is referring to the Chicago school and Robert Merton's functionalism.

4. Daniel P. Moynihan, *Maximum Feasible Misunderstanding: Community Action in the War on Poverty* (New York: The Free Press, 1967).

5. Examples of works of social science dealing with these issues are David J. Armour, *Forced Justice: School Desegregation and the Law* (New York: Oxford University Press, 1995); Sara McLanahan and Gary Sandefur, *Growing Up with a Single Parent: What Hurts, What Works* (Cambridge: Harvard University Press, 1994); John DiIulio, *Governing Prisons: A Comparative Study of Correctional Management* (New York: The Free Press, 1987); and Edward O. Laumann, John H. Gagnon, Robert T. Michael, and Stuart Michaels, *The Social Organization of Sexuality: Sexual Practices in the United States* (Chicago: University of Chicago Press, 1984).

6. Theda Skocpol, *Protecting Soldiers and Mothers: The Political Origins of So-*

cial Policy in the United States (Cambridge: The Belknap Press of Harvard University Press, 1992).

7. The J. David Greenstone Award of the Politics and History Section, American Political Science Association; Outstanding Book Award, Political Sociology Section, American Sociological Association; Allan Sharlin Memorial Award, Social Science History Association; Woodrow Wilson Award, American Political Science Association; Ralph Waldo Emerson Award, Phi Beta Kappa.

8. Theda Skocpol, *Social Policy in the United States: Future Possibilities in Historical Perspective* (Princeton: Princeton University Press, 1995), 6.

9. Ibid, pp. 310, 253.

10. Margaret Weir, Ann Shola Orloff, and Theda Skocpol, "The Future of Social Policy in the United States," in *The Politics of Social Policy in the United States* (Princeton: Princeton University Press, 1988), 421–45.

11. Morton Keller, *Affairs of State: Public Life in Late Nineteenth Century America* (Cambridge: The Belknap Press of Harvard University Press, 1977), 311.

12. In addition to Keller, see Richard F. Bensel, *Sectionalism and American Political Development, 1880–1980* (Madison: University of Wisconsin Press, 1984), 70, and Jill S. Quadagno, *The Transformation of Old Age Security: Class and Politics in the American Welfare State* (Chicago: University of Chicago Press, 1988), 36–47.

13. Sonya Michel, "The Limits of Maternalism: Policies Toward American Wage-Earning Mothers During the Progressive Era," in Seth Koven and Sonya Michel, eds., *Mothers of a New World: Maternalist Politics and the Origins of Welfare States* (New York: Routledge, 1993), 277–320, and Barbara J. Nelson, "The Origins of the Two-Channel Welfare State: Workmen's Compensation and Mothers' Aid," in Linda Gordon, ed., *Women, the State, and Welfare* (Madison: University of Wisconsin Press, 1990), 123–51.

14. Rosalind Rosenberg, *Beyond Separate Spheres: Intellectual Roots of Modern Feminism* (New Haven: Yale University Press, 1982). Rosenberg, who would come to accept the notion that women and men have different needs, wrote a very favorable review of Skocpol's book: "How the Safety Net Got Torn," *New York Times Book Review* (January 31, 1993), 16.

15. Judith A. Baer, *The Chains of Protection: The Judicial Response to Women's Labor Legislation* (Westport: Greenwood Press, 1978). See also Susan Lehrer, *Origins of Protective Labor Legislation for Women, 1905–1925* (Albany: State University of New York Press, 1987).

16. Virginia Sapiro, "The Gender Basis of American Social Policy," in Gordon, *Women, the State, and Welfare*, p. 44.

17. Linda Gordon, *Pitied But Not Envied: Single Mothers and the History of Welfare* (New York: The Free Press, 1994), 37–64.

18. Theda Skocpol, "Soldiers, Workers, and Mothers: Gendered Identities in Early U. S. Social Policy," *Contention* 2 (Spring 1993), 178.

19. Linda Gordon, "Gender, State, and Society: A Debate With Theda Skocpol," *Contention* 2 (Spring 1993), 147.

20. For some sense of the debates within feminism, see Marianne Hirsch and Evelyn Fox Keller, eds., *Conflicts in Feminism* (New York: Routledge, 1990).

21. T. H. Marshall, "Citizenship and Social Class," in *Class, Citizenship and Social Development*, S. M. Lipset, ed. (Garden City: Anchor Books, 1964), 71–134.

22. Theda Skocpol, *States and Social Revolutions: A Comparative Analysis of France, Russia, and China* (New York: Cambridge University Press, 1979), 285.

23. Ann Shola Orloff and Theda Skocpol, "Why Not Equal Protection? Explaining the Politics of Public Social Spending in Britain 1900–1914 and the United States 1880s-1920," *American Sociological Review* 49 (December 1984), 702.

24. Theda Skocpol, "Bringing the State Back In: Strategies of Analysis in Current Research," in Peter B. Evans, Dietrich Rueschemeyer, and Theda Skocpol, eds., *Bringing the State Back In* (New York: Cambridge University Press, 1985), 3–37.

25. Linda Gordon, "Social Insurance and Public Assistance: The Influence of Gender in Welfare Thought in the United States, 1890–1035," *American Historical Review* 97 (February 1992), 21.

26. James Q. Wilson, *The Amateur Democrat: Club Politics in Three Cities* (Chicago: University of Chicago Press, 1966); Robert K. Merton, *Social Theory and Social Structure*, 1968 enlarged edition (New York: The Free Press, 1968), 126–36; Richard Hofstadter, *The Age of Reform: From Bryan to FDR* (New York: Knopf, 1955).

27. Skocpol, "Soldiers, Workers, and Mothers," p. 157.

Chapter Ten

1. For the case in favor of the heritability of homosexuality, offered with modesty and caution, see Simon LeVay, *The Sexual Brain* (Cambridge: MIT Press, 1993), and Dean Hamer and Peter Copeland, *The Science of Desire: The Search for the Gay Gene and the Biology of Behavior* (New York: Simon and Schuster, 1994).

2. Conservatives, wanting to blame gays for their own behavior, tend to argue that they choose their lifestyle, while they once argued for biological destiny. Radicals, influenced by Michel Foucault, argue for the social construction of sexuality, but one who now has doubts is Richard Mohr, *Gay Ideas: Outings and Other Controversies* (Boston: Beacon Press, 1992), 221–42.

3. Talcott Parsons, "Social Science: A Basic National Resource," in Samuel Z. Klausner and Victor M. Lidz, eds., *The Nationalization of the Social Sciences* (Phil

adelphia: University of Pennsylvania Press, 1986), cited in Ellen Herman, *The Romance of American Psychology: Political Culture in the Age of Experts* (Berkeley and Los Angeles: University of California Press, 1995), 128.

4. Ibid.

5. Richard Herrnstein and Charles Murray, *The Bell Curve: Intelligence and Class Structure in American Life* (New York: The Free Press, 1994).

6. Judith Herman, *Trauma and Recovery* (New York: Basic Books, 1992). The debate has been joined by Richard Ofshe and Ethan Watters, *Making Monsters: False Memory, Psychotherapy, and Sexual Hysteria* (New York: Scribner's, 1994), and Elizabeth Loftus and Katherine Ketcham, *The Myth of Repressed Memory: False Memories and Allegations of Sexual Abuse* (New York: St. Martin's, 1994). See also Ian Hacking, *Rewriting the Soul: Multiple Personality and the Sciences of Memory* (Princeton: Princeton University Press, 1995).

7. For a review of the evidence, see Daniel Batson, *The Altruism Question: Towards a Social-Psychological Answer* (Hillsdale: Erlbaum Associates, 1991).

8. James Q. Wilson, *The Moral Sense* (New York: The Free Press, 1993), 12.

9. Nancy Scheper-Hughes, *Death Without Weeping: The Violence of Everyday Life in Brazil* (Berkeley and Los Angeles: University of California Press, 1992).

10. Diane E. Eyer, *Mother-Infant Bonding: A Scientific Fiction* (New Haven: Yale University Press, 1992).

11. John Bowlby, *Forty-Four Juvenile Thieves and Their Characters and Home Life* (London: Ballier, Tyndal, and Cox, 1946).

12. Mary D. Salter Ainsworth, *Infancy in Uganda: Infant Care and the Growth of Attachment* (Baltimore: Johns Hopkins University Press, 1967).

13. Mary D. Salter Ainsworth, Mary C. Blehar, Everett Waters, and Sally Wall, *Patterns of Attachment* (Hillsdale: Erlbaum, 1978).

14. John Bowlby, *Attachment,* volume 1 of *Separation: Anxiety and Anger* (New York: Basic Books, 1969), 37–64.

15. D. Rajecki, Michael E. Lamb, and Pauline Obmascher, "Toward a General Theory of Infantile Attachment: A Comparative Review of Aspects of the Social Bond," *Behavioral and Brain Sciences* 3 (1978), 428.

16. Jerome Kagan, *The Nature of the Child* (New York: Basic Books, 1984), 57–64.

17. James Q. Wilson, "The Family Values Debate," *Commentary* 95 (April 1993), 26.

18. Jerome Kagan, *Galen's Prophecy: Temperament in Human Nature* (New York: Basic Books, 1994).

19. Robert Wright, *The Moral Animal: Evolutionary Psychology and Everyday Life* (New York: Pantheon Books, 1994).

20. See my discussion of this whole issue in *The Human Difference: Animals, Computers, and the Necessity of Social Science* (Berkeley and Los Angeles: University of California Press, 1993).

Chapter Eleven

1. For examples, see Alisdair MacIntyre, *After Virtue: A Study in Moral Theory* (Notre Dame: University of Notre Dame Press, 1981), and Roberto Managabeira Unger, *Knowledge and Politics* (New York:The Free Press, 1985).

2. Daniel Bell, *Communitarianism and Its Critics* (Oxford: Clarendon Press, 1993).

3. Lawrence Susskind and Jeffrey Cruikshank, *Breaking the Impasse: Consensual Approaches to Resolving Public Disputes* (New York: Basic Books, 1987).

4. Deborah Tannen, *That's Not What I Meant! How Conversational Style Makes or Breaks Relationships* (New York: Ballantine Books, 1986), 6.

5. Deborah Tannen, *You Just Don't Understand: Men and Women in Conversation* (New York: Ballantine Books, 1990); Deborah Tannen, *Talking From 9 to 5: How Women's and Men's Conversational Styles Affect Who Gets Heard, Who Gets Credit, and What Gets Done at Work* (New York: William Morrow, 1994).

6. Deborah Tannen, *Gender and Discourse* (New York: Oxford University Press, 1994).

7. John J. Gumperz, "Introduction," in John J. Gumperz and Dell Hymes, eds., *New Directions in Sociolinguistics* (New York: Holt, Rinehart, and Winston, 1972), 9.

8. John J. Gumperz and Jenny Cook-Gumperz, "Introduction: Language and the Communication of Social Identity," in John J. Gumperz, ed., *Language and Social Identity* (Cambridge: Cambridge University Press, 1982), 7.

9. Robin Tomach Lakoff, *Language and Woman's Place* (New York: Harper and Row, 1975).

10. Steven Pinker, *The Language Instinct* (New York: William Morrow, 1994), 63–64.

11. Deborah Tannen, *Conversational Style: Analyzing Talk among Friends* (Norwood: Ablex, 1984).

12. Don H. Zimmerman and Candace West, "Sex Roles, Interruptions, and Silences in Conversation," in Barrie Thorne and Nancy Henley, eds., *Language and Sex: Difference and Domination* (Rowley: Newbury House, 1975), 105–29.

13. Gregory Bateson, *Steps to an Ecology of Mind* (San Francisco: Chandler, 1972), 179.

14. Gregory Bateson, *Naven: A Survey of the Problems Suggested by a Composite Picture of the Culture of a New Guinea Tribe Drawn from Three Points of View*, second edition (Stanford: Stanford University Press, 1958), 257.

15. Mary Catherine Bateson, *With a Daughter's Eye: A Memoir of Margaret Mead and Gregory Bateson* (New York: Morrow, 1984), 93.

16. David Lipset, *Gregory Bateson: The Legacy of a Scientist* (Englewood Cliffs: Prentice-Hall, 1980), 121–59.

17. Bronislaw Malinowski, Preface, to Raymond Firth, *We, the Tikopia* (New York: American Books Company, 1936), vii-viii.

18. Bateson, *Naven*, pp. 196–97.

19. Nicholas Rescher, *Pluralism: Against the Demand for Consensus* (Oxford: Clarendon Press, 1993), 17.

20. Albert O. Hirschman, *Exit, Voice, and Loyalty: Responses to Decline in Firms, Organizations, and States* (Cambridge: Harvard University Press, 1970).

21. Stephen Macedo, *Liberal Virtues: Citizenship, Virtue, and Community in Liberal Constitutionalism* (Oxford: Clarendon Press, 1990).

22. Deborah Tannen, "The Triumph of the Yell," *New York Times*, January 14, 1994, p. A29.

23. Deborah Tannen, "Perspective on Whitewater," *Los Angeles Times*, April 5, 1994, p. B7.

24. Robert T. Handy, *Undermined Establishment: Church-State Relations in America, 1880–1920* (Princeton: Princeton University Press, 1991).

25. Stephen Holmes, *Passions and Constraints: On the Theory of Liberal Democracy* (Chicago: University of Chicago Press, 1995).

26. Mark Hulliung, *The Autocritique of Enlightenment: Rousseau and the Philosophes* (Cambridge: Harvard University Press, 1994).

27. I have in mind Stephen Holmes, *The Anatomy of Antiliberalism* (Cambridge: Harvard University Press, 1993).

28. Judith N. Shklar, *Ordinary Vices* (Cambridge: Belknap Press of Harvard University Press, 1984), 7–44.

Chapter Twelve

1. Noam Chomsky, *American Power and the New Mandarins* (New York: Pantheon, 1967), 325.

2. Mills, *The Power Elite*, p. 356.

3. Raymond Aron, *Memoirs: Fifty Years of Political Reflection*, George Holoch, trans. (New York: Holmes and Meier, 1990).

4. Ibid, p. 42.

5. Raymond Aron, *German Sociology*, Mary and Thomas Bottomore, trans. (Glencoe: The Free Press, 1957); Raymond Aron, *Introduction to the Philosophy of History: An Essay on the Limits of Historical Objectivity*, George J. Irwin, trans. (Boston: Beacon Press, 1961); Raymond Aron, *La philosophie critique de l'histoire: Essai sur une théorie allemande de l'histoire* (Paris: J. Vrin, 1969).

6. Raymond Aron, *Introduction to the Philosophy of History: An Essay on the Limits of Historical Objectivity*, George J. Irwin, trans. (Boston: Beacon Press, 1096), 337.

7. Aron, *German Sociology*, p. 67.

8. Maurice Merleau-Ponty, *Humanism and Terror: An Essay on the Communist*

Problem, John O'Neill, trans. (Boston: Beacon Press, 1969). On efforts to create a "third force," see James D. Wilkinson, *The Intellectual Resistance in Europe* (Cambridge: Harvard University Press, 1981).

9. Raymond Aron *The Century of Total War* (Garden City: Doubleday, 1954), 181, 185, 186.

10. Raymond Aron, *La tragédie algérienne* (Paris: Plon, 1957).

11. Raymond Aron, *Main Currents in Sociological Thought*, Richard Howard and Helen Weaver, trans. (New York: Basic Books, 1965).

12. Raymond Aron, *Dix-huit leçons sur la société industrielle* (Paris: Gallimard, 1941).

13. Raymond Aron, *Clausewitz: Philosopher of War*, Christine Booker and Norman Stone, trans. (Englewood Cliffs: Prentice-Hall, 1985); Raymond Aron, *Peace and War: A Theory of International Relations*, Richard Howard and Annette Baker Fox, trans. (Garden City: Doubleday, 1966).

14. Raymond Aron, *The Opium of the Intellectuals*, Terence Kilmartin, trans. (Garden City: Doubleday, 1957).

15. Raymond Aron, *History and Dialectic of Violence: An Analysis of Sartre's Critique de la Raison Dialectique*, Barry Cooper, trans. (New York: Harper, 1975).

16. Raymond Aron, *In Defense of Decadent Europe*, Stephen Cox, trans. (South Bend: Regnery/Gateway, 1979), 99, 257.

17. Norman O. Brown, *Love's Body* (Berkeley and Los Angeles: University of California Press, 1990), 27. This book was originally published in 1966.

18. Norman O. Brown, *Apocalypse and/or Metamorphosis* (Berkeley and Los Angeles: University of California Press, 1991).

19. Philip Rieff, *The Feeling Intellect: Selected Writings*, edited with an introduction by Jonathan B. Imber (Chicago: University of Chicago Press, 1990), 323.

20. Norman O. Brown, *Life Against Death: The Psychoanalytic Meaning of History* (Middletown: Wesleyan University Press, 1959), 83.

21. Nancy Chodorow, *Feminism and Psychoanalytic Theory* (New Haven: Yale University Press, 1989), 123–29.

22. Betty Friedan, *The Feminine Mystique* (New York: Norton, 1963). Nearly thirty years later another feminist would argue that anorexia is similar to the starvation experienced in the death camps. See Naomi Wolf, *The Beauty Myth* (New York: William Morrow, 1991), 207–8. And, as I pointed out in Chapter 6, feminist Andrea Dworkin argues that what men do to women in pornography is worse than what happened to the Jews under Hitler.

23. Reprinted as Herbert Marcuse, "Love Mystified: A Critique of Norman O. Brown," in *Negations* (Boston: Beacon Press, 1968), 228.

24. Jacques Derrida, "Force of Law: The 'Mystical Foundation of Authority'," in Drucilla Cornell, Michel Rosenfeld, and David Gray Carlson, eds., *Deconstruction and the Possibilities of Justice* (New York: Routledge, 1992), 3–67.

Chapter Thirteen

1. *Contract with America: The Bold Plan by Rep. Newt Gingrich, Rep. Dick Armey and the House of Representatives to Change the Nation* (New York: Times Books, 1994).

2. Newt Gingrich, *To Renew America* (New York: HarperCollins, 1995); Dick Armey, *The Freedom Revolution: The New Republican Majority Leader Tells Why Big Government Failed, Why Freedom Works, and How We Will Rebuild America* (Washington: Regnery, 1995).

3. Louis Hartz, *The Liberal Tradition in America: An Interpretation of American Political Thought Since the Revolution* (New York: Harcourt Brace, 1955).

4. Charles R. Lawrence III, "If He Hollers Let Him Go: Regulating Racist Speech on Campus," in Mari J. Matsuda, Charles R. Lawrence III, Richard Delgado, and Kimberlè Williams Crenshaw, eds., *Words that Wound: Critical Race Theory, Assaultive Speech, and the First Amendment* (Boulder: Westview Press, 1993), 76.

5. Stephen Holmes, *Passions and Constraints: On the Theory of Liberal Democracy* (Chicago: University of Chicago Press, 1995), 11.

6. Michael Piore, *Beyond Individualism: How Social Demands of the New Identity Groups Constrain American Political and Economic Life* (Cambridge: Harvard University Press, 1995), 25.

7. Iris Marion Young, *Justice and the Politics of Difference* (Princeton: Princeton University Press, 1990), 184.

8. Lani Guinier, *The Tyranny of the Majority: Fundamental Fairness in Representative Democracy* (New York: The Free Press, 1994).

9. Martin Anderson, *Impostors in the Temple: American Intellectuals Are Destroying Our Universities and Cheating Our Students of Their Future* (New York: Simon and Schuster, 1992); Roger Kimball, *Tenured Radicals: How Politics Has Corrupted Our Higher Education* (New York: Harper and Row, 1990); and Charles Sykes, *Profscam: Professors and the Demise of Higher Education* (Washington: Regnery Gateway, 1988).

10. Russell Jacoby, *The Last Intellectuals: American Culture in the Age of Academe* (New York: Basic Books, 1987), and *Dogmatic Wisdom: How the Culture Wars Divert Education and Distract America* (New York: Doubleday, 1994).

11. Irving Louis Horowitz, *The Decomposition of Sociology* (New York: Oxford University Press, 1993).

12. I argue this point at greater length, and with many examples, in "Weak Sociology. Strong Sociologists: Consequences and Contradictions of a Field in Turmoil," *Social Research* 59 (Winter 1992), 759–79.

13. Jacques Barzun, *The American University: How It Runs, Where It Is Going* (New York: Harper, 1968); David Damrosch, *We Scholars: Changing the Culture of*

the University (Cambridge: Harvard University Press, 1995); Page Smith, *Killing the Spirit: Higher Education in America* (New York: Viking, 1990).

14. See note 10 above.

15. Steven Brint, *In an Age of Experts: The Changing Role of Professions in Politics and Public Life* (Princeton: Princeton University Press, 1994), 209–10.

16. Robert S. Boynton, "The New Intellectuals," *The Atlantic* 275 (March 1995), 53–56+ and Michael Bérubé, "The Public Academy," *The New Yorker* 70 (January 9, 1995), 73–80.

17. Christopher Jencks, *The Homeless* (Cambridge: Harvard University Press, 1994); Sara McLanahan and Gary Sandefur, *Growing Up With a Single Parent: What Hurts, What Helps* (Cambridge: Harvard University Press, 1994); Herbert Gans, *The War Against the Poor: The Underclass and Anti-Poverty Policy* (New York: Basic Books, 1995).

18. Robert K. Merton and Alan Wolfe, "The Cultural and Social Incorporation of Sociological Knowledge," *The American Sociologist* 26 (Fall 1995), 15–39.